SUPER COOKERY

# Low Fat
# & Salads

DP

DEMPSEY
PARR

This is a Dempsey Parr Book
First published in 2000

Dempsey Parr is an imprint of Parragon
Parragon
Queen Street House
4 Queen Street
Bath BA1 1HE, UK

ISBN: 1-84084-726-3

A copy of the CIP data for this book is available from the British
Library, upon request.

Printed in China

**Note**
Cup measurements used in this book are for American cups.
Tablespoons are assumed to be 15 ml. Unless otherwise stated,
milk is assumed to be full fat, eggs are medium and pepper is
freshly ground black pepper.

# Contents

# Introduction

No-one who has more than a passing interest in their health can be unaware of the problems associated with a diet that contains too much fat. A high level of fat consumption is implicated in obesity—and all that that entails—coronary disease, diabetes, and even cancer. The message that we should all cut down on the fat in our diets is reinforced every time we go shopping, and it is almost impossible to walk around a supermarket without being beset on all sides by labels proclaiming low-fat this, reduced-fat that and no-fat the other.

Cutting the amount of fat in our diets is, of course, an effective way to lose weight, simply because it will reduce the number of calories we consume, as well as reducing the likelihood that we will contract a serious disease. However, before we cut fat out of our lives completely, it is important to remember that we all need to include a certain amount of fat in our daily intake of food if our bodies are to function properly. Essential fatty acids are needed to build cell membranes and for other vital bodily functions. Our brain tissue, nerve sheaths and bone marrow need fat, for example, and we all need fat to protect vital organs such as our liver, kidneys, and heart.

Nutritionists suggest that we should aim to cut our intake of fat to 27-30 per cent of our total daily calorie intake. If your average diet totals 2000 calories, this will mean eating no more than about 2¾ ounces of fat a day. As a guide, bear in mind that most people consume about 40 per cent of their daily calories in the form of fat. Remember, however, that if you are being treated for any medical condition, you must discuss with your family doctor the changes you propose making in your diet before you begin your new regime.

When you are thinking about reducing your intake of fat, it is important to know that fats can be broadly divided into saturated and unsaturated fat. Saturated fats are those that are solid at room temperature, and they are found mainly in animal products— butter and cheese, high-fat meats (sausages, pâté, streaky bacon), cakes, chocolate, potato crisps, biscuits, coconut, and hydrogenated (hardened) vegetable or fish oils. Unsaturated fats are healthier—but they are still fats. Your target should be a reduction to 8 per cent of your daily calories in the form of saturated facts, with the remainder in the form of unsaturated fats. These are usually liquid at room temperature and come from vegetable sources—olive oil, ground nut oil, sunflower oil, safflower oil, and corn oil. Remember, though, that oil is only another name for liquid fat. Using oil instead of margarine or butter to fry onions or garlic will do nothing to reduce your overall intake of fat.

## INGREDIENTS

One of the simplest and most beneficial changes you can make in your diet is to change from full-fat milk, cream, cheese, and yogurt to a low- or reduced-fat equivalent. Semi-skimmed milk, for example, has all the nutritional benefits of whole milk but ½ ounces of fat per pint compared with ¾ ounces of fat per pint in whole milk. Use skimmed milk to make custards and sauces and you will not notice the difference in flavor. Low-fat yogurt or fromage frais mixed with chopped chives is a delicious and healthy alternative to butter or sour cream.

Most vegetables are naturally low in fat and can be used to make a meal of meat or fish go further. Recent nutritional research indicates that we should all aim to eat five portions of fresh fruit and vegetables every day because they contain what are known as antioxidant vitamins, including beta carotene (which creates vitamin A in the body) and vitamins C and E. The antioxidant vitamins in vegetables are thought to help prevent a number of degenerative illnesses (including cancer, heart disease, arthritis, and even ageing of the skin) and to protect the body from the harmful effects of pollution and ultraviolet light, which can damage the body's cells. Phytochemicals, which occur naturally in plants, are thought to be instrumental in the fight against cancer.

Steaming is the best way to cook vegetables to preserve their goodness. Boiling can, for example, destroy up to three-quarters of the vitamin C present in green vegetables. If you have to boil, cook the vegetables as quickly as possible and avoid over-cooking, which also destroys the carotene.

If you have time, it is a good idea to make your own stock to use as the basis of casseroles and soups. The ready-made stocks and stock cubes that are available from shops are often high in salt and artificial flavourings. Instead, use fresh herbs and spices in the water in which vegetables have been cooked or in which dried mushrooms have been soaked. Liquids in which meat and fish of various kinds have been cooked should be saved, too. Chill the liquid in the refrigerator and you will easily be able to remove and discard the fat, which will have risen to the top of the container and solidified.

Pasta, noodles, pulses, and grains can all be used in the low-fat diet, and they are useful for bulking out dishes. Pasta is available in a wide range of shapes, and it is excellent for boosting your carbohydrate intake. Inadequate intake of carbohydrate can result in fatigue and poor energy levels. Whole wheat pasta is also particularly high in fiber, which helps to speed the passage of waste material through the digestive system. Stir cooked brown rice into soups and casseroles to thicken them, or mix one part red lentils with three parts lean ground beef to make a smaller amount of meat go further. Before you buy, check that noodles and pasta have not been enriched with egg. Look out instead for whole wheat or rice varieties.

# EQUIPMENT

Good quality non-stick pans and cookware will directly reduce the amount of fat needed for cooking, and are easier to clean. Use plastic implements or wooden spoons with non-stick pans so that you do not scratch the surface.

A ridged skillet makes it possible to cook with the minimum amount of fat or oil, because the fat drips down between the ridges rather than being absorbed by the food. When you are stir-frying, use a small amount of oil. Keep the heat constant and the food moving to ensure quick, even cooking. Use a non-stick wok, which will help you cut down still further on the amount of oil you need to use in cooking.

Use a perforated spoon to remove food from the skillet, so that cooking juices are left behind. Absorbent kitchen paper is useful for draining surface oil and fat from food that has just been cooked, and it can also be used to mop up fat that rises to the top during cooking. Use plain, unpatterned paper so that no dye is transferred to the food.

# COOKING METHODS

The way we cook our food is one of the most important factors in ensuring a healthy and low-fat diet. In general, steaming is the best way to cook vegetables to preserve their goodness. Boiling can, for example, destroy up to three-quarters of the vitamin C present in green vegetables. This guide will help you to choose the healthiest way to cook your dish, while maintaining optimum flavor and color.

**Frying.** This is the most fat-rich method of cooking. Yet, surprisingly deep-frying the food absorbs less fat than shallow-frying. To cut down on fat intake buy a good quality, non-stick skillet as you will need less fat, and use a vegetable oil, high in polyunsaturates. The preferred method is to stir-fry, as you require little oil as the food is cooked quickly over a high heat.

**Broiling.** This is a good alternative to frying, producing a similar crisp and golden coating while remaining moist and tender inside. Ingredients with a delicate texture and which can easily dry out, such as white fish or chicken breasts, will require brushing with oil. Marinating can reduce the need for oil. Always cook on a rack so that the fat drains away.

**Poaching.** This is ideal for foods with a delicate texture of subtle flavor, such as chicken and fish, but is fat free. Instead of water try alternative liquids such as stock, wine, and acidulated water, flavored with herbs and vegetable. The cooking liquid can make the basis of a nutritious and flavorsome sauce.

**Steaming.** This is also fat-free and is becoming a popular method of cooking meat, fish, chicken, and vegetables. Ingredients maintain their color, flavor, and texture, fewer nutrients are leached out. An additional advantage is that when meat is steamed, the fat melts and drips into the cooking liquid—this should not then be used for gravy.

**Braising and stewing.** Slow cooking techniques produce succulent dishes that are especially welcome in winter. Trim all visible fat from the meat and always remove the skin from the chicken.

**Roasting.** Fat is an integral part of this cooking technique, and without it meat or fish would dry out. Try standing meat on a rack over a roasting tray so that the fat drains off. Do not use the meat juices for gravy.

**Baking.** Many dishes are fat free. Foil-wrapped packets of meat or fish are always delicious. Add fruit juice or wine instead of oil or butter for a moist texture.

**Microwaving.** Food cooked in this way rarely requires additional fat.

# MAKING SALADS

The popular definition of a salad is a dish of raw or cold cooked foods, usually served with a dressing or seasoning to add flavor. Traditionally they are used as a side dish accompaniment to a main course or as a starter. However, several different salads, carefully balanced, can make an excellent main course for a casual meal in the summer. On their own, individual salads are ideal to use as a starter for a more formal occasion or perfect for a light lunch.

More substantial salad dishes can be devised, however, with the addition of cooked or semi-cooked vegetables, and ingredients such as cooked meats can be included. Using cooked vegetables in a salad adds gentle flavor and the mixing of hot and cold ingredients adds interest to the dish. Another idea that is gaining in popularity is to combine vegetables with fruit to make a range of contrasting savory and sweet tastes in a salad. Other ingredients often incorporated in salad dishes include dried fruits, nuts, and seeds.

Salads are generally of high nutritional value. They are not, however, necessarily low in fat content, owing to the rich dressings, sauces, and mayonnaises that are sometimes used to give them flavor. If you are following a low fat-diet, then look at the ingredients in the dressings given with the recipes in this book and choose low-fat alternatives such as butter and margarine instead of oils.

# STORE CUPBOARD

## Rice and pasta

There are a good variety of rices to choose from for incorporating in salads. Try long-grain, basmati, Italian arborio, or wild rice. Brown rice is a good source of vitamin B1 and fiber. Keep a good selection of pasta, preferably in small shapes, such as rigatoni, farfalle, or fusili, and of course, macaroni and spaghetti.

## Legumes

As they provide a valuable source of protein, stock up on red kidney beans, cannellini beans, and garbanzo beans to use in salads.

## Nuts and seeds

As well as adding protein, vitamins, and useful healthy fats to the diet, nuts such as hazelnuts, walnuts, pine kernels, and seeds such as sesame, sunflower, and poppy add flavor and texture to salads.

## Oils and fats

Oils are useful for adding subtle flavorings to food. Use extra-virgin olive oil for salad dressings or try hazelnut and walnut oils for a superb flavor. All fats and oils are high in calories; butter and margarine are lower-fat options.

## Vinegars

Red or white wine vinegar, tarragon, sherry, or balsamic vinegars will all add their own subtle flavors to salad dishes.

# Soups & Starters

*Many favorite snacks and starters—especially those that we buy ready-prepared on supermarket shelves and in cans—are surprisingly high in fat. Next time, before you buy, think instead about making some of the appetizing recipes on the following pages—they will get your meal off to a wonderful low-fat start.*

*Soups are a traditional first course, but, served with crusty bread, they can also be a satisfying meal in their own right. Although it does take a little longer, consider making your own stock by using the liquid left after cooking vegetables, and the juices from fish and meat that have been used as the base of casseroles. Use a potato to thicken your soups rather than stirring in the traditional thickener of flour and water—or, worse, flour and fat.*

*Also included here are a delicious range of salads; if you are following a low-fat diet check the ingredients, in particular the dressing, and replace those high in fat with lower-fat options.*

# *Chicken & Asparagus Soup*

### Serves 4

### INGREDIENTS

8 ounces fresh asparagus
$3\frac{3}{4}$ cups fresh chicken stock
$\frac{2}{3}$ cup dry white wine

1 sprig each fresh parsley, dill,
   and tarragon
1 garlic clove
$\frac{1}{3}$ cup vermicelli rice noodles

12 ounces lean cooked chicken,
   finely shredded
salt and white pepper
1 small leek

1 Wash the asparagus and trim away the woody ends. Cut each spear into pieces about $1\frac{1}{2}$ inches long.

2 Pour the stock and wine into a large saucepan and bring to a boil.

3 Wash the herbs and tie them with clean string. Peel the garlic clove and add, with the herbs, to the saucepan, together with the asparagus and noodles. Cover and simmer for 5 minutes.

4 Stir in the chicken and plenty of seasoning. Simmer gently for a further 3–4 minutes until heated through.

5 Using a sharp knife, trim the leek, slice it down the center, and wash under running water to remove any dirt. Shake dry and shred finely.

6 Remove the herbs and garlic from the pan and discard. Ladle the soup into warm bowls, sprinkle with shredded leek, and serve at once.

## VARIATION

*You can use any of your favorite herbs in this recipe, but choose those with a subtle flavor so that they do not overpower the asparagus. Small, tender asparagus spears give the best results and flavor.*

## COOK'S TIP

*Rice noodles contain no fat and are an ideal substitute for egg noodles.*

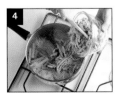

# Beef, Water Chestnut, & Rice Soup

### Serves 4

**INGREDIENTS**

12 ounces lean beef (such as
    rump or sirloin)
4 cups fresh beef stock
1 cinnamon stick, broken
2 star anise
2 tbsp dark soy sauce
2 tbsp dry sherry

3 tbsp tomato paste
4 ounce can water chestnuts,
    drained and sliced
3 cups cooked white rice
1 tsp zested orange rind
6 tbsp orange juice
salt and pepper

TO GARNISH:
strips of orange rind
2 tbsp snipped chives

1 Using a sharp knife, carefully trim away any fat from the beef. Cut the beef into thin strips and then place into a large saucepan.

2 Add the stock, cinnamon, star anise, soy sauce, sherry, tomato paste, and water chestnuts. Bring to a boil, skimming away any surface film with a flat ladle. Cover the pan and simmer gently for about 20 minutes or until the beef is tender.

3 Skim the soup with a flat ladle again to remove any film. Remove and discard the cinnamon and star anise and blot the surface with absorbent paper towels to remove any fat.

4 Stir in the rice, orange rind, and juice. Adjust the seasoning if necessary. Heat through for 2–3 minutes before ladling into warm bowls. Serve garnished with orange rind and snipped chives.

## VARIATION

*Omit the rice for a lighter soup that is an ideal starter for a Chinese meal of many courses. For a more substantial soup that would be a meal in its own right, add diced vegetables such as carrot, bell pepper, corn, or zucchini.*

# *Winter Beef & Vegetable Soup*

### Serves 4

**INGREDIENTS**

| | | |
|---|---|---|
| 1/3 cup pearl barley | 1 large carrot, diced | salt and pepper |
| 5 cups fresh beef stock | 1 leek, shredded | 2 tbsp fresh parsley, chopped, |
| 1 tsp dried mixed herbs | 1 medium onion, chopped | to garnish |
| 8 ounces lean rump or sirloin | 2 celery stalks, sliced | crusty bread, to serve |
| beef | | |

1 Place the pearl barley in a large saucepan. Pour in the stock and add the mixed herbs. Bring to a boil, cover, and simmer for 10 minutes.

2 Meanwhile, trim any fat from the beef and cut the meat into thin strips.

3 Skim away any scum that has risen to the top of the stock with a flat ladle.

4 Add the beef, carrot, leek, onion, and celery to the pan. Bring back to a boil, cover, and simmer for about 20 minutes or until the meat and vegetables are just tender.

5 Skim away any remaining film that has risen to the top of the soup with a flat ladle. Blot the surface with absorbent paper towels to remove any fat. Adjust the seasoning according to taste.

6 Ladle the soup into warm bowls and sprinkle with freshly chopped parsley. Serve accompanied with fresh crusty bread.

## VARIATION

*This soup is just as delicious made with lean lamb or pork tenderloin. A vegetarian version can be made by omitting the beef and beef stock and using vegetable stock instead. Just before serving, stir in 6 ounces fresh bean curd, drained and diced. An even more substantial soup can be made by adding other root vegetables, such as rutabaga or turnip, instead of, or as well as, the carrot.*

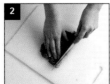

# Mediterranean-Style Fish Soup

### Serves 4

## INGREDIENTS

1 tbsp olive oil
1 large onion, chopped
2 garlic cloves, finely chopped
1³/₄ cups fresh fish stock
²/₃ cup dry white wine
1 bay leaf
1 sprig each fresh thyme,
    rosemary, and oregano

1 pound firm white fish fillets
    (such as cod, monkfish or
    halibut), skinned and cut into
    1-inch cubes
1 pound fresh mussels, prepared
14 ounce can chopped tomatoes
8 ounces peeled shrimp, thawed
    if frozen

salt and pepper
sprigs of thyme, to garnish

TO SERVE:
lemon wedges
4 slices toasted French bread,
    rubbed with cut garlic clove

1 Heat the oil in a pan and gently sauté the onion and garlic for 2–3 minutes, until softened.

2 Pour in the stock and wine and bring to a boil. Tie the bay leaf and herbs together with clean string and add to the saucepan, together with the fish and mussels. Stir well, cover, and simmer for 5 minutes.

3 Stir in the tomatoes and shrimp and continue to cook for a further 3–4 minutes, until piping hot and the fish is cooked through.

4 Discard the herbs and any mussels that have not opened. Season to taste, then ladle into warm bowls. Garnish with fresh thyme and serve with lemon wedges and toasted bread.

## COOK'S TIP

*Traditionally, the toasted bread is placed at the bottom of the bowl and the soup spooned over the top. For convenience, use prepared, cooked shellfish mixtures, instead of fresh fish. Simply add to the soup with the tomatoes in step 3.*

# Tuscan Bean & Vegetable Soup

### Serves 4

**INGREDIENTS**

1 medium onion, chopped

1 garlic clove, finely chopped

2 celery stalks, sliced

1 large carrot, diced

14 ounce can chopped tomatoes

$^2/_3$ cup Italian dry red wine

5 cups fresh vegetable stock

1 tsp dried oregano

15 ounce can mixed beans
    and legumes

2 medium zucchini, diced

1 tbsp tomato paste

salt and pepper

TO SERVE:

low-fat pesto sauce

crusty bread

1 Place the prepared onion, garlic, celery, and carrot in a large saucepan. Stir in the tomatoes, red wine, vegetable stock, and oregano.

2 Bring the vegetable mixture to a boil, cover the pan, and simmer for about 15 minutes. Stir the beans and zucchini into the mixture, and continue to cook, uncovered, for a further 5 minutes.

3 Add the tomato paste and season well with salt and pepper to taste. Then heat through, stirring occasionally, for a further 2–3 minutes, but do not allow the mixture to boil again.

4 Ladle the soup into warm bowls and serve with a spoonful of low-fat pesto (see page 146) on each portion and accompanied with lots of fresh crusty bread.

### VARIATION

*For a more substantial soup, add 12 ounces diced lean cooked chicken or turkey with the tomato paste in step 3.*

# Lentil, Pasta, & Vegetable Soup

### Serves 4

## INGREDIENTS

| | | |
|---|---|---|
| 1 tbsp olive oil | 2¹/₂ cups fresh vegetable stock | 2 tbsp fresh parsley, chopped, |
| 1 medium onion, chopped | 3 cups boiling water | to garnish |
| 4 garlic cloves, finely chopped | 1 cup dried pasta | |
| 12 ounces carrots, sliced | ²/₃ cup natural low-fat | |
| 1 celery stalk, sliced | unsweetened yogurt | |
| 1¹/₄ cups red lentils | salt and pepper | |

1 Heat the oil in a large saucepan and gently sauté the prepared onion, garlic, carrot, and celery, stirring gently, for about 5 minutes or until the vegetables begin to soften.

2 Add the lentils, stock, and boiling water. Season with salt and pepper to taste, stir, and bring back to a boil. Simmer, uncovered, for 15 minutes until the lentils are completely tender. Allow to cool for 10 minutes.

3 Meanwhile, bring another saucepan of water to a boil and cook the pasta according to the instructions on the packet. Drain well and set aside.

4 Place the soup in a blender and process until smooth. Return to a saucepan and add the pasta. Bring back to a simmer and heat for 2–3 minutes, until piping hot. Remove from the heat and stir in the yogurt. Adjust the seasoning if necessary.

5 Serve sprinkled with chopped parsley.

### COOK'S TIP

*Avoid boiling the soup once the yogurt has been added. Otherwise it will separate and become watery, spoiling the appearance of the soup.*

# Creamy Corn Soup

### Serves 4

### INGREDIENTS

| | | |
|---|---|---|
| 1 large onion, chopped | 1 pound canned corn kernels or | salt and pepper |
| 1 large potato, peeled and diced | frozen, drained or thawed | |
| 4 cups skim milk | 1 tbsp cornstarch | TO GARNISH: |
| 1 bay leaf | 3 tbsp cold water | 3 1/2 ounces lean ham, diced |
| 1/2 tsp ground nutmeg | 4 tbsp natural low-fat | 2 tbsp snipped fresh chives |
| | unsweetened yogurt | |

1 Place the onion and potato in a large saucepan and pour in the milk. Add the bay leaf, nutmeg, and half the corn. Bring to a boil, cover, and simmer gently for 15 minutes, until the potato is softened. Stir the soup occasionally and keep the heat low so that the milk does not burn on the bottom of the pan.

2 Discard the bay leaf and leave the liquid to cool for 10 minutes. Transfer to a blender and process briefly. Alternatively, rub through a strainer.

3 Pour the smooth liquid into a saucepan. Blend the cornstarch with the cold water to make a paste and stir it into the soup.

4 Bring the soup back to a boil, stirring until it thickens, and add the remaining corn. Heat through for 2–3 minutes until piping hot.

5 Remove from the heat and season with salt and pepper. Stir in the yogurt. Ladle the soup into bowls, garnish, and serve.

## VARIATION

*For a more substantial soup, add 8 ounces flaked white crabmeat or peeled, cooked shrimp in step 4.*

# Tomato & Red Bell Pepper Soup

### Serves 4

**INGREDIENTS**

2 large red bell peppers
1 large onion, chopped
2 celery stalks, trimmed and
    chopped

1 garlic clove, crushed
2½ cups fresh vegetable stock
2 bay leaves
2 14 ounce cans plum tomatoes

salt and pepper
2 scallions, finely shredded,
    to garnish
crusty bread, to serve

1 Preheat the broiler. Halve and seed the bell peppers, arrange them on the broiler rack and cook, turning occasionally, for 8–10 minutes until softened and charred.

2 Leave to cool slightly, then carefully peel off the charred skin. Reserving a small piece for garnish, chop the bell pepper flesh and place in a large saucepan.

3 Mix in the onion, celery, and garlic. Add the stock and the bay leaves.

Bring to a boil, cover, and simmer for 15 minutes. Remove from the heat.

4 Stir in the tomatoes and transfer to a blender. Process for a few seconds until smooth. Return to the saucepan.

5 Season with salt and pepper to taste and heat for 3–4 minutes until piping hot. Ladle the soup into warm bowls and garnish with the reserved bell pepper cut into strips and the scallion. Serve with lots of fresh crusty bread.

## COOK'S TIP

*If you prefer a coarser, more robust soup, lightly mash the tomatoes with a wooden spoon and omit the blending process in step 4.*

# Carrot, Apple, & Celery Soup

### Serves 4

#### INGREDIENTS

| | | |
|---|---|---|
| 2 pounds carrots, finely diced | 3 medium-size eating | ¼ large lemon |
| 1 medium onion, chopped | apples | salt and pepper |
| 3 celery stalks, trimmed and | 2 tbsp tomato paste | celery leaves, washed and |
| diced | 1 bay leaf | shredded, to garnish |
| 4 cups fresh vegetable stock | 2 tsp superfine sugar | |

1 Place the prepared carrots, onion, and celery in a large saucepan and add the fresh vegetable stock. Bring to a boil, cover and simmer for about 10 minutes.

2 Meanwhile, peel, core, and dice 2 of the apples. Add the pieces of apple, tomato paste, bay leaf, and superfine sugar to the saucepan and bring to a boil. Reduce the heat, half cover the pan, and allow to simmer for 20 minutes. Remove and discard the bay leaf.

3 Meanwhile, wash, core, and cut the remaining apple into thin slices, leaving on the skin. Place the apple slices in a small saucepan and squeeze in the lemon juice. Heat gently and simmer for 1–2 minutes, until tender. Drain and set aside.

4 Place the carrot and apple mixture in a blender or food processor and blend until smooth. Alternatively, press the mixture through a strainer with the back of a wooden spoon, until smooth.

5 Gently reheat the soup if necessary and season with salt and pepper to taste. Ladle the soup into warm bowls and serve topped with the reserved apple slices and shredded celery leaves.

## COOK'S TIP

*Soaking light colored fruit in lemon juice prevents it from turning brown when exposed to the air.*

# *Chilled Piquant Shrimp & Cucumber Soup*

### Serves 4

### INGREDIENTS

1 cucumber, peeled and diced
$1^2/_3$ cups fresh fish stock, chilled
$^2/_3$ cup tomato juice
$1^2/_3$ cup low-fat unsweetened
    yogurt

$4^1/_2$ ounces peeled shrimp,
    thawed if frozen, roughly
    chopped
few drops Tabasco sauce
1 tbsp fresh mint, chopped

salt and white pepper
ice cubes, to serve

TO GARNISH:
sprigs of mint
cucumber slices
whole peeled shrimp

1 Place the diced cucumber in a blender or food processor and work for a few seconds until a smooth purée is formed. Alternatively, chop the cucumber finely and push through a strainer.

2 Transfer the cucumber to a bowl. Stir in the fish stock, tomato juice, yogurt, and shrimp, and mix well. Add the Tabasco sauce and season with salt and pepper to taste.

3 Stir in the chopped mint, cover, and chill in the refrigerator for at least 2 hours.

4 Ladle the soup into glass bowls and add a few ice cubes. Serve garnished with mint, cucumber slices, and whole shrimp.

## VARIATION

*Instead of shrimp, add white crabmeat or cooked ground chicken. For a vegetarian version of this soup, omit the shrimp and add an extra $4^1/_2$ ounces finely diced cucumber. Use fresh vegetable stock instead of fish stock.*

# Celery, Stilton, & Walnut Soup

### Serves 4

### INGREDIENTS

| | | |
|---|---|---|
| 4 tablespoons butter | 2¹/₂ cups vegetable stock | 2 tablespoons walnut halves, |
| 2 shallots, chopped | 1¹/₄ cups milk | roughly chopped |
| 3 celery stalks, chopped | 1¹/₂ cups crumbled blue Stilton | ²/₃ cup unsweetened yogurt |
| 1 garlic clove, crushed | cheese, plus extra to garnish | salt and pepper |
| 2 tablespoons all-purpose flour | | chopped celery leaves, to garnish |

1 Melt the butter in a large saucepan and sauté the shallots, celery, and garlic for 2–3 minutes, stirring constantly, until softened.

2 Add the all-purpose flour and cook, stirring constantly, for 30 seconds.

3 Gradually stir in the stock and milk and bring to a boil.

4 Reduce the heat to a gentle simmer and add the crumbled blue Stilton cheese and walnut halves. Cover and simmer for 20 minutes.

5 Stir in the unsweetened yogurt and heat for a further 2 minutes without boiling.

6 Season the soup to taste with salt and pepper, then transfer to a warm soup tureen or individual serving bowls, garnish with chopped celery leaves and extra crumbled blue Stilton cheese, and serve at once.

## COOK'S TIP

*As well as adding protein, vitamins, and useful fats to the diet, nuts add important flavor and texture to vegetarian meals.*

## VARIATION

*Use an alternative blue cheese, such as Dolcelatte or Gorgonzola, if desired, or a strong vegetarian Cheddar cheese, grated.*

# Spicy Chicken Noodle Soup

### Serves 4

## INGREDIENTS

2 tbsp tamarind paste

4 red Thai chiles, finely chopped

2 cloves garlic, crushed

1-inch piece Thai ginger, peeled and very finely chopped

4 tbsp fish sauce

2 tbsp palm sugar or brown sugar

8 lime leaves, roughly torn

5 cups chicken stock

12 ounces boneless chicken breast

1–2 medium carrots, very thinly sliced

12 ounces sweet potato, diced

3½ ounces baby corn cobs, halved

3 tbsp fresh cilantro, roughly chopped

3½ ounces cherry tomatoes, halved

5½ ounces flat rice noodles

fresh cilantro, chopped, to garnish

1 Place the tamarind paste, Thai chiles, garlic, Thai ginger, fish sauce, sugar, lime leaves, and chicken stock in a large preheated wok and bring to a boil, stirring constantly. Reduce the heat and cook for about 5 minutes.

2 Using a sharp knife, thinly slice the chicken. Add the chicken to the wok and cook for a further 5 minutes, stirring the mixture well.

3 Reduce the heat slightly and add the carrots, sweet potato, and baby corn cobs to the wok. Simmer, uncovered, for about 5 minutes, or until the vegetables are just tender and the chicken is completely cooked through.

4 Stir in the cilantro, cherry tomatoes and noodles. Simmer for about 5 minutes, or until the noodles are tender. Transfer to warm bowls, garnish and serve hot.

## COOK'S TIP

*Tamarind paste is produced from the seed pod of the tamarind tree. It adds both a brown color and tang to soups and gravies. If unavailable, dilute brown sugar or molasses with lime juice.*

# *Chili Fish Soup*

### Serves 4

**INGREDIENTS**

| | | |
|---|---|---|
| ¹/₂ ounce Chinese dried mushrooms | 1¹/₂ cups bamboo shoots | 2 tbsp fresh cilantro |
| 2 tbsp sunflower oil | 3 tbsp sweet chili sauce | 1 pound cod fillet, skinned and cubed |
| 1 onion, sliced | 5 cups fish or vegetable stock | |
| 1¹/₂ cups snow peas | 3 tbsp light soy sauce | |

1 Place the mushrooms in a large bowl. Pour over enough boiling water to cover and let stand for 5 minutes. Drain the mushrooms thoroughly. Using a sharp knife, remove the stalks and roughly chop the caps.

2 Heat the sunflower oil in a preheated wok. Add the onion to the wok and stir-fry for 5 minutes, or until softened.

3 Add the snow peas, bamboo shoots, chili sauce, stock, and soy sauce to the wok and bring to a boil.

4 Add the cilantro and cubed fish to the wok. Lower the heat slightly and simmer for about 5 minutes, or until the fish is cooked through.

5 Transfer the soup to warm bowls, garnish with extra cilantro, if wished, and serve hot.

## VARIATION

*Cod is used in this recipe, as it is a meaty white fish. For real luxury, use monkfish tail instead.*

## COOK'S TIP

*There are many different varieties of dried mushrooms, but shiitake are best. They are not cheap, but a small quantity will go a long way.*

# Hot & Sour Mushroom Soup

### Serves 4

**INGREDIENTS**

2 tbsp tamarind paste
4 red Thai chiles, very finely chopped
2 cloves garlic, crushed
1-inch piece of Thai ginger, peeled
    and very finely chopped

4 tbsp fish sauce
2 tbsp palm or brown sugar
8 lime leaves, roughly torn
5 cups vegetable stock
1–.2 medium carrots, very
    thinly sliced

3¼ cups button mushrooms, halved
12 ounces shredded white cabbage
¾ cup fine green beans, halved
3 tbsp fresh cilantro, roughly
    chopped
3½ ounces cherry tomatoes, halved

1 Place the tamarind paste, Thai chiles, garlic, Thai ginger, fish sauce, palm or brown sugar, lime leaves, and stock in a large preheated wok. Bring the mixture to a boil, stirring occasionally.

2 Reduce the heat slightly and add the carrots, mushrooms, cabbage, and green beans. Simmer the soup, uncovered, for about 10 minutes, or until the vegetables are just tender.

3 Stir the cilantro and cherry tomatoes into the mixture in the wok and heat through for 5 minutes.

4 Transfer the soup to warm bowls and serve hot.

## COOK'S TIP

*Tamarind is one of the ingredients that gives Thai cuisine its special sweet and sour flavor.*

## VARIATION

*Instead of the white cabbage, try using Chinese cabbage for a sweeter flavor. Add the Chinese cabbage with the cilantro and cherry tomatoes in step 3.*

# Chicken & Leek Soup

### Serves 6

**INGREDIENTS**

12 ounces boneless chicken

12 ounces leeks

2 tablespoons butter

5 cups chicken stock

1 bouquet garni packet

8 pitted prunes, halved

salt and white pepper

cooked rice and diced bell

peppers (optional)

1 Using a sharp knife, cut the chicken and leeks into 1-inch pieces.

2 Melt the butter in a large saucepan, add the chicken and leeks, and fry for 8 minutes, stirring occasionally.

3 Add the chicken stock and bouquet garni to the mixture in the pan, and season with salt and pepper to taste.

4 Bring the soup to a boil and simmer over gentle heat for 45 minutes.

5 Add the pitted prunes with some cooked rice and diced bell peppers (if using), and simmer for 20 minutes. Remove the bouquet garni packet and discard. Pour the soup into a warm tureen or warm individual soup bowls and serve at once.

## COOK'S TIP

*If you have time, make the chicken stock yourself, using the recipe on page 5. Alternatively, you can buy good fresh stock from supermarkets.*

## COOK'S TIP

*Instead of the bouquet garni packet, you can use a bunch of fresh, mixed herbs, tied together with string. Choose herbs such as parsley, thyme, and rosemary.*

# *Thai Chicken Noodle Soup*

### Serves 4–6

### INGREDIENTS

1 sheet of dried egg noodles
from a 9 ounce pack
1 tablespoon oil
4 skinless, boneless
chicken thighs, diced
1 bunch scallions, sliced

2 garlic cloves, chopped
3/4-inch piece fresh
ginger root, finely chopped
3 3/4 cups chicken stock
scant 1 cup coconut milk
1 tablespoon red Thai curry paste

3 tablespoons peanut butter
2 tablespoons light soy sauce
1 small red bell pepper, chopped
1/2 cup frozen peas
salt and pepper

1 Put the noodles in a shallow dish and soak in boiling water following the instructions on the packet.

2 Heat the oil in a large saucepan or wok, add the chicken, and fry for 5 minutes, stirring until lightly browned. Add the white part of the scallions, the garlic, and ginger and fry for 2 minutes, stirring constantly. Add the stock, coconut milk, curry paste, peanut butter, and soy sauce. Season with salt and pepper to taste. Bring to a

boil, stirring constantly, then simmer for 8 minutes, stirring occasionally. Add the red bell pepper, peas, and green scallion tops and cook for 2 minutes.

3 Add the drained noodles and heat through. Spoon into individual bowls and serve with a spoon and fork.

## VARIATION

*Green Thai curry paste can be used for a less fiery flavor. It is available from specialty gourmet stores.*

# Chicken Consommé

### Serves 8–10

**INGREDIENTS**

| | | |
|---|---|---|
| 8 cups chicken stock | 4 egg whites, plus egg shells | salt and pepper |
| 2/3 cup medium sherry | 4 ounces cooked chicken, thinly sliced | |

1 Place the chicken stock and sherry in a large saucepan and heat gently for 5 minutes.

2 Add the egg whites and the egg shells to the chicken stock and whisk until the mixture begins to boil.

3 Remove the pan from the heat and allow the mixture to subside for 10 minutes. Repeat this process three times. This allows the egg white to trap the sediments in the chicken stock to clarify the soup. Let the consommé cool for 5 minutes.

4 Carefully place a piece of fine cheesecloth over a clean saucepan. Ladle the soup over the cheesecloth and strain into the saucepan.

5 Repeat this process twice, then gently reheat the consommé. Season with salt and pepper to taste, then add the cooked chicken slices. Pour the soup into a warm serving dish or individual bowls.

6 Garnish the consommé with any of the suggestions in the Cook's Tip, right.

## COOK'S TIP

*Consommé is usually garnished with freshly cooked pasta shapes, noodles, rice, or lightly cooked vegetables. Alternatively, you could garnish it with omelet strips, drained first on paper towels.*

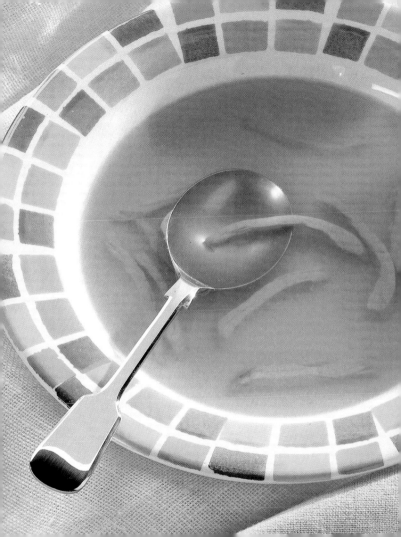

# Chicken Wonton Soup

### Serves 4–6

**INGREDIENTS**

FILLING:

12 ounces ground chicken

1 tablespoon soy sauce

1 teaspoon grated, fresh ginger root

1 garlic clove, crushed

2 teaspoons sherry

2 scallions, chopped

1 teaspoon sesame oil

1 egg white

1/2 teaspoon cornstarch

1/2 teaspoon sugar

about 35 wonton wrappers

SOUP:

6 cups chicken stock

1 tablespoon light soy sauce

1 scallion, shredded

1 small carrot, cut into
    very thin slices

1 Combine all the ingredients for the filling and mix well.

2 Place a small spoonful of the filling in the center of each wonton wrapper.

3 Dampen the edges and gather up the wonton wrapper to form a pouch enclosing the filling.

4 Cook the filled wontons in boiling water for 1 minute, or until they float to the top.

5 Remove with a slotted spoon. Bring the chicken stock to a boil.

6 Add the soy sauce, shredded scallion, carrot, and wontons to the soup. Simmer gently for 2 minutes, then serve.

## VARIATION

*Instead of the chicken, you can use ground pork.*

## COOK'S TIP

*Look for wonton wrappers in Chinese or Asian supermarkets. Fresh wrappers can be found in the chilled compartment and they can be frozen if desired. Wrap them in plastic wrap before freezing.*

# Rosy Melon & Strawberries

### Serves 4

**INGREDIENTS**

| | | |
|---|---|---|
| ¼ honeydew melon | ⅔ cup rosé wine | 6 ounces small strawberries, |
| ½ Charentais or Cantaloupe melon | 2–3 tsp rosewater | washed and hulled |
| | | rose petals, to garnish |

1 Scoop out the seeds from both melons with a spoon. Then carefully remove the skin, taking care not to remove too much flesh.

2 Cut the melon flesh into thin strips and place in a bowl. Pour in the wine and sufficient rosewater to taste. Mix together gently, cover, and chill in the refrigerator for at least 2 hours.

3 Halve the strawberries and carefully mix into the melon. Allow the melon and strawberries to stand at room temperature

for about 15 minutes for the flavors to develop fully.

4 Arrange the melon and strawberries on individual serving plates and serve sprinkled with a few rose petals.

## COOK'S TIP

*Rosewater is a distillation of rose petals. It is generally available from large pharmacies and leading supermarkets, as well as from more specialty food suppliers.*

## VARIATION

*It does not matter whether the rosé wine is sweet or dry—although sweet wine contains more calories. Experiment with different types of melon. Varieties such as "Sweet Dream" have whitish-green flesh, while Charentais melons, which have orange flesh, are fragrant and go better with a dry wine. If you wish, soak the strawberries in the wine with the melon, but always allow the fruit to return to room temperature before serving.*

# *Italian Platter*

### Serves 4

**INGREDIENTS**

4¹/₂ ounces reduced-fat
  mozzarella cheese, drained
2 ounces lean prosciutto
14 ounce can artichoke
  hearts, drained
4 ripe figs

1 small mango
plain bread sticks, to serve

DRESSING:
1 small orange
1 tbsp sieved tomatoes

1 tsp wholegrain mustard
4 tbsp low-fat unsweetened
  yogurt
fresh basil leaves
salt and pepper

1 Cut the cheese into 12 sticks, 2¹/₂ inches long. Remove the fat from the prosciutto and slice the meat into 12 strips.

2 Carefully wrap a strip of prosciutto around each stick of cheese and arrange them neatly on a serving platter.

3 Halve the artichoke hearts and cut the figs into quarters. Arrange them on the serving platter in groups.

4 Peel the mango, then slice it down each side of the large, flat central pit. Slice the flesh into strips and arrange them so that they form a fan shape on the serving platter.

5 To make the dressing, pare the rind from half of the orange using a vegetable peeler. Cut the rind into small strips and place them in a bowl. Extract the juice from the orange and add it to the bowl containing the rind.

6 Add the sieved tomatoes, mustard, yogurt, and seasoning to the bowl and mix together. Shred the basil leaves and mix them into the dressing.

7 Spoon the dressing into a small dish and serve with the Italian Platter, accompanied with bread sticks.

# *Breakfast Muffins*

### Serves 4

### INGREDIENTS

| | | |
|---|---|---|
| 2 whole wheat English muffins | 2 large tomatoes | salt and pepper |
| 8 slices lean bacon | 2 large flat mushrooms | 1 small bunch fresh chives, |
| 4 medium eggs | 4 tbsp fresh vegetable stock | snipped, to garnish |

1 Preheat the broiler. Cut the muffins in half and toast them for 1–2 minutes on the open side. Set aside and keep warm.

2 Trim off all visible fat from the bacon and broil for 2–3 minutes on each side. Drain on absorbent paper towels and keep warm.

3 Place 4 egg-poaching rings in a skillet and pour in enough water to cover the base of the pan. Bring to a boil and reduce the heat to a simmer. Carefully break one egg into each ring and poach gently for 5–6 minutes until set.

4 Meanwhile, cut the tomatoes into 8 thick slices and arrange on a piece of kitchen foil on the broiler rack. Broil for 2–3 minutes, until just cooked. Season to taste.

5 Peel and thickly slice the mushrooms. Place in a pan with the stock, bring to a boil, cover, and simmer for 4–5 minutes until cooked. Drain thoroughly, set aside, and keep warm.

6 To serve, arrange the tomato and mushroom slices on the toasted muffins and top each with 2 slices of bacon. Arrange an egg on top of each and sprinkle with pepper. Garnish with snipped chives and serve.

## VARIATION

*Omit the bacon for a vegetarian version and use more tomatoes and mushrooms instead. Alternatively, include a broiled low-fat bean curd or soy protein burger.*

# Cheesy Ham & Celery Savory

### Serves 4

## INGREDIENTS

4 celery stalks

12 thin slices of lean ham

1 bunch scallions

6 ounces low-fat soft cheese
with garlic and herbs

6 tbsp low-fat unsweetened
yogurt

4 tbsp Parmesan cheese,
freshly grated

celery salt and pepper

TO SERVE:

tomato salad

crusty bread

1 Wash the celery, remove the leaves, and slice the celery stalks into 3 equal portions.

2 Cut any visible fat off the ham and lay the slices on a chopping board. Place a piece of celery on each piece of ham and roll up. Place 3 ham and celery rolls in each of 4 small, heatproof dishes.

3 Trim the scallions, then finely shred both the white and green parts. Sprinkle the shredded scallions over the ham and celery rolls and season with celery salt and pepper.

4 Mix together the soft cheese and yogurt and spoon over the ham and celery rolls.

5 Preheat the broiler. Sprinkle each portion with 1 tbsp grated Parmesan cheese and broil for 6–7 minutes until hot and the cheese has formed a crust. If the cheese starts to brown too quickly, lower the broiler setting slightly.

6 Serve with a tomato salad and lots of fresh crusty bread.

## COOK'S TIP

*Parmesan is useful in low-fat recipes because its intense flavor means you need to use only a small amount.*

# *Parsleyed Chicken & Ham Pâté*

### Serves 4

**INGREDIENTS**

| | | |
|---|---|---|
| 8 ounces lean, skinless chicken, cooked | 2 tbsp lime juice | 1 tsp lime zest, to garnish |
| 3½ ounces lean ham, trimmed | 1 garlic clove, peeled | |
| small bunch fresh parsley | ½ cup low-fat unsweetened yogurt | TO SERVE: |
| 1 tsp lime rind, grated | salt and pepper | wedges of lime |
| | | crispbread |

1 Dice the chicken and ham and place in a blender or food processor. Add the parsley, lime rind and juice, and garlic and process well until finely ground. Alternatively, finely chop the chicken, ham, parsley, and garlic and place in a mixing bowl. Mix gently with the lime rind and juice.

2 Transfer the mixture to a bowl and mix in the yogurt. Season with salt and pepper to taste, cover, and set aside to chill in the refrigerator for about 30 minutes.

3 Transfer the pâté into individual serving dishes and garnish with lime zest. Serve the pâtés with lime wedges and crispbread.

## VARIATION

*This pâté can be made equally successfully with other kinds of ground, lean, cooked meat, such as turkey, beef, and pork. Alternatively, replace the chicken and ham with peeled shrimp and/or white crabmeat or with canned tuna in water, drained. Remember that removing the skin from poultry reduces the fat content of any dish.*

# Spinach Cheese Molds

### Serves 4

**INGREDIENTS**

3½ ounces fresh spinach leaves
10½ ounces skim milk soft
   cheese
2 garlic cloves, crushed

sprigs of fresh parsley, tarragon,
   and chives, finely chopped
salt and pepper

TO SERVE:
salad greens and fresh herbs
pita bread

1 Trim the stalks from the spinach leaves. Rinse the leaves under running water. Pack the leaves into a saucepan while still wet, cover, and cook for 3–4 minutes until wilted—they will cook in the steam from the wet leaves (do not overcook). Drain well and pat dry with absorbent paper towels.

2 Base-line 4 small pudding basins or individual ramekin dishes with baking parchment. Line the basins or ramekins with spinach leaves so that the leaves overhang the edges if they are large enough to do so.

3 Place the cheese in a bowl and add the garlic and herbs. Mix together thoroughly and season to taste.

4 Spoon the cheese and herb mixture into the basins or ramekins and pull over the overlapping spinach to cover the cheese, or lay extra leaves to cover the top. Place a baking paper round on top of each dish and weigh down with a 4 ounce weight. Chill in the refrigerator for 1 hour.

5 Remove the weights and peel off the paper. Loosen the molds by running a small spatula around the edges of each dish and turn them out onto individual plates.

6 Serve with a mixture of salad greens and fresh herbs, and warm pita bread.

# Soufflé Omelet

### Serves 4

**INGREDIENTS**

| | | |
|---|---|---|
| 6 ounces cherry tomatoes | 4 tbsp fresh vegetable stock | 4 tsp olive oil |
| 8 ounces mixed mushrooms | small bunch fresh thyme | 1 ounce arugula leaves |
| (such as button, chestnut, | 4 medium eggs, separated | salt and pepper |
| shiitake, oyster) | 4 medium egg whites | fresh thyme sprigs, to garnish |

1. Halve the tomatoes and place them in a saucepan. Wipe the mushrooms with paper towels, trim if necessary, and slice if large. Place in the saucepan.

2. Add the stock and thyme to the pan. Bring to a boil, cover, and simmer for 5–6 minutes until tender. Drain, remove the thyme and discard, and keep the mixture warm.

3. Meanwhile, whisk the egg yolks with 8 tablespoons of water until frothy. In a clean, greasefree bowl, mix the 8 egg whites until stiff and dry.

4. Spoon the egg yolk mixture into the egg whites and, using a metal spoon, fold the whites and yolks into each other until well mixed. Do not knock out too much of the air.

5. For each omelet, brush a small omelet pan with 1 tsp oil and heat until hot. Pour in a quarter of the egg mixture and cook for 4–5 minutes, until the mixture has set.

6. Preheat the broiler and finish cooking the omelet for 2–3 minutes.

7. Transfer the omelet to a warm serving plate. Fill the omelet with a few arugula leaves, and a quarter of the mushroom and tomato mixture. Flip over the top of the omelet, garnish with sprigs of thyme, and serve.

# Broiled Rice & Tuna Bell Peppers

### Serves 4

## INGREDIENTS

⅓ cup wild rice
⅓ cup brown rice
4 assorted medium bell peppers
7 ounce can tuna fish in water,
    drained and flaked

11½ ounce can corn kernels (with
    no added sugar or salt), drained
3½ ounces reduced-fat Cheddar
    cheese, grated
1 bunch fresh basil leaves,
    shredded

2 tbsp dry white bread crumbs
1 tbsp Parmesan cheese,
    freshly grated
salt and pepper
fresh basil leaves, to garnish
crisp salad leaves, to serve

1 Place the wild rice and brown rice in two different saucepans, cover with water, and cook according to the instructions on the packet. Drain well.

2 Meanwhile, preheat the broiler. Halve the bell peppers, remove the seeds and stalks, and arrange the bell peppers on the broiler rack, cut side down. Cook for 5 minutes, turn over, and cook for 4–5 minutes.

3 Transfer the cooked rice to a mixing bowl and add the flaked tuna and drained corn. Gently fold in the grated Cheddar. Mix in the basil leaves and season to taste.

4 Divide the tuna and rice mixture into 8 equal portions. Pile each portion into each cooked bell pepper half. Mix together the bread crumbs and Parmesan cheese and sprinkle the mixture over each bell pepper.

5 Place the bell peppers back under the broiler for 4–5 minutes, until hot and golden-brown. Serve immediately, garnished with fresh basil leaves and accompanied with fresh, crisp salad leaves.

# Baked Potatoes with a Spicy Filling

### Serves 4

**INGREDIENTS**

4 baking potatoes, each about
  10¹⁄₂ ounces
1 tbsp vegetable oil (optional)
14 ounce can garbanzo
  beans, drained

1 tsp ground coriander
1 tsp ground cumin
4 tbsp fresh cilantro, chopped
²⁄₃ cup low-fat unsweetened
  yogurt

salt and pepper
salad, to serve

1 Preheat the oven to 400°F. Scrub the potatoes and pat them dry on absorbent paper towels. Prick them all over with a fork, brush with oil (if using), and season to taste with salt and pepper.

2 Place the potatoes on a cookie sheet and bake for 1–1¼ hours, or until cooked through. Cool for 10 minutes.

3 Meanwhile, mash the garbanzo beans with a fork or potato masher. Stir in the spices and half the

chopped cilantro. Cover and set aside.

4 Halve the cooked potatoes and scoop the flesh into a bowl, keeping the shells intact. Mash the flesh until smooth and gently mix into the garbanzo bean mixture with the yogurt. Season well with salt and pepper.

5 Fill the potato shells with the potato and garbanzo bean mixture and place on a cookie sheet. Return the potatoes to the oven and bake for

10–15 minutes, until heated through.

6 Serve sprinkled with the remaining chopped cilantro and a fresh salad.

## COOK'S TIP

*For an even lower fat version of this recipe, bake the potatoes without oiling them first.*

# Spinach Crêpes with Curried Crab

### Serves 4

**INGREDIENTS**

| | | |
|---|---|---|
| 4 ounces buckwheat flour | FILLING: | 2 tbsp fresh cilantro, chopped |
| 1 large egg, beaten | 12 ounces white crabmeat | |
| 1¼ cups skim milk | 1 tsp mild curry powder | TO SERVE: |
| 4½ ounces frozen spinach, thawed, well-drained, and chopped | 1 tbsp mango chutney | salad greens |
| | 1 tbsp reduced-calorie mayonnaise | lemon wedges |
| 2 tsp vegetable oil | 2 tbsp low-fat unsweetened yogurt | |

1 Sift the flour into a bowl and remove any husks that remain in the strainer.

2 Make a well in the center of the flour and add the egg. Gradually whisk in the milk, then blend in the spinach. Transfer the batter to a pitcher and allow to stand for 30 minutes.

3 To make the filling, mix together all the ingredients, except the cilantro, in a bowl, cover, and chill until required.

4 Whisk the batter. Brush a crêpe pan with a little oil, heat until hot, and pour in enough batter to cover the base thinly. Cook for 1–2 minutes until set, turn over, and cook for 1 minute until golden. Transfer to a warmed plate. Repeat to make 8 pancakes, layering them on the plate with baking parchment.

5 Stir the cilantro into the crab mixture. Fold each pancake into quarters. Open one fold and fill with the crab mixture. Serve warm, with salad greens and lemon wedges.

## VARIATION

*Try lean diced chicken in a light white sauce or peeled shrimp instead of the crab.*

# Crispy Potato Skins

### Serves 4

---

**INGREDIENTS**

4 large baking potatoes
2 tablespoons vegetable oil
4 teaspoons salt
snipped chives, to garnish
$^2/_3$ cup sour cream and
    2 tablespoons chopped
    chives, to serve

BEAN SPROUT SALAD:
$^1/_2$ cup bean sprouts
1 celery stalk, sliced
1 orange, peeled and segmented
1 red eating apple, chopped
$^1/_2$ red bell pepper, chopped
1 tablespoon chopped parsley
1 tablespoon light soy sauce
1 tablespoon clear honey
1 small garlic clove, crushed

BEAN FILLING:
$1^1/_2$ cups canned, mixed
    beans, drained
1 onion, halved and sliced
1 tomato, chopped
2 scallions, chopped
2 teaspoons lemon juice
salt and pepper

---

1 Scrub the potatoes and place them on a cookie sheet. Prick the potatoes all over with a fork and rub the vegetable oil and salt into their skins.

2 Cook in a preheated oven at 400°F for 1 hour, or until they are soft.

3 Cut the potatoes in half lengthwise and scoop out the flesh, leaving a $^1/_2$-inch thick shell. Put the shells, skin side uppermost, in the oven for 10 minutes until crisp.

4 Mix the ingredients for the bean sprout salad in a bowl, tossing in the soy sauce, honey, and garlic to coat.

5 Mix the ingredients for the bean filling in a separate bowl.

6 Mix the sour cream and chives in another bowl.

7 Serve the potato skins hot, with the two salad fillings, garnished with snipped chives, together with the sour cream and chive sauce.

# *Lentil Pâté*

### Serves 4

**INGREDIENTS**

| | | |
|---|---|---|
| 1 tablespoon vegetable oil, plus extra for greasing | ½ teaspoon ground coriander | 2 tablespoons mango chutney |
| 1 onion, chopped | 1¼ cups vegetable stock | 2 tablespoons chopped parsley, plus extra to garnish |
| 2 garlic cloves, crushed | ¾ cup red lentils | salad greens and warm toast, to serve |
| 1 teaspoon garam masala | 1 small egg | |
| | 2 tablespoons milk | |

1 Heat the oil in a large saucepan and sauté the onion and garlic for 2–3 minutes, stirring. Add the spices and cook for a further 30 seconds.

2 Stir in the stock and lentils and bring the mixture to a boil. Reduce the heat and simmer for 20 minutes, until the lentils are cooked and softened. Remove the pan from the heat and drain off any excess moisture.

3 Put the mixture in a food processor and add the egg, milk, mango chutney, and 2 tablespoons parsley. Process until completely smooth.

4 Grease and line the base of a 1-pound loaf pan and spoon the mixture into it, leveling and smoothing the surface. Cover and cook in a preheated oven at 400°F for 40–45 minutes, or until the pâté is firm to the touch.

5 Allow the pâté to cool in the pan for about 20 minutes, then transfer to the refrigerator to cool completely.

6 Turn out the pâté onto a serving plate, slice, and garnish with chopped parsley. Serve with salad greens and toast.

## VARIATION

*Use other spices, such as chili powder or Chinese five-spice powder, to flavor the pâté and add tomato relish or chili relish instead of the mango chutney, if desired.*

# Roasted Vegetables on Muffins

### Serves 4

**INGREDIENTS**

| | | |
|---|---|---|
| 1 red onion, cut into eight pieces | 2 garlic cloves, crushed | 1 tablespoon flour |
| 1 eggplant, halved and sliced | 1 tablespoon chopped thyme | ²⁄₃ cup milk |
| 1 yellow bell pepper, sliced | 2 teaspoons light brown sugar | ¹⁄₃ cup vegetable stock |
| 1 zucchini, sliced | 4 muffins, halved | ³⁄₄ cup grated vegetarian Cheddar cheese |
| 4 tablespoons olive oil | salt and pepper | 1 teaspoon whole-grain mustard |
| 1 tablespoon garlic vinegar | | 3 tablespoons chopped mixed herbs |
| 2 tablespoons vermouth | SAUCE: | |
| | 2 tablespoons butter | |

1 Arrange the vegetables in a shallow ovenproof dish. Mix together the oil, vinegar, vermouth, garlic, thyme, and sugar and pour over the vegetables, tossing well to coat. Marinate for 1 hour.

2 Transfer the vegetables to a cookie sheet. Cook in a preheated oven at 400°F for 20–25 minutes, or until the vegetables have softened.

3 Meanwhile, make the sauce. Melt the butter in a small pan and add the flour. Cook for 1 minute and remove from the heat. Stir in the milk and stock and return the pan to the heat. Bring to a boil, stirring, until thickened. Stir in the cheese, mustard, and mixed herbs and season well.

4 Preheat the broiler. Cut the muffins in half and broil for 2–3 minutes, until golden brown, then remove, and arrange on a warm serving plate.

5 Spoon the roasted vegetables onto the muffins and pour the sauce over the top. Serve at once.

# Sardines with Olives & Tomatoes

### Serves 4

**INGREDIENTS**

| | | |
|---|---|---|
| 12 fresh sardines, gutted and cleaned | 1 tbsp butter | TO GARNISH: |
| fresh basil leaves | 1 tbsp olive oil | plum tomatoes, sliced |
| 4 plum tomatoes | 2 tbsp lemon juice | pitted olives, sliced |
| 8 pitted black olives | salt and pepper | 1 fresh basil sprig |

1 Season the sardines inside and out with salt and pepper to taste. Insert 1–2 basil leaves inside the cavity of each fish. Using a sharp knife, make a few slashes in the body of each fish.

2 Cut the tomatoes and olives into slices and transfer to a large bowl. Tear 4 basil leaves into small pieces and toss together with the tomatoes and olives.

3 Divide the tomato and olive mixture among

4 large sheets of foil, and place 3 sardines on top of each portion.

4 Melt the butter and oil together in a small pan. Stir in the lemon juice and pour the mixture over.

5 Carefully wrap up the fish in the foil. Cook the fish over medium hot coals for 15–20 minutes until the fish is firm and cooked through.

6 Transfer the fish to individual serving plates and remove the foil.

Garnish the fish with slices of tomato and olive, and with a fresh sprig of basil. Serve at once.

## COOK'S TIP

*Slashing the body of the fish helps the flesh to absorb the flavors. It is particularly important if you do not have time to allow the fish to marinate before cooking.*

# Bacon & Scallop Skewers

## Makes 4

### INGREDIENTS

| | | |
|---|---|---|
| grated rind and juice of ¹/₂ lemon | ¹/₂ tsp dried dill | 1 green bell pepper |
| | 12 scallops | 1 yellow bell pepper |
| 4 tbsp sunflower oil | 1 red bell pepper | 6 slices bacon |

1 Mix together the lemon rind and juice, sunflower oil, and dried dill in a nonmetallic dish. Add the scallops and mix thoroughly to coat in the marinade. Marinate for 1–2 hours in the refrigerator.

2 Cut the red, green, and yellow bell peppers in half and seed them. Cut the bell pepper halves into 1-inch pieces and then set aside in a small bowl until required.

3 Carefully stretch the bacon slices with the back of a knife blade, then cut each bacon slice in half.

4 Remove the scallops from the marinade, reserving any excess marinade. Wrap a piece of bacon around each scallop.

5 Thread the bacon-wrapped scallops onto skewers, alternating with the bell pepper pieces.

6 Broil the bacon and scallop skewers over hot coals for about 5 minutes, basting frequently with the lemon and oil marinade.

7 Transfer the bacon and scallop skewers to serving plates and serve at once.

## VARIATION

*Peel 4–8 raw shrimp and add them to the marinade with the scallops. Thread them onto the skewers alternately with the scallops and bell peppers.*

# Salt & Pepper Shrimp

### Serves 4

**INGREDIENTS**

| | | |
|---|---|---|
| 2 tsp salt | 1 pound peeled raw jumbo shrimp | 3 cloves garlic, crushed |
| 1 tsp black pepper | 2 tbsp peanut oil | scallions, sliced, to garnish |
| 2 tsp Szechuan peppercorns | 1 red chili, seeded and finely chopped | shrimp crackers, to serve |
| 1 tsp sugar | 1 tsp freshly grated ginger | |

1 Finely grind the salt, black pepper and Szechuan peppercorns in a mortar with a pestle. Mix the salt and pepper mixture with the sugar and set aside until required.

2 Rinse the shrimp under cold running water and pat dry with absorbent paper towels.

3 Heat the oil in a preheated wok. Add the shrimp, chili, ginger, and garlic and stir-fry for 4–5 minutes, or until the shrimp are cooked through and have changed color.

4 Add the salt and pepper mixture to the wok and stir-fry for 1 minute.

5 Transfer to warm serving bowls and garnish with sliced scallion. Serve immediately with shrimp crackers.

## COOK'S TIP

*Szechuan peppercorns are also known as farchiew. These wild reddish-brown peppercorns from the Szechuan region of China add an aromatic flavor to a dish.*

## COOK'S TIP

*Jumbo shrimp are widely available and are not only colorful and tasty, but they have a meaty texture, too. If cooked jumbo shrimp are used, add them with the salt and pepper mixture in step 4 – if the cooked shrimp are added any earlier they will toughen up and be inedible.*

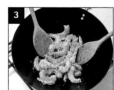

# Herb & Garlic Shrimp

### Serves 4

### INGREDIENTS

| | | |
|---|---|---|
| 12 ounces raw shrimp, peeled | 4 tbsp lemon juice | 2 cloves garlic, chopped |
| 2 tbsp chopped, fresh parsley | 2 tbsp olive oil | salt and pepper |
| | 5 tbsp butter | |

1 Place the prepared shrimp in a shallow, nonmetallic dish with the parsley, lemon juice, and salt and pepper to taste. Stir gently to mix. Marinate the shrimp in the herb mixture for at least 30 minutes in the refrigerator.

2 Heat the oil and butter in a small pan, together with the garlic, until the butter melts. Stir to mix thoroughly.

3 Remove the shrimp from the marinade with a slotted spoon and add them to the pan containing the garlic butter.

Stir the shrimp into the garlic butter until well coated all over, then thread the shrimp onto several skewers.

4 Broil the kabobs over hot coals for 5–10 minutes, turning the skewers occasionally, until the shrimp turn pink and are cooked through. Generously brush the shrimp with the remaining garlic butter during the cooking time.

5 Transfer the herb and garlic shrimp kabobs to warm serving plates. Drizzle over any of the remaining garlic butter and serve at once.

## VARIATION

*If raw shrimp are unavailable, use cooked shrimp, but reduce the cooking time. Small cooked shrimp can also be cooked in a foil packet instead of on the skewers. Marinate and toss the cooked shrimp in the garlic butter, wrap in foil, and cook for about 5 minutes, shaking the packets once or twice.*

# Meat & Poultry

The increased interest in healthy eating means
that most supermarkets and butchers now offer
special cuts of lean meat. Although they are often
slightly more expensive than standard cuts, it is
worth buying this meat and spending a little extra
time cooking it carefully to enhance the flavor.
You will not need to buy as much if you combine
the meat with thoughtfully chosen
and prepared vegetables.

Look out, too, for packs of low- or reduced-fat
ground meat in your local supermarket, and include
it in burgers, serve it in a flavor-filled sauce
with rice, or your favorite pasta.

Cut any visible fat from beef and pork before
you cook it. Chicken and turkey are lower in fat
than red meats, and you can make them even
healthier by removing the skin. Duck is a rich meat
with a distinctive flavor, and you need only a small
amount to create apparently extravagant,
flavorsome dishes that are healthy, too.

# Pan-Cooked Pork with Fennel & Aniseed

### Serves 4

## INGREDIENTS

4 lean pork chops,
    4$\frac{1}{2}$ ounces each
$\frac{1}{3}$ cup brown rice, cooked
1 tsp orange rind, grated
4 scallions, trimmed and
    finely chopped

$\frac{1}{2}$ tsp aniseed
1 tbsp olive oil
1 fennel bulb, trimmed and
    thinly sliced
2 cups unsweetened orange juice
1 tbsp cornstarch

2 tbsp Pernod
salt and pepper
fennel fronds, to garnish
cooked vegetables, to serve

1 Trim away any excess fat from the pork chops. Using a small, sharp knife, make a slit in the center of each chop to create a pocket.

2 Mix the cooked rice, orange rind, scallions, salt and pepper to taste, and aniseed together in a bowl. Press the mixture into the pocket of each pork chop, then press gently to seal together.

3 Heat the oil in a skillet and fry the pork chops on each side for 2–3 minutes, until golden.

4 Add the sliced fennel and orange juice to the skillet, bring to a boil, and simmer for 15–20 minutes or until the meat is tender and cooked through. Remove the pork and fennel with a slotted spoon and transfer to a warm serving plate.

5 Blend the cornstarch and Pernod together in a small bowl. Add the cornstarch mixture to the pan and stir into the pan juices. Cook for 2–3 minutes, stirring, until the sauce thickens.

6 Pour the Pernod sauce over the pork chops, garnish with fennel fronds, and serve with a selection of cooked vegetables, if you wish.

# Pork Stroganoff

### Serves 4

**INGREDIENTS**

12 ounces lean pork tenderloin
1 tbsp vegetable oil
1 medium onion, chopped
2 garlic cloves, crushed
1 ounce all-purpose flour
2 tbsp tomato paste
1³/₄ cups fresh chicken or
    vegetable stock

4¹/₂ ounces button
    mushrooms, sliced
1 large green bell pepper, seeded
    and diced
¹/₂ tsp ground nutmeg
4 tbsp low-fat unsweetened
    yogurt, plus extra to serve
salt and pepper

white rice, freshly boiled,
    to serve

TO GARNISH:
chopped fresh parsley
ground nutmeg

1 Using a sharp knife, trim away any excess fat and silver skin from the pork, then cut the meat into slices ¹/₂ inch thick.

2 Heat the oil in a large skillet and gently fry the pork, onion, and garlic for 4–5 minutes until lightly browned.

3 Stir in the flour and tomato paste, pour in the stock, and stir to mix thoroughly.

4 Add the mushrooms, bell pepper, seasoning, and nutmeg. Bring to a boil, cover, and simmer for 20 minutes, until the pork is tender and cooked through.

5 Remove the saucepan from the heat and stir in the yogurt.

6 Serve the pork and sauce on a bed of rice, garnished with chopped parsley. Spoon the extra yogurt on top of the pork

and mushrooms and dust with ground nutmeg.

## COOK'S TIP

*You can buy ready-made meat, vegetable, and fish stocks from leading supermarkets. Although more expensive, they are better nutritionally than stock cubes, which are high in salt and artificial flavorings. Homemade stock is best of all.*

# *Pan-Cooked Pork Medallions with Apples & Cider*

### Serves 4

**INGREDIENTS**

8 lean pork medallions, about
   1¾ ounces each
2 tsp vegetable oil
1 medium onion, finely sliced
1 tsp superfine sugar
1 tsp dried sage

⅔ cup hard cider
⅔ cup fresh chicken or
   vegetable stock
1 green-skinned apple
1 red-skinned apple
1 tbsp lemon juice

salt and pepper
fresh sage leaves, to garnish
freshly cooked vegetables,
   to serve

1 Discard the string from the pork and trim away any excess fat. Re-tie with clean string and set aside until required.

2 Heat the oil in a skillet and gently sauté the onion for 5 minutes, until softened. Add the sugar and cook for 3–4 minutes until golden.

3 Add the pork to the pan and cook for 2 minutes on each side, until browned. Add the sage, cider, and stock. Bring to a boil and then simmer for 20 minutes.

4 Meanwhile, core and cut each apple into 8 wedges. Toss the apple wedges in lemon juice so that they do not discolor and turn brown.

5 Add the apples to the pork and mix gently. Season and cook for 3–4 minutes, until tender.

6 Remove the string from the pork and serve immediately, garnished with fresh sage and accompanied with freshly cooked vegetables.

## COOK'S TIP

*If pork medallions are not available, buy 14 ounces pork tenderloin and slice it into evenly-sized medallions yourself.*

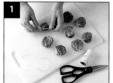

# Red Roast Pork with Bell Peppers

### Serves 4

**INGREDIENTS**

| | | |
|---|---|---|
| 1 pound lean pork tenderloin | 1-inch piece fresh ginger root, finely chopped | 4 tbsp superfine sugar |
| 6 tbsp dark soy sauce | 1 large red bell pepper | 2 tbsp red wine vinegar |
| 2 tbsp dry sherry | 1 large yellow bell pepper | |
| 1 tsp five-spice powder | 1 large orange bell pepper | TO GARNISH: |
| 2 garlic cloves, crushed | | scallions, shredded |
| | | fresh chives, snipped |

1 Trim away any excess fat and silver skin from the pork and place in a shallow dish.

2 Mix together the soy sauce, sherry, five-spice powder, garlic, and ginger. Spoon over the pork, cover, and marinate in the refrigerator for at least 1 hour.

3 Preheat the oven to 375°F. Drain the pork, reserving the marinade. Place the pork on a roasting rack over a roasting pan. Cook in the oven, occasionally basting with the marinade, for 1 hour or until cooked through.

4 Meanwhile, halve and seed the bell peppers. Cut each bell pepper half into 3 equal portions. Arrange them on a cookie sheet and bake alongside the pork for the last 30 minutes of cooking time.

5 Place the superfine sugar and vinegar in a small saucepan and heat gently over a low heat until the sugar has completely dissolved. Bring to a boil and simmer for 3–4 minutes, until syrupy.

6 As soon as the pork is cooked, remove from the oven and brush with the sugar syrup. Allow to stand for 5 minutes, then slice, and arrange on a warm platter with the bell peppers. Garnish and serve.

# Pork with Ratatouille Sauce

### Serves 4

**INGREDIENTS**

4 lean, boneless pork chops,
   about 4$\frac{1}{2}$ ounces each
1 tsp dried mixed herbs
salt and pepper
baked potatoes, to serve

SAUCE:
1 medium onion
1 garlic clove
1 small green bell pepper
1 small yellow bell pepper
1 medium zucchini

3$\frac{1}{2}$ ounces button mushrooms
14 ounce can chopped tomatoes
2 tbsp tomato paste
1 tsp dried mixed herbs
1 tsp superfine sugar

1 To make the sauce, peel and chop the onion and garlic. Seed and dice the bell peppers. Trim and dice the zucchini. Wipe and halve the mushrooms.

2 Place all of the vegetables in a saucepan and stir in the chopped tomatoes and tomato paste. Add the dried herbs, sugar, and plenty of seasoning. Bring to a boil, cover, and simmer for 20 minutes.

3 Meanwhile, preheat the broiler. Trim away any excess fat from the chops, then season on both sides, and rub in the dried mixed herbs. Cook the chops for 5 minutes, then turn over, and cook for a further 6–7 minutes until cooked through.

4 Drain the pork chops on absorbent paper towels and serve accompanied with the sauce and baked potatoes, if wished.

## COOK'S TIP

*This vegetable sauce could be served with any other broiled or baked meat or fish. It would also make an excellent alternative filling for the Spinach Crêpes on page 64.*

# Beef & Orange Curry

### Serves 4

## INGREDIENTS

1 tbsp vegetable oil
8 ounces shallots, halved
2 garlic cloves, crushed
1 pound lean rump or sirloin
  beef, trimmed and cut
  into ³/₄ inch cubes
3 tbsp curry paste

2 cups fresh beef stock
4 medium oranges
2 tsp cornstarch
salt and pepper
2 tbsp fresh cilantro, chopped,
  to garnish
Basmati rice, freshly boiled, to serve

RAITA:
¹/₂ cucumber, finely diced
3 tbsp fresh mint, chopped
²/₃ cup low-fat unsweetened
  yogurt

1 Heat the oil in a large saucepan. Gently fry the shallots, garlic, and the cubes of beef for 5 minutes, stirring occasionally, until the beef is evenly browned all over.

2 Blend together the curry paste and stock. Add the mixture to the beef and stir to mix. Bring to a boil, cover, and simmer for 1 hour, or until the meat is tender.

3 Grate the rind of one orange. Extract the juice from the orange and from a second orange. Peel the two remaining oranges, removing as much pith as possible. Slice between each segment and remove the flesh.

4 Blend the cornstarch with the orange juice. At the end of the cooking time, stir the orange rind into the beef, along with the orange and cornstarch mixture. Bring to a boil and simmer, stirring, for 3–4 minutes, until the sauce thickens. Season and stir in the orange segments.

5 To make the raita, mix the cucumber with the mint, and stir in the yogurt. Season to taste.

6 Garnish the curry and serve with rice and the cucumber raita.

# Pan-Seared Beef with Ginger, Pineapple, & Chili

### Serves 4

**INGREDIENTS**

4 lean beef steaks (such as rump,
    sirloin, or fillet), 3½ ounces
    each
2 tbsp ginger wine
1-inch piece fresh ginger root,
    finely chopped
1 garlic clove, crushed

1 tsp ground chili
1 tsp vegetable oil
salt and pepper
red chili strips, to garnish

TO SERVE:
freshly cooked noodles
2 scallions, shredded

RELISH:
8 ounces fresh pineapple
1 small red bell pepper
1 red chili
2 tbsp light soy sauce
1 piece preserved ginger in
    syrup, drained and chopped

1 Trim any excess fat from the beef. Using a meat mallet or covered rolling pin, pound the steaks until ½ inch thick. Season on both sides and place in a shallow dish.

2 Mix the ginger wine, ginger root, garlic, and chili and pour over the meat. Cover and chill for 30 minutes.

3 Meanwhile, make the relish. Peel and finely chop the pineapple and place it in a bowl. Halve, seed, and finely chop the bell pepper and chili. Stir into the pineapple, together with the soy sauce and preserved ginger. Cover and chill until required.

4 Brush a ridged skillet with the oil and heat until very hot. Drain the beef and add to the pan, pressing down to seal. Lower the heat and cook for 5 minutes. Turn the steaks over and cook for 5 minutes.

5 Drain the steaks on paper towels and transfer to serving plates. Garnish with chili strips, and serve with noodles, scallions, and the relish.

# Beef & Tomato Gratin

### Serves 4

## INGREDIENTS

| | | |
|---|---|---|
| 12 ounces lean ground beef | 2 large tomatoes, thinly sliced | 1 medium egg yolk |
| 1 large onion, finely chopped | 4 medium zucchini, thinly sliced | 4 tbsp Parmesan cheese, |
| 1 tsp dried mixed herbs | 2 tbsp cornstarch | freshly grated |
| 1 tbsp all-purpose flour | 1¼ cups skim milk | salt and pepper |
| 1¼ cups beef stock | ⅔ cup low-fat unsweetened | |
| 1 tbsp tomato paste | yogurt | TO SERVE: |
| | | crusty bread |
| | | steamed vegetables |

1 Preheat the oven to 375°F. In a large pan, dry-fry the beef and onion for 4–5 minutes until browned.

2 Stir in the herbs, flour, stock, and tomato paste, and season. Bring to a boil and simmer for 30 minutes until thickened.

3 Transfer the beef mixture to an ovenproof gratin dish.

Cover with a layer of the sliced tomatoes and then add a layer of sliced zucchini. Set aside until required.

4 Blend the cornstarch with a little milk in a small bowl. Pour the remaining milk into a saucepan and bring to a boil. Add the cornstarch mixture and cook, stirring, for 1–2 minutes, until thickened. Remove from the heat and beat in the

yogurt and egg yolk. Season with salt and pepper to taste.

5 Place the dish on a cookie sheet. Spread the white sauce over the layer of zucchini and sprinkle with grated Parmesan. Bake in the oven for 25–30 minutes, until golden brown. Serve with lots of fresh crusty bread and steamed vegetables.

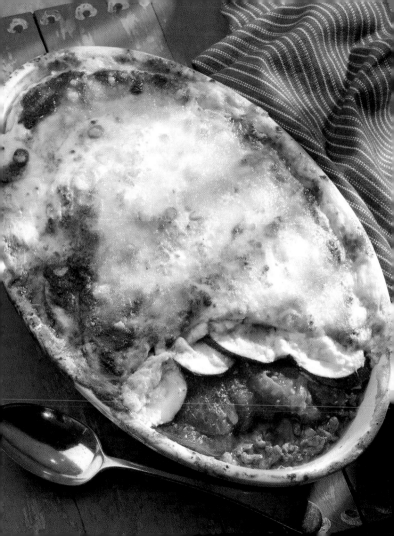

# Sweet & Sour Venison Stir-Fry

### Serves 4

## INGREDIENTS

1 bunch scallions
1 red bell pepper
3½ ounces snow peas
3½ ounces baby corn cobs
12 ounces lean venison steak
1 tbsp vegetable oil
1 clove garlic, crushed

1-inch piece fresh ginger root,
  finely chopped
3 tbsp light soy sauce, plus extra
  for serving
1 tbsp white wine vinegar
2 tbsp dry sherry
2 tsp clear honey

8 ounce can pineapple pieces in
  natural juice, drained
1 ounce bean sprouts
freshly cooked rice, to serve

1 Trim the scallions and cut into 1-inch pieces. Halve and seed the bell pepper and cut it into 1-inch pieces. Top and tail the snow peas and trim the baby corn cobs.

2 Using a sharp knife, trim the excess fat from the meat and cut it into thin strips. Heat the oil in a large skillet or preheated wok until hot and stir-fry the meat, garlic, and ginger for 5 minutes.

3 Add the prepared scallion, bell pepper, snow peas, and baby corn cobs to the pan, then add the soy sauce, vinegar, sherry, and honey. Stir-fry for a further 5 minutes, keeping the heat high.

4 Carefully stir in the pineapple pieces and bean sprouts and cook for a further 1–2 minutes to heat through. Serve with freshly cooked rice and extra soy sauce for dipping.

## VARIATION

*For a quick and nutritious meal-in-one, cook 8 ounces egg noodles in boiling water for 3–4 minutes. Drain well and add to the pan in step 4, together with the pineapple and bean sprouts. Stir well to mix. You will have to add an extra 2 tbsp soy sauce with the pineapple and bean sprouts so that the stir-fry does not dry out.*

# Venison & Garlic Mash

### Serves 4

**INGREDIENTS**

8 medallions of venison,
2³/₄ ounces each
1 tbsp vegetable oil
1 red onion, chopped
²/₃ cup fresh beef stock
²/₃ cup red wine

3 tbsp redcurrant jelly
3¹/₂ ounces dried, pitted prunes
2 tsp cornstarch
2 tbsp brandy
salt and pepper

GARLIC MASH:
2 pounds potatoes, peeled and
diced
¹/₂ tsp garlic paste
2 tbsp low-fat unsweetened
yogurt
4 tbsp fresh parsley, chopped

1 Trim off any excess fat from the meat and season with salt and pepper on both sides.

2 Heat the oil in a pan and fry the medallions with the onions on a high heat for 2 minutes on each side until browned all over.

3 Lower the heat and pour in the stock and wine. Add the redcurrant jelly and prunes and stir until the jelly melts. Bring to a boil, cover, and simmer for 10 minutes until cooked through.

4 To make the garlic mash, place the potatoes in a pan and add enough water to cover. Bring to a boil and cook for 8–10 minutes, until tender. Drain.

5 Mash the potatoes. Add the garlic paste, yogurt, and parsley and blend thoroughly. Season, set aside, and keep warm.

6 Remove the medallions from the skillet with a slotted spoon and keep warm.

7 Blend the cornstarch with the brandy in a small bowl and add to the pan juices. Heat, stirring, until thickened. Season with salt and pepper to taste.

8 Transfer the venison to serving plates and serve with the redcurrant and prune sauce and garlic mash.

# Venison Meatballs with Sherried Kumquat Sauce

### Serves 4

### INGREDIENTS

1 pound lean ground venison
1 small leek, finely chopped
1 medium carrot, finely grated
¹/₂ tsp ground nutmeg
1 medium egg white, lightly
 beaten

salt and pepper

TO SERVE:
freshly cooked pasta or noodles
freshly cooked vegetables

SAUCE:
3¹/₂ ounces kumquats
¹/₂ ounce superfine sugar
²/₃ cup water
4 tbsp dry sherry
1 tsp cornstarch

1 Place the venison in a mixing bowl, together with the leek, carrot, seasoning, and nutmeg. Add the egg white and bind the ingredients together with your hands until the mixture is well molded and firm.

2 Divide the mixture into 16 equal portions. Using your fingers, form each portion into a small, round ball.

3 Bring a large saucepan of water to a boil. Arrange the meatballs on a layer of baking parchment in a steamer or large strainer and place over the boiling water. Cover and steam for 10 minutes, until cooked through.

4 Meanwhile, make the sauce. Wash and thinly slice the kumquats. Place them in a saucepan with the sugar and water and

bring to a boil. Simmer for 2–3 minutes until tender.

5 Blend the sherry and cornstarch together and add to the pan. Heat through, stirring, until the sauce thickens. Season.

6 Drain the meatballs and transfer to a serving plate. Spoon the sauce on top and serve with pasta and vegetables, if wished.

# Fruity Lamb Casserole

### Serves 4

## INGREDIENTS

1 pound lean lamb, trimmed and
   cut into 1-inch cubes
1 tsp ground cinnamon
1 tsp ground coriander
1 tsp ground cumin
2 tsp olive oil

1 medium red onion, finely
   chopped
1 garlic clove, crushed
14 ounce can chopped tomatoes
2 tbsp tomato paste
4¹⁄₂ ounces dried apricots

1 tsp superfine sugar
1¹⁄₄ cups vegetable stock
salt and pepper
1 small bunch fresh cilantro,
   to garnish
brown rice, steamed couscous, or
   bulgar wheat, to serve

1 Preheat the oven to 350°F. Place the meat in a bowl and add the cinnamon, coriander, cumin, and oil. Mix so that the lamb is well coated in the spices.

2 Heat a nonstick skillet for a few seconds until it is hot, then add the spiced lamb. Reduce the heat and cook for 4–5 minutes, stirring, until browned all over. Using a slotted spoon, remove the lamb and transfer to a large casserole.

3 In the same skillet, cook the onion, garlic, tomatoes, and tomato paste for 5 minutes. Season to taste. Stir in the apricots and sugar, add the stock, and bring to a boil.

4 Spoon the sauce over the lamb and mix well. Cover and cook in the oven for 1 hour, removing the lid for the last 10 minutes.

5 Roughly chop the cilantro and sprinkle over the casserole to garnish. Serve with boiled brown rice, steamed couscous, or bulgar wheat.

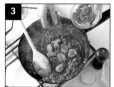

# Lamb, Bell Pepper, & Couscous

### Serves 4

## INGREDIENTS

2 medium red onions, sliced
juice of 1 lemon
1 large red bell pepper, seeded
    and thickly sliced
1 large green bell pepper, seeded
    and thickly sliced
1 large orange bell pepper,
    seeded and thickly sliced

pinch of saffron strands
cinnamon stick, broken
1 tbsp clear honey
1¼ cups vegetable stock
2 tsp olive oil
12 ounces lean lamb fillet,
    trimmed and sliced
1 tsp harissa paste

7 ounce can chopped tomatoes
15 ounce can garbanzo
    beans, drained
12 ounces couscous
2 tsp ground cinnamon
salt and pepper

1 Toss the red onions in the lemon juice and put in a pan. Add the bell peppers, saffron, cinnamon stick, and honey. Pour in the vegetable stock, bring to a boil, cover, and leave to simmer for 5 minutes.

2 Meanwhile, heat the olive oil in a skillet and gently fry the lamb for 3–4 minutes, until it is well browned all over.

3 Using a slotted spoon, drain the lamb and transfer it to the pan with the onions and peppers. Season and stir in the harissa paste, tomatoes, and garbanzo beans. Mix well, bring back to a boil, and simmer, uncovered, for 20 minutes.

4 Meanwhile, soak the couscous, following the instructions on the packet. Bring a saucepan of

water to a boil. Transfer the couscous to a steamer or strainer lined with cheesecloth and place over the pan of boiling water. Cover and steam as directed.

5 Transfer the couscous to a warm serving platter and dust with ground cinnamon. Discard the cinnamon stick and serve the stew with the couscous.

# Hot Pot Chops

### Serves 4

**INGREDIENTS**

4 lean, boned lamb leg steaks,
about 4½ ounces each
1 small onion, thinly sliced
1 medium carrot, thinly sliced

1 medium potato, thinly sliced
1 tsp olive oil
1 tsp dried rosemary
salt and pepper

fresh rosemary, to garnish
freshly steamed green
vegetables, to serve

1 Preheat the oven to 350°F. Using a sharp knife, trim any excess fat from the lamb steaks.

2 Season both sides of the steaks well with salt and pepper and arrange them on a cookie sheet or ovenproof dish.

3 Alternate layers of sliced onion, carrot, and potato on top of each lamb steak.

4 Brush the tops of the potato lightly with oil, season well with salt and pepper to taste, and then sprinkle with a little dried rosemary.

5 Bake the hot pot chops in the oven for about 25–30 minutes, until the lamb is tender and cooked through.

6 Drain the lamb on absorbent paper towels and transfer to a warmed serving plate.

7 Garnish with fresh rosemary and serve with a selection of green vegetables.

## VARIATION

*This recipe would work equally well with boneless chicken breasts. Pound the chicken slightly with a meat mallet or covered rolling pin so that the pieces are the same thickness throughout.*

# *Minty Lamb Burgers*

### Serves 4

## INGREDIENTS

12 ounces lean lamb, ground
1 medium onion, finely chopped
4 tbsp dry whole wheat
    bread crumbs
2 tbsp mint jelly
salt and pepper

TO SERVE:
4 whole wheat rolls, split
2 large tomatoes, sliced
small piece of cucumber, sliced
lettuce leaves

RELISH:
4 tbsp low-fat unsweetened yogurt
1 tbsp mint jelly, softened
2-inch piece of cucumber,
    finely diced
1 tbsp fresh mint, chopped

1 Place the lamb in a large bowl and mix in the onion, bread crumbs, and jelly. Season well, then mold the ingredients together with your hands to form a firm mixture.

2 Divide the mixture into 4 and shape each portion into a round measuring 4 inches across. Place the rounds on a plate lined with baking parchment and leave to chill for 30 minutes.

3 Preheat the broiler. Line a broiler rack with baking parchment, securing the ends under the rack, and place the burgers on top. Cook for 8 minutes, then turn over the burgers, and cook for a further 7 minutes, or until completely cooked through.

4 Meanwhile, make the relish. Mix together the unsweetened yogurt, mint jelly, cucumber, and freshly chopped mint in a bowl. Cover and chill in the refrigerator until it is required.

5 Drain the burgers on absorbent paper towels. Serve the burgers inside the rolls with sliced tomatoes, cucumber, lettuce, and relish.

# Jerk Chicken

### Serves 4

### INGREDIENTS

4 chicken portions
1 bunch scallions, trimmed
1–2 Scotch Bonnet chiles, seeded
1 garlic clove

2-inch piece fresh ginger root,
    peeled and roughly chopped
$\frac{1}{2}$ tsp dried thyme
$\frac{1}{2}$ tsp paprika
$\frac{1}{4}$ tsp ground allspice

pinch ground cinnamon
pinch ground cloves
4 tbsp white wine vinegar
3 tbsp light soy sauce
pepper

1 Rinse the chicken portions and pat them dry on absorbent paper towels. Place them in a shallow dish.

2 Place the scallions, chiles, garlic, ginger, thyme, paprika, allspice, cinnamon, cloves, white wine vinegar, light soy sauce, and pepper to taste in a food processor and process to make a smooth mixture.

3 Pour the spicy mixture over the chicken. Turn the chicken portions so that they are well coated in the marinade. Transfer the chicken to the refrigerator and leave to marinate for up to 24 hours.

4 Remove the chicken from the marinade and broil over medium hot coals for 30 minutes, turning the chicken over and basting occasionally with any remaining marinade, until it is cooked through.

5 Transfer the chicken portions to individual serving plates and serve at once.

## COOK'S TIP

*As Jamaican cuisine becomes increasingly popular, you will find jars of ready-made jerk marinade, which you can use when time is short. Allow the chicken to marinate for as long as possible for maximum flavor.*

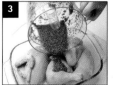

# *Favorite Barbecued Chicken*

### Serves 4

#### INGREDIENTS

| | | |
|---|---|---|
| 8 chicken wings or 1 chicken cut into 8 portions | 3 tbsp brown fruity ketchup | 1 tbsp olive oil |
| 3 tbsp tomato paste | 1 tbsp white wine vinegar | 1 clove garlic, crushed (optional) |
| | 1 tbsp clear honey | salad greens, to serve |

1 Remove the skin from the chicken if you want to reduce the fat in the dish.

2 To make the barbecue glaze, place the tomato paste, brown fruity ketchup, white wine vinegar, honey, oil, and garlic in a small bowl. Stir all of the ingredients together until they are thoroughly blended.

3 Brush the barbecue glaze over the chicken and broil over hot coals for 15–20 minutes. Turn the chicken portions over occasionally and baste frequently with the barbecue glaze. If the chicken begins to blacken before it is cooked thoroughly, raise the barbecue rack if possible or move the chicken to a cooler part of the barbecue in order to slow down the cooking process.

4 Transfer the barbecued chicken to warm serving plates and serve immediately with fresh salad greens.

## VARIATION

*This barbecue glaze also makes a very good baste to brush over pork chops.*

## COOK'S TIP

*When poultry is cooked over a very hot barbecue the heat immediately seals in all of the juices, leaving the meat succulent. For this reason you must make sure that the coals are hot enough before starting to cook.*

# *Indian Charred Chicken*

### Serves 4

**INGREDIENTS**

| | | |
|---|---|---|
| 4 skinless, boneless chicken breasts | $^1/_2$ tsp ground cumin | CUCUMBER RAITA: |
| 2 tbsp curry paste | | $^1/_4$ cucumber |
| 1 tbsp sunflower oil | TO SERVE: | salt |
| 1 tbsp light brown sugar | naan bread | $^2/_3$ cup unsweetened yogurt |
| 1 tsp ground ginger | salad greens | $^1/_4$ tsp chili powder |

1 Place the chicken breasts between 2 sheets of baking parchment or plastic wrap. Pound them with the flat side of a meat mallet or with a rolling pin to flatten them.

2 Mix together the curry paste, oil, sugar, ginger, and cumin in a small bowl. Spread the mixture over both sides of the chicken and set aside until required.

3 To make the raita, peel the cucumber and scoop out the seeds with a spoon. Grate the cucumber flesh, sprinkle with salt, place in a strainer, and let stand for 10 minutes. Rinse off the salt and squeeze out any moisture by pressing the cucumber with the base of a glass or back of a spoon.

4 To make the raita, mix the cucumber with the yogurt and stir in the chili powder. Chill until required.

5 Transfer the chicken breasts to an oiled rack and broil over hot coals for about 10 minutes, turning once.

6 Warm the naan bread at the side of the barbecue. Serve the chicken with the naan bread and raita, and accompanied with fresh salad greens.

## COOK'S TIP

*Flattening the chicken breasts makes them thinner, so that they cook more quickly.*

# Tricolor Chicken & Spinach Lasagne

## Serves 4

### INGREDIENTS

12 ounces frozen chopped
  spinach, thawed and drained
$\frac{1}{2}$ tsp ground nutmeg
1 pound lean, cooked chicken,
  skinned and diced
4 sheets precooked lasagne verde
1$\frac{1}{2}$ tbsp cornstarch
1$\frac{3}{4}$ cups skim milk

4 tbsp Parmesan cheese,
  freshly grated
salt and pepper

TOMATO SAUCE:
14 ounce can chopped tomatoes
1 medium onion, finely chopped
1 garlic clove, crushed

$\frac{2}{3}$ cup white wine
3 tbsp tomato paste
1 tsp dried oregano

1 Preheat the oven to 400°F. To make the tomato sauce, place the tomatoes in a saucepan and stir in the onion, garlic, wine, tomato paste, and oregano. Bring to a boil and simmer for 20 minutes, until thick. Season well.

2 Drain the spinach again and spread it out on absorbent paper towels to make sure that as much water as possible has been removed. Layer the spinach in the base of an ovenproof baking dish. Sprinkle with nutmeg and season.

3 Arrange the chicken over the spinach, and spoon the tomato sauce on top. Arrange the sheets of lasagne over the sauce.

4 Blend the cornstarch with a little of the milk to make a paste. Pour the remaining milk into a pan and stir in the cornstarch paste. Heat for 2–3 minutes, stirring, until the sauce thickens. Season.

5 Spoon the sauce over the lasagne and transfer the dish to a cookie sheet. Sprinkle the grated cheese over the sauce and bake in the oven for 25 minutes, until golden-brown.

# Chicken Pasta Bake with Fennel & Raisins

### Serves 4

## INGREDIENTS

2 bulbs fennel
2 medium red onions, finely
    shredded
1 tbsp lemon juice
4¹/₂ ounces button mushrooms
1 tbsp olive oil

8 ounces penne (pasta quills)
¹/₃ cup raisins
8 ounces lean, boneless cooked
    chicken, skinned and shredded
13 ounces low-fat soft cheese
    with garlic and herbs

4¹/₂ ounces low-fat mozzarella
    cheese, thinly sliced
2 tbsp Parmesan cheese, grated
salt and pepper

1 Preheat the oven to 400°F. Trim the fennel and reserve the green fronds for garnishing. Slice the fennel bulbs thinly. Coat the onion in the lemon juice. Quarter the mushrooms.

2 Heat the oil in a large skillet and sauté the fennel, onion, and mushrooms for 4–5 minutes, stirring, until just softened. Season and transfer the vegetable mixture to a large bowl.

3 Bring a pan of lightly salted water to a boil and cook the penne according to the instructions on the packet until "al dente". Drain and mix the pasta with the vegetables.

4 Stir the raisins and chicken into the pasta mixture. Soften the soft cheese by beating it, then mix into the pasta and chicken—the heat from the pasta should make the cheese melt slightly.

5 Put the mixture into an ovenproof dish and transfer to a cookie sheet. Arrange the mozzarella over the top and sprinkle with the grated Parmesan. Bake in the oven for 20–25 minutes, until golden. Garnish with chopped fennel fronds and serve hot.

# Baked Southern-Style Chicken & Fries

### Serves 4

### INGREDIENTS

| | | |
|---|---|---|
| 4 baking potatoes, 8 ounces each | ¹/₂ tsp dried thyme | salt and pepper |
| 1 tbsp sunflower oil | 8 chicken drumsticks, skin | |
| 2 tsp coarse sea salt | removed | TO SERVE: |
| 2 tbsp all-purpose flour | 1 medium egg, beaten | low-fat coleslaw salad |
| pinch of cayenne pepper | 2 tbsp cold water | corn relish |
| ¹/₂ tsp paprika | 6 tbsp dry white bread crumbs | |

1 Preheat the oven to 400°F. Wash and scrub the potatoes and cut each into 8 equal portions. Place in a clean plastic bag and add the oil. Seal and shake the bag well to coat.

2 Arrange the potato wedges, skin side down, on a nonstick cookie sheet, sprinkle with the sea salt, and bake in the oven for 30–35 minutes, until they are tender and golden.

3 Meanwhile, mix the flour, cayenne pepper,

paprika, thyme, and salt and pepper to taste on a plate. Press the chicken drumsticks into the seasoned flour to coat.

4 On one plate mix together the egg and water. On another plate sprinkle the bread crumbs. Dip the chicken drumsticks first in the egg, and then in the bread crumbs. Place on a nonstick cookie sheet.

5 Bake the chicken drumsticks alongside the potato wedges for

30 minutes, turning after 15 minutes, until they are tender and cooked through.

6 Drain the potato wedges thoroughly on absorbent paper towels to remove any excess fat. Serve with the chicken, accompanied with low-fat coleslaw and corn relish, if desired.

# Lime Chicken Skewers with Mango Salsa

## Serves 4

### INGREDIENTS

4 boneless, skinless chicken
  breasts, about 4½ ounces each
3 tbsp lime marmalade
1 tsp white wine vinegar
½ tsp lime rind, finely grated
1 tbsp lime juice

salt and pepper

TO SERVE:
lime wedges
boiled white rice, sprinkled with
  chili powder

SALSA:
1 small mango
1 small red onion
1 tbsp lime juice
1 tbsp chopped fresh cilantro

1 Slice the chicken breasts into thin pieces and thread onto 8 skewers so that the meat forms an S-shape down each skewer.

2 Preheat the broiler. Arrange the chicken kabobs on the broiler rack. Mix together the marmalade, vinegar, lime rind, and juice. Season with salt and pepper to taste. Brush the dressing generously over the chicken and broil for 5 minutes. Turn the chicken over, brush with the dressing again, and broil for a further 4-5 minutes, until the chicken is cooked through.

3 Meanwhile, prepare the salsa. Peel the mango and slice the flesh off the smooth, central pit, using a sharp knife. Dice the flesh into small pieces and place in a small bowl.

4 Peel and finely chop the onion and mix into the mango, together with the lime juice and chopped cilantro. Season with salt and pepper, cover, and chill until it is required.

5 Transfer the chicken kabobs to serving plates and serve with the salsa, accompanied with wedges of lime and boiled rice sprinkled with a little chili powder.

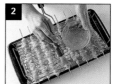

# *Sage Chicken & Rice*

### Serves 4

**INGREDIENTS**

1 large onion, chopped
1 garlic clove, crushed
2 celery stalks, sliced
2 carrots, diced
2 sprigs fresh sage
1¼ cups chicken stock
12 ounces boneless, skinless
    chicken breasts

1⅓ cups mixed brown and wild
    rice
14 ounce can chopped tomatoes
dash of Tabasco sauce
2 medium zucchini, trimmed and
    thinly sliced
3½ ounces lean ham, diced
salt and pepper

fresh sage, to garnish

TO SERVE:
salad greens
crusty bread

1 Place the onion, garlic, celery, carrots, and sprigs of fresh sage in a large saucepan and pour in the chicken stock. Bring to a boil, cover the pan, and simmer for 5 minutes.

2 Cut the chicken into 1-inch cubes. Add the chicken to the pan containing the vegetables, cover the pan, and continue to cook for a further 5 minutes.

3 Stir in the rice and chopped tomatoes. Add a dash of Tabasco sauce to taste and season with salt and pepper to taste. Bring to a boil, cover, and simmer for 25 minutes.

4 Stir in the sliced zucchini and diced ham and continue to cook, uncovered, for a further 10 minutes, stirring occasionally, until the rice is just tender.

5 Remove and discard the sprigs of sage. Garnish with a few sage leaves and serve with a salad greens and fresh crusty bread.

## COOK'S TIP

*If you do not have fresh sage, use 1 tsp of dried sage in step 1.*

# Chili Chicken & Corn Meatballs

### Serves 4

## INGREDIENTS

1 pound lean ground chicken

4 scallions, trimmed and finely chopped, plus extra to garnish

1 small red chili, seeded and finely chopped

1-inch piece fresh ginger root, finely chopped

3½ ounce can corn (no added sugar or salt), drained

salt and white pepper

boiled jasmine rice, to serve

SAUCE:

²⁄₃ cup fresh chicken stock

3½ ounces cubed pineapple in natural juice, drained, with 4 tbsp reserved juice

1 medium carrot, cut into thin strips

1 small red bell pepper, seeded and diced, plus extra to garnish

1 small green bell pepper, seeded and diced

1 tbsp light soy sauce

2 tbsp rice vinegar

1 tbsp superfine sugar

1 tbsp tomato paste

2 tsp cornstarch mixed to a paste with 4 tsp cold water

1 To make the meatballs, place the chicken in a bowl and add the scallions, chili, ginger, seasoning, and corn. Mix with your hands.

2 Divide the mixture into 16 portions and form each into a ball. Bring a pan of water to a boil. Put the meatballs on a sheet of parchment in a steamer, set over the water, cover, and steam for 10–12 minutes.

3 To make the sauce, pour the stock and pineapple cubes and juice into a pan and bring to a boil. Add the carrot and bell peppers, cover, and simmer for 5 minutes.

4 Stir in the remaining ingredients and heat through, stirring, until thickened. Season and set aside until required.

5 Drain the meatballs and transfer to a serving plate. Garnish and serve with boiled rice and the sauce.

# *Crispy-Topped Stuffed Chicken*

### Serves 4

**INGREDIENTS**

4 boneless, skinless chicken
breasts, about 5½ ounces
each
4 sprigs fresh tarragon
½ small orange bell pepper,
seeded and sliced

½ small green bell pepper,
seeded and sliced
½ ounce whole wheat
bread crumbs
1 tbsp sesame seeds
4 tbsp lemon juice

1 small red bell pepper, halved
and seeded
7 ounce can chopped tomatoes
1 small red chili, seeded and
chopped
¼ tsp celery salt
salt and pepper
fresh tarragon, to garnish

1 Preheat the oven to
400°F. Slit the chicken
breasts with a small, sharp
knife to create a pocket in
each. Season inside
each pocket with salt and
pepper to taste.

2 Place a sprig of
tarragon and a few
slices of orange and green
bell peppers in each pocket.
Place the chicken breasts
on a nonstick cookie sheet
and sprinkle with the bread
crumbs and sesame seeds.

3 Spoon 1 tablespoon of
lemon juice over each
chicken breast and bake
in the oven for 35–40
minutes, or until the
chicken is tender and
cooked through.

4 Meanwhile, preheat
the broiler. Arrange the
red bell pepper halves, skin
side up, on the rack and
cook for 5–6 minutes, until
the skin blisters. Leave to
cool for 10 minutes, then
peel off the skins.

5 Put the red bell pepper
in a blender, add the
tomatoes, chili, and celery
salt, and process for a few
seconds. Season to taste.
Alternatively, chop the red
bell pepper and press
through a strainer with the
tomatoes and chili.

6 When the chicken is
cooked, heat the sauce,
spoon a little onto a warm
plate, and arrange a chicken
breast in the center.
Garnish and serve.

# Chicken with a Curried Yogurt Crust

### Serves 4

### INGREDIENTS

| | | |
|---|---|---|
| 1 garlic clove, crushed | 1 tsp ground turmeric | RELISH: |
| 1-inch piece fresh ginger root, finely chopped | 1 tsp garam masala | 4 medium tomatoes |
| | 1 tbsp lime juice | $\frac{1}{4}$ cucumber |
| 1 fresh green chili, seeded and finely chopped | 4 boneless, skinless chicken breasts, each $4\frac{1}{2}$ ounces | 1 small red onion |
| 6 tbsp low-fat unsweetened yogurt | salt and pepper | 2 tbsp chopped fresh cilantro |
| 1 tbsp tomato paste | wedges of lime or lemon, to serve | |

1 Preheat the oven to 375°F. In a small bowl mix together the garlic, ginger, chili, yogurt, tomato paste, turmeric, garam masala, lime juice, and seasoning.

2 Wash and pat dry the chicken breasts with paper towels and place them on a cookie sheet. Brush or spread the spicy yogurt mix over the chicken and bake in the oven for 30–35 minutes until the meat is tender and cooked through.

3 To make the relish, finely chop the tomatoes, cucumber, and onion and mix together with the cilantro. Season with salt and pepper, cover, and chill until required.

4 Drain the cooked chicken on absorbent paper towels and serve hot with the relish. Alternatively, allow to cool, chill for at least 1 hour, and serve sliced as part of a salad.

## VARIATION

*The spicy yogurt coating would work just as well if spread on a chunky white fish, such as cod fillet. The cooking time should be reduced to 15–20 minutes.*

# Broiled Chicken with Lemon & Honey

### Serves 4

## INGREDIENTS

4 boneless, skinless chicken
    breasts, about 4¹/₂ ounces
    each
2 tbsp clear honey
1 tbsp dark soy sauce
1 tsp finely grated lemon rind

1 tbsp lemon juice
salt and pepper

TO GARNISH:
1 tbsp fresh chives, chopped
lemon rind, grated

NOODLES:
8 ounces rice noodles
2 tsp sesame oil
1 tbsp sesame seeds
1 tsp finely grated lemon rind

1 Preheat the broiler. Trim the chicken breasts to remove any excess fat, then wash, and pat dry with absorbent paper towels. Using a sharp knife, score the chicken breasts with a criss-cross pattern on both sides (making sure that you do not cut all the way through the meat).

2 Carefully mix together the honey, soy sauce, lemon rind, and juice in a small bowl, and then season well with a little black pepper.

3 Arrange the chicken breasts on the broiler rack and brush with half of the honey mixture. Cook for 10 minutes, turn over, and brush with the remaining mixture. Cook for a further 8–10 minutes, or until cooked through.

4 Meanwhile, prepare the noodles according to the instructions on the packet. Drain well and transfer to a warm serving bowl. Mix the noodles with the sesame oil, sesame seeds, and the lemon rind.

Season with salt and pepper to taste and keep warm.

5 Drain the chicken and serve with a small mound of noodles, garnished with freshly chopped chives and grated lemon rind.

# Chicken & Plum Casserole

### Serves 4

### INGREDIENTS

2 slices lean bacon, chopped

1 tbsp sunflower oil

1 pound skinned, boned chicken
    thighs, cut into 4 equal strips

1 garlic clove, crushed

6 ounces shallots, halved

8 ounces plums, halved or
    quartered (if large) and pitted

1 tbsp light brown sugar

$^2/_3$ cup dry sherry

2 tbsp plum sauce

2 cups fresh chicken stock

2 tsp cornstarch mixed with
    4 tsp cold water

2 tbsp chopped flat-leaf parsley,
    to garnish

crusty bread, to serve

1 In a large, nonstick skillet, dry-fry the bacon for 2–3 minutes, until the juices run out. Remove the bacon from the pan with a slotted spoon, set aside, and keep warm.

2 In the same skillet, heat the sunflower oil and fry the strips of chicken with the garlic and shallots for 4–5 minutes, stirring occasionally, until well browned all over.

3 Return the bacon to the skillet and stir in the plums, sugar, sherry, plum sauce, and stock. Bring to a boil and simmer for 20 minutes, or until the plums have softened and the chicken is completely cooked through.

4 Add the cornstarch mixture to the skillet and cook, stirring occasionally, for a further 2–3 minutes, until the mixture has thickened.

5 Spoon the casserole onto warm serving plates and garnish with chopped parsley. Serve with chunks of bread to mop up the fruity gravy.

## VARIATION

*Chunks of lean turkey or pork would also go well with this combination of flavors. The cooking time will remain the same.*

# Oat Chicken Pieces

### Serves 4

**INGREDIENTS**

| | | |
|---|---|---|
| $1/3$ cup rolled oats | 1 egg white | salt and pepper |
| 1 tablespoon chopped fresh rosemary | $1/2$ cup ricotta cheese | grated carrot salad, to serve |
| 4 skinless chicken quarters | 2 teaspoons wholegrain mustard | |

1 Mix together the rolled oats, fresh rosemary, and salt and pepper.

2 Brush each piece of chicken evenly with egg white, then coat in the oat mixture. Place on a cookie sheet and bake in a preheated oven at 400°F for about 40 minutes, or until the juices run clear when the chicken is pierced with the point of a sharp knife.

3 In a bowl, mix together the ricotta cheese and wholegrain mustard, season with salt and pepper to taste, then serve with the chicken, hot or cold, with a grated carrot salad.

## VARIATION

*To make oat chicken nuggets, chop up 4 skinless, boneless chicken breasts into small pieces. Reduce the cooking time by about 10 minutes and test for doneness. These nuggets would be ideal at a picnic, buffet, or children's party.*

## VARIATION

*Add 1 tablespoon sesame or sunflower seeds to the oat mixture for an even crunchier texture. Experiment with different herbs, instead of the rosemary.*

# *Solomongundy*

### Serves 4

**INGREDIENTS**

| | | |
|---|---|---|
| 1 large lettuce | $^2/_3$ cup sliced cooked ham | 12 shallots, boiled |
| 4 chicken breasts, cooked and thinly sliced | $2^2/_3$ cups sliced roast beef | $^1/_2$ cup slivered almonds |
| 8 rollmop herrings and their marinade | $^2/_3$ cup sliced roast lamb | $^1/_3$ cup golden raisins |
| 6 hard-cooked eggs, quartered | 1 cup snow peas, cooked | 2 oranges |
| | $^3/_4$ cup seedless black grapes | sprig of mint |
| | 20 stuffed olives, sliced | salt and pepper |
| | | fresh crusty bread, to serve |

1 Spread out the lettuce leaves to cover a large oval platter.

2 Arrange the chicken in three sections on the platter.

3 Place the rollmops, eggs, and meats in lines or sections over the remainder of the platter.

4 Use the snow peas, grapes, olives, shallots, almonds, and golden raisins to fill in the spaces between the lines or sections.

5 Grate the rind from the oranges and sprinkle it over the whole platter. Peel and slice the oranges and add the orange slices and mint sprig to the platter. Season to taste with salt and pepper. Sprinkle with the rollmop herring marinade and serve.

## VARIATION

*Should you wish, serve the Solomongundy with cold, cooked vegetables, such as sliced beans, baby corn, and cooked beets.*

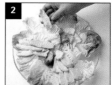

# Spiced Chicken Casserole

### Serves 4–6

**INGREDIENTS**

3 tablespoons olive oil
2 pounds chicken meat, sliced
10 shallots or pickling onions
3 carrots, chopped
$\frac{1}{2}$ cup waterchestnuts, sliced
$\frac{1}{2}$ cup slivered almonds, toasted
1 teaspoon freshly grated nutmeg

1 tablespoon ground cinnamon
$1\frac{1}{4}$ cups white wine
$1\frac{1}{4}$ cups chicken stock
$\frac{3}{4}$ cup white wine vinegar
1 tablespoon chopped fresh tarragon
1 tablespoon chopped fresh flat
    leaf parsley

1 tablespoon chopped fresh thyme
grated rind of 1 orange
1 tablespoon brown sugar
$\frac{3}{4}$ cup seedless black grapes, halved
sea salt and pepper
fresh herbs, to garnish
wild rice or puréed potato, to serve

1 Heat the olive oil in a large saucepan and fry the chicken, shallots or pickling onions, and carrots for about 6 minutes, or until browned.

2 Add the remaining ingredients, except the grapes, and simmer over low heat for 2 hours, until the meat is very tender. Stir the casserole occasionally.

3 Add the grapes just before serving and serve with wild rice or puréed potato. Garnish with herbs.

## VARIATION

*Experiment with different types of nuts and fruits—try sunflower seeds instead of the almonds, and add 2 fresh apricots, chopped.*

## COOK'S TIP

*This casserole would also be delicious served with thick slices of crusty whole-wheat bread to soak up the sauce.*

# Country Chicken Bake

### Serves 4

### INGREDIENTS

2 tablespoons sunflower oil
4 chicken quarters
16 small whole onions, peeled
3 stalks celery, sliced

14 ounce can red kidney beans
4 medium tomatoes, quartered
scant 1 cup hard cider or stock
4 tablespoons chopped fresh parsley

1 teaspoon paprika
4 tablespoons butter
12 slices French bread
salt and pepper

1 Heat the oil in a flameproof casserole and fry the chicken quarters, two at a time, until golden. Using a slotted spoon, remove the chicken from the pan and set aside until required.

2 Add the onions and fry, turning occasionally, until golden brown. Add the celery and fry for 2–3 minutes. Return the chicken to the pan, then stir in the beans, tomatoes, cider, and half the parsley, and season to taste. Sprinkle with the paprika.

3 Cover and cook in a preheated oven at 400°F for 20–25 minutes, until the juices run clear when the chicken is pierced with the point of a sharp knife.

4 Mix the remaining parsley with the butter and spread it evenly over the French bread.

5 Uncover the casserole, arrange the bread slices overlapping on top, and bake for a further 10–12 minutes, until golden and crisp.

## VARIATION

*For a more Italian-tasting dish, replace the garlic and parsley bread topping with Pesto Toasts.*

## COOK'S TIP

*Add a crushed garlic clove to the parsley butter for extra flavor.*

# Chicken in Exotic Mushroom & Ginger Sauce

### Serves 6-8

**INGREDIENTS**

6 tablespoons sesame oil

2 pounds chicken meat

$1/2$ cup all-purpose flour, seasoned

6 cups roughly chopped exotic
    mushrooms

32 baby onions, sliced

$1 1/4$ cups chicken stock

2 tablespoons Worcestershire sauce

2 tablespoons grated fresh
    ginger root

1 tablespoon clear honey

$2/3$ cup unsweetened yogurt

salt and pepper

flat leaf parsley, to garnish

wild rice and white rice, to serve

1 Heat the oil in a large skillet. Coat the chicken in the seasoned flour and cook for about 4 minutes, until browned all over. Transfer to a large deep casserole and keep warm until required.

2 Add the baby onions and mushrooms to the juices in the skillet and fry over a low heat.

3 Add the chicken stock, Worcestershire sauce, honey, and fresh ginger, then season to taste with salt and pepper.

4 Pour the mixture over the chicken, and cover the casserole with a lid or cooking foil.

5 Cook in the center of a preheated oven at 300°F for about $1 1/2$ hours, until the meat is very tender. Add the yogurt and cook for a further 10 minutes. Serve the casserole with a mixture of wild rice and white rice, and garnish with fresh parsley.

## COOK'S TIP

*Mushrooms can be stored in the refrigerator for 24–36 hours. Keep them in paper bags as they "sweat" in plastic. You do not need to peel mushrooms, but wild mushrooms must be washed thoroughly.*

# Honey & Mustard Baked Chicken

### Serves 4–6

**INGREDIENTS**

8 chicken pieces

4 tablespoons butter, melted

4 tablespoons mild mustard

4 tablespoons clear honey

2 tablespoons lemon juice

1 teaspoon paprika

3 tablespoons poppy seeds

salt and pepper

tomato and corn salad, to serve

1 Place the chicken pieces, skinless side down, on a large cookie sheet.

2 Place all the ingredients, except the poppy seeds, into a large bowl and blend together thoroughly.

3 Brush the mixture over the chicken portions.

4 Bake in the center of a preheated oven at 400°F for 15 minutes.

5 Carefully turn over the chicken pieces and coat the top side of the chicken with the remaining honey and mustard mixture.

6 Sprinkle the chicken with poppy seeds and return to the oven for a further 15 minutes.

7 Arrange the chicken on a large, warm serving dish, pour over the cooking juices, and serve with a tomato and corn salad, if desired.

## COOK'S TIP

*Mexican rice makes an excellent accompaniment to this dish: boil the rice for 10 minutes, drain, then fry for 5 minutes. Add chopped onions, garlic, tomatoes, carrots, and chili and cook for 1 minute before adding stock. Bring to a boil, cover, and simmer for 20 minutes, adding more stock if necessary. Add peas 5 minutes before the end of the cooking time.*

# *Cheddar Baked Chicken*

### Serves 4

## INGREDIENTS

1 tablespoon milk

2 tablespoons prepared
English mustard

1 cup grated sharp Cheddar cheese

3 tablespoons all-purpose flour

2 tablespoons chopped fresh chives

4 skinless, boneless chicken breasts

1 Mix together the milk and mustard in a bowl. In another bowl, combine the cheese, flour, and chives.

2 Dip the chicken into the milk and mustard mixture, brushing to coat evenly.

3 Dip the chicken breasts into the cheese mixture, pressing to coat evenly. Place on a cookie sheet and spoon any spare cheese coating over the top.

4 Bake in a preheated oven at 400°F for 30–35 minutes, or until golden brown and the juices run clear, not pink, when it is pierced with the point of a sharp knife. Serve hot, with baked potatoes and fresh vegetables, or serve cold, with a crisp salad.

## COOK'S TIP

*There are several varieties of mustard available. For a sharper flavor try French varieties–Meaux mustard has a grainy texture with a warm, spicy flavor, while Dijon mustard is medium-hot and tangy.*

## COOK'S TIP

*It is a good idea to freeze herbs, as they retain their color, flavor, and nutrients very well. Chives are particularly suitable for freezing–store them in labeled plastic bags and shake them dry before use. Dried chives are not an adequate substitute for fresh.*

# Spicy Sesame Chicken

### Serves 4

**INGREDIENTS**

| | | |
|---|---|---|
| 4 chicken quarters | finely grated rind and juice | 1 tablespoon sesame seeds |
| 1/2 cup plain yogurt | of 1 small lemon | lemon wedges, to garnish |
| | 2 teaspoons medium-hot curry paste | salad and naan bread, to serve |

1 Remove the skin from the chicken and make cuts in the flesh at intervals with a sharp knife.

2 In a small bowl, thoroughly combine the plain yogurt, lemon rind, lemon juice, and curry paste to form a smooth mixture.

3 Spoon the mixture over the chicken quarters and arrange them on a foil-lined broiler pan or cookie sheet.

4 Place the chicken quarters under a preheated broiler and broil for about 12–15 minutes, turning once. Broil until golden brown and thoroughly cooked. Just before the end of the cooking time, sprinkle the chicken with the sesame seeds.

5 Serve at once, garnished with lemon wedges, with a salad and naan bread.

## COOK'S TIP

*If you have time, leave the chicken and the sauce in the refrigerator to marinate overnight so the flavors are fully absorbed.*

## VARIATION

*Poppy seeds, fennel seeds, or cumin seeds, or a mixture of all three, can also be used to sprinkle over the chicken.*

# Broiled Chicken
# & Vegetable Salad

### Serves 4

## INGREDIENTS

| | | |
|---|---|---|
| 1 small eggplant, sliced | 4 boneless chicken breasts | 1 large red onion, sliced thickly |
| 2 garlic cloves, crushed | 2 medium zucchini, sliced | 1 small Italian loaf or |
| finely grated rind of $1/2$ lemon | 1 medium red bell | 1 French baguette, sliced |
| 1 tablespoon chopped fresh mint | pepper, quartered | extra olive oil |
| 6 tablespoons olive oil | 1 small bulb fennel, sliced thickly | salt and pepper |

1 Place the eggplant slices in a colander and sprinkle with salt. Leave over a bowl to drain for 30 minutes, then rinse, and dry. This will get rid of the bitter juices.

2 Mix together the garlic, lemon rind, mint, and olive oil and season.

3 Slash the chicken breasts at intervals with a sharp knife. Stir the oil mixture to combine and spoon half over the chicken breasts.

4 In a separate bowl, combine the eggplants and the remaining vegetables, then toss in the remaining oil mixture. Set the chicken and vegetables aside to marinate for about 30 minutes.

5 Place the chicken breasts and vegetables on a preheated hot broiler or barbecue, turning occasionally, until they are golden brown and tender. Alternatively, cook on a ridged griddle pan on the stove.

6 Brush the bread slices with olive oil and broil until they are golden.

7 Drizzle a little olive oil over the chicken and broiled vegetables and serve hot or cold with the crusty bread toasts.

# *Tropical Chicken Skewers*

### Serves 6

**INGREDIENTS**

| | | |
|---|---|---|
| 1 pound 10 ounces boneless chicken breasts | 3 mangoes | 2 tablespoons coarsely shredded coconut |
| 2 tablespoons medium sherry | bay leaves | pepper |
| | 2 tablespoons oil | |

1 Remove the skin from the chicken, cut the flesh into 1-inch cubes, and toss in the sherry, together with a little pepper, coating them well.

2 Using a sharp knife, cut the mango into wedges. Peel and cut the wedges into 1-inch cubes

3 Thread the chicken, mango cubes, and bay leaves alternately onto long skewers, then brush lightly with oil.

4 Broil the skewers on a preheated broiler for about 8–10 minutes, turning occasionally, until golden.

5 Sprinkle the skewers with the coconut and broil for a further 30 seconds. Serve with a crisp salad.

### COOK'S TIP

*Use mangoes that are ripe, but still firm so that they hold together on the skewers during cooking. Another firm fruit that would be suitable is pineapple.*

### COOK'S TIP

*Remember that if you are using metal skewers, they will get very hot, so be sure to use potholders or tongs to turn them. Wooden skewers should be soaked in water for 30 minutes before use to prevent them from burning on the barbecue, and the exposed ends should be covered with pieces of kitchen foil.*

# Skewered Spicy Tomato Chicken

### Serves 4

## INGREDIENTS

| | | |
|---|---|---|
| 1 pound 2 ounces skinless, boneless chicken breasts | 2 tablespoons clear honey | 9 ounces cherry tomatoes |
| 3 tablespoons tomato paste | 2 tablespoons Worcestershire sauce | sprigs of rosemary, to garnish |
| | 1 tablespoon chopped fresh rosemary | couscous or rice, to serve |

1 Using a sharp knife, cut the chicken into 1-inch chunks and place in a bowl.

2 Mix together the tomato paste, honey, Worcestershire sauce, and rosemary. Add to the chicken, stirring to coat evenly and thoroughly.

3 Alternating the chicken pieces and tomatoes, thread them onto eight wooden skewers.

4 Spoon over any remaining glaze. Cook under a preheated broiler for about 8–10 minutes, turning occasionally, until the chicken is thoroughly cooked. Serve on a bed of couscous or rice and garnish with sprigs of rosemary.

### COOK'S TIP

*Cherry tomatoes are ideal for barbecues as they can be threaded straight onto skewers. As they are kept whole, the skins keep in the tomatoes natural juices.*

### COOK'S TIP

*Couscous is made from semolina that has been made into separate grains. It is very easy to prepare–simply soak it in a bowl of boiling water and then fluff up the grains with a fork. Flavorings, such as lemon or nutmeg, can be added.*

# *Minty Lime Chicken*

### Serves 6

**INGREDIENTS**

3 tablespoons finely chopped mint

4 tablespoons clear honey

4 tablespoons lime juice

12 boneless chicken thighs

salad, to serve

SAUCE:

1/2 cup plain thick yogurt

1 tablespoon finely chopped mint

2 teaspoons finely grated lime rind

1 Combine the mint, honey, and lime juice in a bowl.

2 Use toothpicks to keep the chicken thighs in neat shapes and add the chicken to the marinade, turning to coat evenly.

3 Leave to marinate for at least 30 minutes, preferably overnight. Cook the chicken on a moderately hot barbecue or under a preheated broiler, turning frequently and basting with the marinade. The chicken is cooked if the juices run clear when the chicken is pierced in the thickest part with the point of a knife.

4 Meanwhile, mix together the sauce ingredients.

5 Remove the toothpicks and serve the chicken with a salad and the sauce.

## COOK'S TIP

*Mint can be grown very easily in a garden or window box. It is a useful herb for marinades and salad dressings. Other useful herbs to grow are parsley and basil.*

## VARIATION

*Use this marinade for chicken kabobs, alternating the chicken with lime and red onion wedges.*

# Skewered Chicken with Blackberry Sauce

### Serves 4

**INGREDIENTS**

| | | |
|---|---|---|
| 4 chicken breasts or 8 thighs | pepper | SAUCE: |
| 4 tablespoons dry white wine or cider | rosemary sprigs | 2 cups blackberries |
| 2 tablespoons chopped | and blackberries, to garnish | 1 tablespoon cider vinegar |
| fresh rosemary | salad greens, to serve | 2 tablespoons red currant jelly |
| | | 1/4 teaspoon grated nutmeg |

1 Using a sharp knife, cut the chicken into 1-inch pieces and place in a bowl. Sprinkle it with the white wine and rosemary, and season well with pepper. Cover and set aside to marinate for at least an hour.

2 Drain the chicken pieces thoroughly, reserving the marinade, and thread the meat onto 8 metal or presoaked wooden skewers.

3 Cook on a preheated broiler for about 8–10 minutes, turning occasionally, until golden brown and evenly cooked through.

4 Meanwhile, to make the sauce, place the marinade in a pan with the blackberries and simmer gently until soft. Press the mixture though a strainer using the back of a spoon.

5 Return the blackberry purée to the pan, add the cider vinegar and red currant jelly, and bring to a boil. Boil uncovered until the sauce is reduced by about one third.

6 Spoon a little bramble sauce onto each plate and place a chicken skewer on top. Sprinkle with nutmeg and serve hot. Garnish with rosemary and blackberries and serve

### COOK'S TIP

*If you use canned fruit, omit the red currant jelly.*

# Broiled Rock Cornish Hens with Lemon & Tarragon

### Serves 2

## INGREDIENTS

| | | |
|---|---|---|
| 2 rock Cornish hens | 2 tablespoons butter | 1 garlic clove, crushed |
| 4 sprigs fresh tarragon | rind of ½ lemon | salt and pepper |
| 1 teaspoon oil | 1 tablespoon lemon juice | tarragon and orange slices, to garnish |
| | | new potatoes, to serve |

1 Prepare the rock Cornish hens, turn them breast side down on a chopping board, and cut them through the backbones using kitchen scissors. Crush each bird gently to break the bones, so that they lie flat while cooking. Season each with salt.

2 Turn them over and insert a sprig of tarragon under the skin over each side of the breast.

3 Brush the rock Cornish hens with oil, using a pastry brush, and place under a preheated broiler about 5 inches from the heat. Broil for about 15 minutes, turning half way, until they are lightly browned.

4 Meanwhile, to make the glaze, melt the butter in a small saucepan, add the lemon rind, lemon juice, and garlic, and season with salt and pepper.

5 Brush the rock Cornish hens with the glaze and cook for a further 15 minutes, turning them once and brushing regularly so that they stay moist. Garnish the rock Cornish hens with tarragon and orange slices and serve with new potatoes.

## COOK'S TIP

*Once the rock Cornish hens are flattened, insert 2 metal skewers through them to keep them flat.*

# Barbecued Chicken Quarters
# with Warm Aïoli

### Serves 4

## INGREDIENTS

4 chicken quarters

2 tablespoons oil

2 tablespoons lemon juice

2 teaspoons dried thyme

salt and pepper

salad greens and lemon slices,
    to serve

AIOLI:

5 garlic cloves, crushed

2 egg yolks

$^1/_2$ cup olive oil

$^1/_2$ cup sunflower oil

2 teaspoons lemon juice

2 tablespoons boiling water

1 Using a skewer, prick the chicken quarters in several places, then place them in a shallow dish.

2 Combine the oil, lemon juice, thyme, and seasoning, then pour it over the chicken, turning to coat the chicken evenly. Set aside for 2 hours.

3 To make the aïoli, beat together the garlic and a pinch of salt to make a paste. Add the egg yolks and beat well. Gradually add the oils, drop by drop, beating vigorously, until the mayonnaise becomes creamy and smooth. Add the oils in a thin steady trickle and continue beating until the aïoli is thick. Stir in the lemon juice and season with pepper. Set aside.

4 Place the chicken on a hot barbecue and cook for 25–30 minutes. Brush with the marinade and turn the portions to cook evenly. Remove and arrange on a serving plate.

5 Beat the water into the aïoli and turn into a warm serving bowl. Serve the barbecued chicken with the aïoli, salad greens, and lemon slices.

## COOK'S TIP

*To make a quick aïoli, add the garlic to 1$^1/_4$ cups good-quality mayonnaise, then place in a bowl over a pan of warm water and beat together. Just before serving add 1–2 tablespoons hot water.*

# Chicken with Bell Peppers & Black Bean Sauce

### Serves 4

**INGREDIENTS**

14 ounces chicken breasts, thinly sliced

pinch of cornstarch

2 tablespoons oil

1 garlic clove, crushed

1 tablespoon black bean sauce

1 small red bell pepper, cut into strips

1 small green bell pepper, cut into strips

1 red chili, finely chopped

1 cup sliced mushrooms

1 onion, chopped

6 scallions, chopped

salt and pepper

fresh noodles, to serve

SEASONING:

1/2 teaspoon salt

1/2 teaspoon sugar

3 tablespoons chicken stock

1 tablespoon dark soy sauce

2 tablespoons beef stock

2 tablespoons rice wine

1 teaspoon cornstarch, blended with a little rice wine

1 Put the chicken strips in a bowl. Add a pinch of salt and a pinch of cornstarch and cover with water. Leave for 30 minutes.

2 Heat 1 tablespoon of the oil in a wok or deep-sided skillet and stir-fry the chicken for 4 minutes. Transfer the chicken to a warm serving dish and clean the wok or skillet.

3 Heat the remaining oil in the wok and add the garlic, black bean sauce, green and red bell peppers, chili, mushrooms, onions and scallions. Stir-fry the vegetables for 2 minutes, then return the chicken strips to the wok.

4 Add the seasoning ingredients, fry for 3 minutes, and thicken with a little of the cornstarch paste. Serve at once with fresh noodles.

## COOK'S TIP

*Black bean sauce can be found in specialty shops and in many supermarkets. Use dried noodles if you can't find fresh noodles.*

# *Teppanyaki*

### Serves 4

**INGREDIENTS**

| | | |
|---|---|---|
| 4 boneless chicken breasts | 8 baby corn | 4 tablespoons mirin |
| 1 red bell pepper | ½ cup bean sprouts | 1 tablespoon grated fresh ginger root |
| 1 green bell pepper | 1 tablespoon sesame or sunflower oil | |
| 4 scallions | 4 tablespoons soy sauce | |

1 Remove the skin from the chicken and slice at a slight angle, to a thickness of about ¼ inch.

2 Seed and thinly slice the bell peppers and trim and slice the scallions and corn. Arrange the bell peppers, scallions, corn, and bean sprouts on a plate with the sliced chicken.

3 Heat a large griddle or heavy-based skillet, then lightly brush with oil. Add the prepared vegetables and chicken slices, in small batches, allowing plenty of space between them so that they cook thoroughly.

4 In a small bowl, mix together the soy sauce, mirin, and ginger and serve as a dip with the chicken and vegetables.

## VARIATION

*If you cannot find mirin add one tablespoons of light brown sugar to the sauce instead.*

## VARIATION

*Instead of serving the sauce as a dip, you could use it as a marinade. However, do not leave the chicken to marinate for more than 2 hours, as the soy sauce will cause it to dry out and become rather tough. Use other vegetables, such as snow peas or thinly sliced carrots, if desired.*

# Thai Stir-Fried Chicken with Vegetables

### Serves 4

**INGREDIENTS**

3 tablespoons sesame oil

12 ounces chicken breast, thinly sliced

8 shallots, sliced

2 garlic cloves, finely chopped

1-inch piece fresh ginger

root, grated

1 green chili, finely chopped

1 red bell pepper, thinly sliced

1 green bell pepper, thinly sliced

3 zucchini, thinly sliced

2 tablespoons ground almonds

1 teaspoon ground cinnamon

1 tablespoon oyster sauce

1/4 cup creamed coconut, grated

salt and pepper

1 Heat the sesame oil in a wok, add the chicken, season with salt and pepper, and stir fry for about 4 minutes.

2 Add the shallots, garlic, ginger, and chili and stir-fry for 2 minutes.

3 Add the bell peppers and zucchini and cook for about 1 minute.

4 Finally, add the remaining ingredients and seasoning. Stir-fry for 1 minute and serve.

## COOK'S TIP

*Creamed coconut is sold in blocks by supermarkets and oriental stores. It is a useful storecupboard standby, as it adds richness and depth of flavor.*

## COOK'S TIP

*Since most of the heat of chiles comes from the seeds, remove them before cooking if you want a milder flavor. Be very careful when handling chiles—do not touch your face or eyes, as the chili juice can be very painful. Always wash your hands after preparing chiles.*

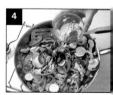

# *Cumin-Spiced Apricot Chicken*

### Serves 4

**INGREDIENTS**

4 large, skinless chicken leg quarters

finely grated rind of 1 lemon

1 cup dried apricots

1 tablespoon ground cumin

1 teaspoon ground turmeric

$^1/_2$ cup reduced fat unsweetened
    yogurt

salt and pepper

TO SERVE:

$1^1/_2$ cups brown rice

2 tablespoons slivered hazelnuts
    or almonds, toasted

2 tablespoons sunflower seeds, toasted

lemon wedges

salad

1 Remove any excess fat from the chicken legs.

2 Use a small sharp knife to carefully cut the flesh away from the thigh bone.

3 Scrape the meat away down as far as the knuckle. Grasp the thigh bone firmly and twist it to break it away from the drumstick.

4 Open out the boned part of the chicken and sprinkle with lemon rind and pepper. Pack the dried apricots into each piece of chicken. Fold over to enclose, and secure with toothpicks.

5 Mix together the cumin, turmeric, yogurt, and salt and pepper, then brush this mixture over the chicken to coat evenly. Place the chicken in an ovenproof dish or roasting pan and bake in a preheated oven at 375°F for about 35–40 minutes, or until the juices run clear, not pink, when the chicken is pierced through the thickest part with the point of a sharp knife.

6 Meanwhile, cook the rice in boiling, lightly salted water until just tender, then drain well. Stir the hazelnuts or almonds and sunflower seeds into the rice. Serve the chicken at once with the nutty rice, lemon wedges and a fresh salad.

# Orange Turkey with Rice & Green Vegetables

### Serves 4

## INGREDIENTS

1 tbsp olive oil
1 medium onion, chopped
1 pound skinless lean turkey
   (such as fillet), cut into
   thin strips

1¼ cups unsweetened orange
   juice
1 bay leaf
8 ounces small broccoli florets
1 large zucchini, diced

1 large orange
6 cups cooked brown rice
salt and pepper
1 ounce pitted black olives in
   brine, drained and quartered,
   to garnish

1 Heat the oil in a large skillet and fry the onion and turkey, stirring, for 4–5 minutes, until lightly browned.

2 Pour in the orange juice and add the bay leaf and seasoning. Bring to a boil and simmer for 10 minutes.

3 Meanwhile, bring a large pan of water to a boil and cook the broccoli, covered, for 2 minutes. Add the diced zucchini, bring back to a boil, cover, and cook for 3 minutes (do not overcook). Drain and set aside.

4 Using a sharp knife, peel off the skin and white pith from the orange. Slice down the orange to make thin, round slices, then cut each slice in half.

5 Stir the broccoli, zucchini, rice, and orange slices into the turkey mixture. Gently mix together and heat through for a further 3–4 minutes, until piping hot.

6 Transfer the turkey rice to serving plates and garnish with black olives.

# Curried Turkey with Apricots & Golden Raisins

### Serves 4

**INGREDIENTS**

1 tbsp vegetable oil

1 large onion, chopped

1 pound skinless turkey breast, cut into 1 inch cubes

3 tbsp mild curry paste

1¼ cups fresh chicken stock

6 ounces frozen peas

14 ounce can apricot halves in natural juice

⅓ cup golden raisins

6 cups Basmati rice, freshly cooked

1 tsp ground coriander

4 tbsp fresh cilantro, chopped

1 green chili, seeded and sliced

salt and pepper

1 Heat the oil in a large saucepan and fry the onion and turkey for 4–5 minutes, until the onion has softened and the turkey is a light golden color.

2 Stir in the curry paste. Pour in the stock, stirring, and bring to a boil. Cover and simmer for 15 minutes. Stir in the peas and bring back to a boil. Cover and simmer for 5 minutes.

3 Drain the apricots, reserving the juice, and cut into thick slices. Add the apricots to the curry, stirring in a little of the juice if the mixture is becoming dry. Add the golden raisins and cook for 2 minutes.

4 Mix the rice with the ground coriander and fresh cilantro, stir in the chili, and season with salt and pepper. Transfer the rice to warm plates and top with the curry.

## VARIATION

*Peaches can be used instead of the apricots if you prefer. Cook in exactly the same way.*

# Turkey Loaf with Zucchini & Tomato

## Serves 6

### INGREDIENTS

| | | |
|---|---|---|
| 1 medium onion, finely chopped | 1 tbsp chopped fresh chives | 1 medium and 1 large zucchini |
| 1 garlic clove, crushed | 1 tbsp chopped fresh tarragon | 2 medium tomatoes |
| 2 pounds lean ground turkey | 1 medium egg white, lightly | salt and pepper |
| 1 tbsp chopped fresh parsley | beaten | tomato and herb sauce, to serve |

1 Preheat the oven to 375°F and line a nonstick loaf pan with baking parchment. Place the onion, garlic, and turkey in a bowl, add the herbs, and season to taste. Mix together with your hands, then add the egg white to bind.

2 Press half of the turkey mixture into the base of the pan. Thinly slice the medium zucchini and the tomatoes and arrange the slices over the meat. Top with the rest of the turkey and press down firmly.

3 Cover with a layer of foil and place in a roasting pan. Pour in enough boiling water to come halfway up the sides of the pan. Bake in the oven for 1–1¼ hours, removing the foil for the last 20 minutes of cooking. Test the loaf by inserting a skewer into the center—the juices should run clear.

4 Using a vegetable peeler or hand-held metal cheese slicer, cut the large zucchini into thin slices. Bring a saucepan of water to a boil and blanch the zucchini slices for 1–2 minutes, until just tender. Drain, set aside, and keep warm.

5 Transfer the turkey loaf to a warm platter. Drape the zucchini slices over the loaf and serve with a tomato and herb sauce.

# Duck with Kiwi Fruit & Raspberries

## Serves 4

### INGREDIENTS

1 pound boneless, skinless duck breasts

2 tbsp raspberry vinegar

2 tbsp brandy

1 tbsp clear honey

1 tsp sunflower oil

salt and pepper

SAUCE:

8 ounces raspberries, thawed if frozen

1¼ cups rosé wine

2 tsp cornstarch blended with 4 tsp cold water

1 Trim the duck breasts to remove any excess fat. Using a sharp knife, score the flesh in diagonal lines and then pound it with a meat mallet or a covered rolling pin until it is about ¾ inch thick.

2 Place the duck breasts in a shallow dish. Mix together the vinegar, brandy, and honey in a small bowl and spoon it over the duck. Cover and chill in the refrigerator for 1 hour. Preheat the broiler.

3 Drain the duck, reserving the marinade, and place on the broiler rack. Season and brush with oil. Cook for 10 minutes, turn over, season, brush with oil again, and cook for 8–10 minutes, until the meat is cooked through.

4 To make the sauce, reserve 2 ounces raspberries and place the rest in a pan. Add the marinade and the wine. Bring to a boil and simmer for 5 minutes, until reduced.

5 Strain the sauce through a strainer, pressing the raspberries with the back of a spoon. Return the liquid to the pan and add the cornstarch paste. Heat through, stirring, until thickened. Add the reserved raspberries and season.

6 Thinly slice the duck breast and arrange fanned out on serving plates, alternating with slices of kiwi fruit. Pour on the sauce and serve.

# Roast Duck with Apples & Apricots

### Serves 4

## INGREDIENTS

4 duckling portions, 12 ounces
  each
4 tbsp dark soy sauce
2 tbsp light brown sugar
2 red-skinned apples
2 green-skinned apples

juice of 1 lemon
2 tbsp clear honey
few bay leaves
salt and pepper
assorted fresh vegetables,
  to serve

SAUCE:
14 ounce can apricots, in
  natural juice
4 tbsp sweet sherry

1 Preheat the oven to 375°F. Wash the duck and trim away any excess fat. Place on a wire rack over a roasting pan and prick all over with a fork.

2 Brush the duck with the soy sauce. Sprinkle on the sugar and season with pepper. Cook in the oven, basting occasionally, for 50–60 minutes, until the meat is cooked through—the juices should run clear when a skewer is inserted into the thickest part of the meat.

3 Meanwhile, core the apples and cut each into 6 wedges. Place in a bowl and mix with the lemon juice and honey. Transfer to a small roasting pan, add a few bay leaves, and season. Cook alongside the duck, basting occasionally, for 20–25 minutes, until tender. Discard the bay leaves.

4 To make the sauce, place the apricots in a blender or food processor, together with the juice from the can and the

sherry. Process for a few seconds until smooth. Alternatively, mash the apricots with a fork until smooth and mix with the juice and sherry.

5 Just before serving, heat the apricot paste in a pan. Remove the skin from the duck (if wished) and pat the flesh with paper towels to absorb any fat.

6 Serve the duck with the apple wedges and the sauce, and accompanied with vegetables.

# Moroccan Lamb Kabobs

### Makes 4

**INGREDIENTS**

1 pound lean lamb
1 lemon
1 red onion
4 small zucchini
couscous, to serve (see Cook's
    Tip)

MARINADE:
grated rind and juice of
    1 lemon
2 tbsp olive oil
1 clove garlic, crushed
1 red chili, sliced (optional)

1 tsp ground cinnamon
1 tsp ground ginger
½ tsp ground cumin
½ tsp ground coriander

1 Cut the lamb into large, even chunks.

2 To make the marinade, combine the lemon rind and juice, oil, garlic, chili (if using), ground cinnamon, ginger, cumin, and coriander in a large nonmetallic dish.

3 Add the meat to the marinade, tossing to coat the meat completely. Cover and marinate in the refrigerator for a minimum of 2 hours or preferably overnight.

4 Cut the lemon into 8 pieces. Cut the onion into wedges, then separate each wedge into 2 pieces.

5 Using a canelle knife or potato peeler, cut thin strips of peel from the zucchini, then cut the zucchini into chunks.

6 Remove the meat from the marinade, reserving the liquid for basting. Thread the meat onto skewers alternating with the onion wedges, lemon pieces, and zucchini.

7 Broil over hot coals for 8–10 minutes, turning and basting with the reserved marinade.

## COOK'S TIP

*Serve these kabobs with couscous or tabouleh. Allowing ⅓ cup couscous per person, soak the couscous in cold water for 20 minutes, until the grains have softened. Drain and steam for 10 minutes, or until hot.*

# *Shish Kabobs*

### Makes 4

**INGREDIENTS**

| | | |
|---|---|---|
| 1 pound lean lamb | 4 tbsp olive oil | TO SERVE: |
| 1 red onion, cut into wedges | grated rind and juice of | 4 pita breads |
| 1 green bell pepper, seeded | ¹/₂ lemon | few crisp lettuce leaves, |
| | 1 clove garlic, crushed | shredded |
| MARINADE: | ¹/₂ tsp dried oregano | 2 tomatoes, sliced |
| 1 onion | ¹/₂ tsp dried thyme | chili sauce (optional) |

1 Cut the lamb into large, even-size chunks.

2 To make the marinade, grate the onion or chop it very finely in a food processor. Remove the juice by squeezing the onion between two plates set over a small bowl to collect the juice.

3 Combine the onion juice with the remaining marinade ingredients in a nonmetallic dish and add the meat. Toss the meat in the marinade, cover, and marinate in the refrigerator for at least 2 hours.

4 Divide the onion wedges into 2. Cut the bell peppers into chunks.

5 Remove the meat from the marinade, reserving the liquid for basting. Thread the meat onto skewers, alternating with the onion and bell peppers. Broil over hot coals for 8–10 minutes, turning and basting frequently.

6 Split the bread; fill with lettuce. Push the meat and vegetables off the skewers into the bread. Top with tomatoes.

## VARIATION

*These kabobs are delicious served with saffron-flavored rice. For easy saffron rice, simply use saffron stock cubes when cooking the rice.*

# *Lamb Cutlets with Rosemary*

### Serves 4

**INGREDIENTS**

8 lamb cutlets
5 tbsp olive oil
2 tbsp lemon juice
1 clove garlic, crushed
$\frac{1}{2}$ tsp lemon pepper
salt

8 sprigs rosemary
baked potatoes, to serve

SALAD:
4 tomatoes, sliced
4 scallions, sliced diagonally

DRESSING:
2 tbsp olive oil
1 tbsp lemon juice
1 clove garlic, chopped
$\frac{1}{4}$ tsp fresh rosemary, finely
    chopped

1 Trim the lamb cutlets by cutting away the flesh with a sharp knife to expose the tips of the bones.

2 Place the olive oil, lemon juice, garlic, lemon pepper, and salt in a shallow, nonmetallic dish and whisk with a fork to combine.

3 Lay the sprigs of rosemary in the dish and place the lamb on top. Marinate for at least

1 hour in the refrigerator, turning the cutlets once.

4 Remove the cutlets from the marinade and wrap a little foil around the bones to stop them from burning.

5 Place the sprigs of rosemary on the rack and place the lamb on top. Broil for about 10–15 minutes, turning once.

6 Meanwhile, make the salad and dressing.

Arrange the tomatoes on a serving dish and scatter the scallions on top. Place all the ingredients for the dressing in a screw-top jar, shake well, and pour over the salad. Serve with the broiled lamb cutlets and baked potatoes.

# Lamb with Mango & Chili

### Serves 4

**INGREDIENTS**

4 loin of lamb or English chops
4 tbsp mango chutney
2 tsp chili sauce
broiled vegetables, to serve

SPICY MANGO RELISH:
1 ripe mango
2 tbsp cider vinegar
2 tbsp light muscovado sugar

½ tsp ground cinnamon
½ tsp ground ginger

1 To make the spicy mango relish, cut the mango lengthwise down both sides of the large, flat pit and discard the pit. Peel the mango and cut the flesh into even-size chunks.

2 Place the cider vinegar, sugar, cinnamon, and ginger in a small pan and heat gently, stirring continuously, until the sugar has completely dissolved.

3 Stir the mango into the mixture in the pan and cook gently at the side of

the barbecue for about 5 minutes, or until the mango is soft.

4 Barbecue the chops on an oiled rack for about 4 minutes on each side.

5 Combine the mango chutney and chili sauce in a small bowl and brush the glaze over both sides of the chops.

6 Continue to barbecue for a further 2–5 minutes on each side, until the lamb is cooked, turning and basting frequently with the chutney and chili glaze.

7 Serve the lamb with a selection of broiled vegetables and the spicy mango relish.

## VARIATION

*The spicy mango relish can also be served cold. Simmer the combined ingredients for 5 minutes, then remove from the heat and allow to cool. Chill in the refrigerator until required. You can also use the mango chutney and chili glaze on other cuts of lamb or on pork chops.*

# *Indian Kofta*

### Makes 8

**INGREDIENTS**

1 small onion
1 pound minced lamb
2 tbsp curry paste
2 tbsp unsweetened yogurt
oil, to baste
sprigs of fresh cilantro, to garnish

TOMATO SAMBAL:
3 tomatoes, seeded and diced
pinch of ground coriander
pinch of ground cumin
2 tsp chopped, fresh cilantro
salt and pepper

TO SERVE:
poppadam
chutney

1 Put the onion in a food processor and chop finely. Add the lamb and process briefly to chop the ground meat further. Chopping the lamb again will help the meat mixture to hold together during cooking. If you do not have a food processor, grate the onion finely before mixing it with the ground lamb.

2 Add the curry paste and yogurt and mix well. Divide the mixture into 8 equal portions.

3 Press and shape the mixture into 8 sausage shapes and push each one onto a skewer, pressing the mixture together firmly so that it holds its shape. Chill the kabobs for at least 30 minutes or until required.

4 To make the tomato sambal, mix together the tomatoes, coriander, cumin, chopped cilantro, and salt and pepper to taste in a bowl. Let stand for at least 30 minutes for the flavors to combine.

5 Broil the kabobs on an oiled rack over hot coals for 10–15 minutes, turning frequently. Baste the kabobs with a little oil if required.

6 Transfer to serving plates and garnish with fresh cilantro. Serve accompanied with poppadam, chutney, and the tomato sambal.

# Pork & Apple Skewers with Mustard

### Makes 4

## INGREDIENTS

1 pound pork tenderloin

2 eating apples

a little lemon juice

1 lemon

2 tsp wholegrain mustard

2 tsp Dijon mustard

2 tbsp apple or orange juice

2 tbsp sunflower oil

crusty brown bread, to serve

MUSTARD SAUCE:

1 tbsp wholegrain mustard

1 tsp Dijon mustard

6 tbsp light cream

1 To make the mustard sauce, combine the wholegrain and Dijon mustards in a bowl and blend in the cream. Set aside while you prepare the pork and apple skewers.

2 Cut the pork tenderloin into bite-size pieces and set aside.

3 Core the apples, then cut them into thick wedges. Toss the apple wedges in a little lemon juice—this will prevent any discoloration. Cut the lemon into slices.

4 Thread the pork, apple, and lemon slices alternately onto 4 skewers.

5 Mix together the mustards, fruit juice, and oil in a bowl until well combined. Brush the mixture over the kabobs and broil over hot coals for 10–15 minutes, turning and basting frequently with the mustard marinade.

6 Transfer the kabobs to warm serving plates and spoon a little of the mustard sauce on top. Serve hot.

## COOK'S TIP

*There are many varieties of mustard available, including English, which is very hot, Dijon, which is milder, and wholegrain, which contains whole mustard seeds. Mustards flavored with other ingredients, such as honey or chili, are also available.*

# *Fruity Pork Skewers*

### Makes 4

**INGREDIENTS**

4 boneless pork loin steaks
8 ready-to-eat prunes
8 ready-to-eat dried apricots

4 bay leaves
slices of orange and lemon,
    to garnish

MARINADE:
4 tbsp orange juice
2 tbsp olive oil
1 tsp ground bay leaves
salt and pepper

1 Trim the visible fat from the pork and cut the meat into even-size chunks.

2 Place the pork in a shallow, nonmetallic dish and add the prunes and apricots.

3 To make the marinade, mix together the orange juice, oil, bay leaves, and salt and pepper to taste in a bowl.

4 Pour the marinade over the pork and fruit and toss until well coated.

Marinate in the refrigerator for at least 1 hour or preferably overnight.

5 Soak 4 wooden skewers in cold water to prevent them from catching fire on the barbecue during cooking.

6 Remove the pork and fruit from the marinade, using a slotted spoon, reserving the marinade for basting. Thread the pork and fruit onto the skewers, alternating with the bay leaves.

7 Broil the skewers on an oiled rack over medium hot coals for 10–15 minutes, turning and frequently basting with the reserved marinade, or until the pork is cooked through.

8 Transfer the pork and fruit skewers to warm serving plates. Garnish with slices of orange and lemon and serve hot.

# Honey-Glazed Pork Chops

### Serves 4

---
**INGREDIENTS**
---

4 lean pork loin chops

4 tbsp clear honey

1 tbsp dry sherry

4 tbsp orange juice

1-inch piece fresh ginger root, grated

2 tbsp olive oil

salt and pepper

---

1 Season the pork chops with salt and pepper to taste. Set aside while you make the glaze.

2 To make the glaze, place the honey, sherry, orange juice, oil, and ginger in a small pan and heat gently, stirring continuously, until the ingredients are blended.

3 Broil the chops on an oiled rack over hot coals for about 5 minutes on each side.

4 Brush the chops with the glaze and broil for another 2–4 minutes on each side, basting frequently with the glaze.

5 Transfer the chops to warm serving plates and serve hot.

## COOK'S TIP

*To give the recipe a little more punch, stir ½ teaspoon of chili sauce or 1 tablespoon of wholegrain mustard into the basting glaze.*

## VARIATION

*This recipe works equally well with lamb chops and with chicken portions, such as thighs or drumsticks. Broil the meat in exactly the same way as in this recipe, basting frequently with the honey glaze—the result will be just as delicious!*

# Fish & Seafood

*Naturally low in fat, yet rich in minerals and
proteins, white fish and seafood should be regular
and important ingredients in any low-fat diet.
There are so many flavors and textures available
that the possible combinations are endless.*

*White fish, such as monkfish, haddock, cod,
and turbot, are widely available and easy to cook.
Shellfish, too, are low in fat and rich in flavor, and
they can be cooked in a variety of ways to produce
mouthwatering, low-fat dishes. Some fish—
salmon, tuna, trout, and mackerel, for example—
are oily and should be eaten in moderation. They
are rich in the fat-soluble vitamins A and D,
however, and it is also believed that the oil in
these fish is beneficial in breaking down
cholesterol in the bloodstream.*

# Shrimp & Tuna Pasta Bake

### Serves 4

**INGREDIENTS**

8 ounces tricolor pasta shapes
1 tbsp vegetable oil
1 bunch scallions, trimmed
    and chopped
6 ounces button mushrooms,
    sliced

14 ounce can tuna in water,
    drained and flaked
6 ounces peeled shrimp, thawed
    if frozen
2 tbsp cornstarch
1³/₄ cups skim milk

4 medium tomatoes, sliced thinly
1 ounce fresh bread crumbs
1 ounce reduced-fat cheddar
    cheese, grated
salt and pepper

1 Preheat the oven to 375°F. Bring a large pan of water to a boil and cook the pasta according to the instructions on the packet, until it is tender but still firm to the bite. Drain thoroughly.

2 Meanwhile, heat the oil in a skillet and sauté all but a handful of the scallions and all of the mushrooms, stirring, for 4–5 minutes until softened.

3 Place the cooked pasta in a bowl and mix in the scallions, mushrooms, tuna, and shrimp. Set aside and keep warm until required.

4 Blend the cornstarch with a little milk to make a paste. Pour the remaining milk into a saucepan and stir in the paste. Heat, stirring, until the sauce begins to thicken. Season with salt and pepper.

5 Pour the sauce over the pasta mixture and stir until well combined. Transfer to the base of an ovenproof gratin dish and place on a cookie sheet.

6 Arrange the tomato slices over the pasta and sprinkle with the bread crumbs and cheese. Bake for 25–30 minutes until golden. Serve sprinkled with the reserved chopped scallions.

# Fish Cakes with Piquant Tomato Sauce

### Serves 4

**INGREDIENTS**

1 pound potatoes, diced
8 ounces haddock fillet
8 ounces trout fillet
1 bay leaf
1³/₄ cups fresh fish stock
2 tbsp low-fat unsweetened
    yogurt
4 tbsp fresh snipped chives

2³/₄ ounces dry white
    bread crumbs
1 tbsp sunflower oil
salt and pepper
snipped chives, to garnish

TO SERVE:
lemon wedges

salad greens

PIQUANT TOMATO SAUCE:
³/₄ cup sieved tomatoes
4 tbsp dry white wine
4 tbsp low-fat unsweetened
    yogurt
chili powder

1 Place the potatoes in a saucepan and cover with water. Bring to a boil and cook for 10 minutes, or until tender. Drain well and mash.

2 Meanwhile, place the fish in a pan with the bay leaf and stock. Bring to a boil and simmer for 7–8 minutes, or until tender. Remove the fish with a slotted spoon and flake the flesh away from the skin.

3 Gently mix the cooked fish with the potato, yogurt, chives, and seasoning. Cool, then cover, and chill for 1 hour.

4 Sprinkle the bread crumbs on a plate. Divide the fish mixture into 8 and form each portion into a patty, about 3 inches in diameter. Press each fish cake into the bread crumbs, coating it all over.

5 Brush a skillet with oil and fry the fish cakes for 6 minutes on each side, or until golden. Drain on paper towels and keep warm.

6 To make the sauce, heat the sieved tomatoes and wine. Season, remove from the heat, and stir in the yogurt. Return to the heat, sprinkle with chili powder, and serve with the fish cakes.

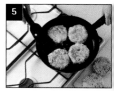

# *Provençal-Style Mussels*

### Serves 4

**INGREDIENTS**

1 tbsp olive oil
1 large onion, finely chopped
1 garlic clove, finely chopped
1 small red bell pepper, seeded
    and finely chopped
sprig of rosemary
2 bay leaves
14 ounce can chopped
    tomatoes

²/₃ cup white wine
1 zucchini, diced finely
2 tbsp tomato paste
1 tsp superfine sugar
1³/₄ ounces pitted black
    olives in brine, drained,
    and chopped
1¹/₂ pounds cooked New Zealand
    mussels in their shells

1 tsp orange rind
salt and pepper
crusty bread, to serve
2 tbsp chopped, fresh parsley, to
    garnish

1 Heat the oil in a large saucepan and gently sauté the onion, garlic, and bell pepper for 3–4 minutes, until just softened.

2 Add the sprig of rosemary and the bay leaves to the saucepan with the tomatoes and ¹/₃ cup of wine. Season with salt and pepper to taste, then bring to a boil, and simmer for about 15 minutes.

3 Stir in the zucchini, tomato paste, sugar, and olives. Simmer for 10 minutes.

4 Meanwhile, bring a pan of water to a boil. Arrange the mussels in a steamer or a large strainer and place over the water. Sprinkle with the remaining wine and the orange rind. Cover and steam until the mussels open (discard any that remain closed).

5 Remove the mussels with a slotted spoon and arrange on a warm serving plate. Discard the herbs and spoon the sauce over the mussels. Garnish with chopped parsley and serve with crusty bread.

# Fish & Rice with Dark Rum

### Serves 4

#### INGREDIENTS

| | | |
|---|---|---|
| 1 pound firm white fish fillets (such as cod or monkfish), skinned and cut into 1-inch cubes | 3 garlic cloves, finely chopped | 2 cups long-grain rice |
| | 1 large onion, chopped | salt and pepper |
| | 1 medium red bell pepper, seeded and sliced into rings | crusty bread, to serve |
| 2 tsp ground cumin | | |
| 2 tsp dried oregano | 1 medium green bell pepper, seeded and sliced into rings | TO GARNISH: |
| 2 tbsp lime juice | | fresh oregano leaves |
| $^2/_3$ cup dark rum | 1 medium yellow bell pepper, seeded and sliced into rings | lime wedges |
| 1 tbsp dark brown sugar | 5 cups fish stock | |

1 Place the cubes of fish in a bowl and add the cumin, oregano, salt, pepper, lime juice, rum, and sugar. Mix well, cover the bowl, and chill for about 2 hours.

2 Meanwhile, place the garlic, onion, and bell peppers in a large saucepan. Pour in the stock and stir in the rice. Bring to a boil, cover, and cook for 15 minutes.

3 Gently add the fish and the marinade juices to the pan. Bring back to a boil and simmer, uncovered, stirring occasionally but taking care not to break up the fish, for 10 minutes, or until the fish is cooked and the rice is tender.

4 Season and transfer to a serving plate. Garnish with oregano and lime wedges and serve.

## VARIATION

*If you prefer, use unsweetened orange juice in the marinade instead of the rum.*

# Seafood Stir-Fry

### Serves 4

**INGREDIENTS**

3½ ounces small, thin asparagus
  spears, trimmed
1 tbsp sunflower oil
1-inch piece fresh ginger root,
  cut into thin strips
1 medium leek, shredded
2 medium carrots, julienned

3½ ounces baby corn cobs,
  quartered lengthwise
2 tbsp light soy sauce
1 tbsp oyster sauce
1 tsp clear honey
1 pound cooked, assorted
  shellfish, thawed if frozen

freshly cooked egg noodles,
  to serve

TO GARNISH:
4 large cooked shrimp
small bunch fresh chives, freshly
  snipped

1 Bring a small pan of water to a boil and blanch the asparagus for 1–2 minutes. Drain, set aside, and keep warm.

2 Heat the oil in a wok or large skillet and stir-fry the ginger, leek, carrot, and corn for 3 minutes.

3 Add the soy sauce, oyster sauce, and honey to the wok or skillet. Stir in the shellfish and continue to stir-fry for

2–3 minutes until the vegetables are just tender and the shellfish is thoroughly heated through. Add the blanched asparagus to the wok or skillet and stir-fry for about 2 minutes.

4 To serve, pile the cooked noodles onto 4 warm serving plates and spoon the seafood and vegetable stir-fry on top. Serve garnished with a large shrimp and freshly snipped chives.

## COOK'S TIP

*When you are preparing dense vegetables, such as carrots and other root vegetables, for stir-frying, slice them into thin, evenly sized pieces so that they cook quickly and at the same rate. Delicate vegetables, such as bell peppers, leeks, and scallions, do not need to be cut as thinly.*

# *Smoky Fish Pie*

### Serves 4

### INGREDIENTS

| | | |
|---|---|---|
| 2 pounds smoked haddock or cod fillets | 4 ounces frozen corn kernels | 3 tbsp cornstarch |
| 2½ cups skim milk | 1½ pounds potatoes, diced | 1 ounce smoked cheese, grated |
| 2 bay leaves | 5 tbsp low-fat unsweetened yogurt | salt and pepper |
| 4 ounces button mushrooms, quartered | 4 tbsp chopped fresh parsley | |
| 4 ounces frozen peas | 2 ounces smoked salmon, sliced into thin strips | |

1 Preheat the oven to 400°F. Place the fish in a pan and add the milk and bay leaves. Bring to a boil, cover, and then simmer for 5 minutes.

2 Add the mushrooms, peas, and corn to the pan, bring back to a simmer, cover, and cook for 5–7 minutes. Let cool.

3 Place the potatoes in a pan, cover with water, boil, and cook for 8 minutes. Drain and mash with a fork or a masher. Stir in the yogurt, parsley, and seasoning. Set aside.

4 Using a slotted spoon, remove the fish from the pan. Flake the cooked fish away from the skin and place in an ovenproof gratin dish. Reserve the cooking liquid.

5 Drain the vegetables, reserving the cooking liquid, and gently stir into the fish, together with the salmon strips.

6 Blend a little cooking liquid into the cornstarch to make a paste. Transfer the rest of the liquid to a saucepan and add the paste. Heat through, stirring, until thickened. Discard the bay leaves and season to taste.

7 Pour the sauce over the fish and vegetables. Spoon the mashed potato on top, covering the fish, sprinkle with cheese, and bake for 25–30 minutes. Serve.

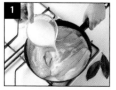

# Seafood Spaghetti

### Serves 4

**INGREDIENTS**

2 tsp olive oil
1 small red onion, finely chopped
1 tbsp lemon juice
1 garlic clove, crushed
2 celery stalks, finely chopped
²⁄₃ cup fresh fish stock
²⁄₃ cup dry white wine

small bunch fresh tarragon
1 pound fresh mussels, prepared
8 ounces fresh shrimp, peeled
    and deveined
8 ounces baby squid, cleaned,
    trimmed, and sliced into
    rings

8 small cooked crab claws,
    cracked and peeled
8 ounces spaghetti
salt and pepper
2 tbsp chopped fresh tarragon,
    to garnish

1 Heat the oil in a pan and sauté the onion with the lemon juice, garlic, and celery for 3–4 minutes, until softened.

2 Pour in the stock and wine. Bring to a boil and add the tarragon and mussels. Cover and simmer for 5 minutes. Add the shrimp, squid, and crab claws to the pan, mix together, and cook for 3–4 minutes, until the mussels have opened, the shrimp are pink, and the squid is opaque. Discard any mussels that have not opened, and the tarragon.

3 Meanwhile, cook the spaghetti in a saucepan of boiling water according to the instructions on the packet. Drain well.

4 Add the spaghetti to the shellfish mixture and toss together. Season.

5 Transfer to warm serving plates and spoon the cooking juices on top. Serve garnished with freshly chopped tarragon.

## COOK'S TIP

*Crab claws contain lean crabmeat. Ask your fish store to crack the claws for you, leaving the pincers intact, because the shell is very tough.*

# Chili- & Crab-Stuffed Red Snapper

### Serves 4

**INGREDIENTS**

| | | |
|---|---|---|
| 4 red snappers, cleaned and scaled, 6 ounces each | STUFFING: | 3¹/₂ ounces white crabmeat, flaked |
| 2 tbsp dry sherry | 1 small red chili | |
| salt and pepper | 1 garlic clove | TO GARNISH: |
| stir-fried shredded vegetables, to serve | 1 scallion | wedges of lime |
| | ¹/₂ tsp finely grated lime rind | red chili strips |
| | 1 tbsp lime juice | |

1 Rinse the fish and pat dry on absorbent paper towels. Season inside and out and place in a shallow dish. Spoon the sherry over the fish and set aside.

2 Meanwhile, make the stuffing. Carefully halve, seed, and finely chop the chili. Place the chili in a small bowl.

3 Peel and finely chop the garlic. Trim and finely chop the scallion. Add to the chili together with the grated lime rind,

lime juice, and the flaked crabmeat. Season with salt and pepper to taste and combine. Spoon some of the stuffing into the cavity of each fish.

4 Bring a large saucepan of water to a boil. Arrange the fish in a steamer lined with baking parchment or in a large strainer and place over a boiling water. Cover and steam for 10 minutes. Turn the fish over and steam for a further 10 minutes, or until the fish is cooked.

5 Drain the fish and transfer to serving plates. Garnish with wedges of lime and serve with stir-fried vegetables.

## COOK'S TIP

*Always wash your hands thoroughly after handling chiles, as they can irritate your skin and eyes.*

# *Citrus Fish Skewers*

### Serves 4

**INGREDIENTS**

| | | |
|---|---|---|
| 1 pound firm white fish fillets (such as cod or monkfish) | 1 bunch fresh bay leaves | salt and pepper |
| 1 pound thick salmon fillet | 1 tsp finely grated lemon rind | TO SERVE: |
| 2 large oranges | 3 tbsp lemon juice | crusty bread |
| 1 pink grapefruit | 2 tsp clear honey | mixed salad |
| | 2 garlic cloves, crushed | |

1 Skin the white fish and the salmon, rinse, and pat dry on absorbent paper towels. Cut each fillet into 16 pieces.

2 Using a sharp knife, remove the skin and pith from the oranges and grapefruit. Cut out the segments of flesh, removing all remaining traces of the pith and dividing membrane.

3 Thread the pieces of fish alternately with the orange and grapefruit

segments and the bay leaves onto 8 skewers. Place the Skewers in a shallow dish.

4 Mix together the lemon rind and juice, the honey, and garlic. Pour over the Skewers and season. Cover and chill for 2 hours, turning occasionally.

5 Preheat the broiler. Remove the kabobs from the marinade and place on the rack. Cook for 7–8 minutes, turning once, until completely cooked through.

6 Drain the Skewers thoroughly, transfer to serving plates, and serve with crusty bread and a fresh salad.

## VARIATION

*This dish makes an unusual starter. Try it with any firm fish—shark or swordfish, for example—or with tuna for a meatier texture.*

# *Seafood Pizza*

### Serves 4

**INGREDIENTS**

5 ounces standard
   pizza base mix
4 tbsp chopped fresh dill
   or 2 tbsp dried dill
fresh dill, to garnish

SAUCE:
1 large red bell pepper

14 ounce can chopped tomatoes
   with onion and herbs
3 tbsp tomato paste
salt and pepper

TOPPING:
12 ounces assorted cooked
   seafood, thawed if frozen

1 tbsp capers in brine, drained
1 ounce pitted black olives in
   brine, drained
1 ounce low-fat mozzarella
   cheese, grated
1 tbsp grated, fresh Parmesan
   cheese

1 Preheat the oven to 400°F. Place the pizza base mix in a bowl and stir in the dill. Make the dough according to the instructions on the packet.

2 Press the dough into a round measuring 10 inches across on a cookie sheet lined with parchment. Set aside to rise.

3 Preheat the broiler. To make the sauce, halve and seed the bell pepper and arrange on a broiler rack. Cook for 8–10 minutes, until softened and charred. Leave to cool slightly, peel off the skin, and chop the flesh.

4 Place the tomatoes and bell pepper in a saucepan. Bring to a boil and simmer for 10 minutes. Gradually stir in the tomato paste and season with salt and pepper to taste.

5 Spread the sauce over the pizza base and top with the seafood. Sprinkle with the capers and olives, top with the grated cheeses, and bake for 25–30 minutes. Garnish with sprigs of dill and serve hot.

# Pan-Seared Halibut with Red Onion Relish

### Serves 4

**INGREDIENTS**

1 tsp olive oil
4 halibut steaks, skinned,
   6 ounces each
$\frac{1}{2}$ tsp cornstarch mixed with 2
   tsp cold water
salt and pepper

2 tbsp fresh chives, snipped,
   to garnish

RED ONION RELISH:
2 medium red onions
6 shallots

1 tbsp lemon juice
2 tsp olive oil
2 tbsp red wine vinegar
2 tsp superfine sugar
$\frac{2}{3}$ cup fresh fish stock

1 To make the relish, peel and thinly shred the onions and shallots. Place in a small bowl and toss in the lemon juice.

2 Heat the oil in a pan and sauté the onions and shallots for 3–4 minutes, or until just softened.

3 Add the vinegar and sugar and continue to cook for 2 minutes over a high heat. Pour in the stock and season with salt and pepper to taste. Bring to a boil and simmer gently for a further 8–9 minutes, until the sauce has thickened and is slightly reduced.

4 Brush a nonstick, ridged skillet with oil and heat until hot. Press the fish steaks into the pan to seal, lower the heat, and cook for 4 minutes. Turn the fish over and cook for 4–5 minutes, until cooked through. Drain on paper towels and keep warm.

5 Stir the cornstarch paste into the onion sauce and heat through, stirring, until thickened. Season to taste.

6 Pile the relish onto 4 warm serving plates and place a halibut steak on top of each. Garnish with chives and pepper.

# Five-Spice Salmon with Ginger Stir-Fry

### Serves 4

---
**INGREDIENTS**
---

4 salmon fillets, skinned,
    4 ounces each
2 tsp five-spice powder
1 large leek
1 large carrot
4 ounces snow peas

1-inch piece fresh ginger root
2 tbsp ginger wine
2 tbsp light soy sauce
1 tbsp vegetable oil
salt and pepper

TO GARNISH:
leek, shredded
fresh ginger root, shredded
carrot, shredded

---

1 Wash the salmon and pat dry on absorbent paper towels. Rub the five-spice powder into both sides of the fish and season with salt and pepper to taste. Set aside until required.

2 Using a sharp knife, trim the leek, slice it down the center, and rinse under cold water to remove any dirt. Finely shred the leek. Peel the carrot and cut it into very thin strips. Top and tail the snow peas and cut them into shreds. Peel the ginger and slice thinly into strips.

3 Place all of the vegetables into a large bowl and toss in the ginger wine and 1 tablespoon of soy sauce. Set aside.

4 Preheat the broiler. Place the salmon fillets on the rack and brush with the remaining soy sauce. Cook for 2–3 minutes on each side, until completely cooked through.

5 While the salmon is cooking, heat the oil in a nonstick wok or large skillet and stir-fry the vegetables for 5 minutes, until just tender. Ensure that you do not overcook the vegetables—they should still have bite. Transfer to serving plates.

6 Drain the salmon on paper towels and serve on a bed of stir-fried vegetables. Garnish with shredded leek, ginger, and carrot and serve.

# Skewered Oriental Shellfish

### Makes 12

**INGREDIENTS**

12 ounces raw tiger shrimp,
   peeled leaving tails intact
12 ounces scallops, cleaned,
   trimmed, and halved
   (quartered if large)
1 bunch scallions, sliced into
   1-inch pieces
1 medium red bell pepper, seeded
   and cubed

3¹/₂ ounces baby corn cobs,
   trimmed and sliced into 1/2-
   inch pieces
3 tbsp dark soy sauce
¹/₂ tsp hot chili powder
¹/₂ tsp ground ginger
1 tbsp sunflower oil
1 red chili, seeded and sliced

DIP:
4 tbsp dark soy sauce
4 tbsp dry sherry
2 tsp clear honey
1-inch piece fresh ginger root,
   peeled and grated
1 scallion, trimmed and sliced
   very finely

1 Soak 12 wooden skewers in cold water for 10 minutes to prevent them from burning.

2 Divide the shrimp, scallops, scallions, bell pepper, and baby corn cobs into 12 portions and thread onto the cooled wooden skewers. Cover the ends with foil so that they do not burn, and place in a shallow dish.

3 Mix the soy sauce, chili powder, and ground ginger and coat the shellfish and vegetable kabobs. Cover and chill for about 2 hours.

4 Preheat the broiler. Arrange the kabobs on the rack, brush the shellfish and vegetables with oil, and cook for 2–3 minutes on each side, until the shrimp turn pink, the scallops become opaque, and the vegetables are soft.

5 Mix together the dip ingredients and set aside.

6 Remove the foil and transfer the kabobs to a warm serving platter. Garnish with sliced chili and serve with the dip.

# Tuna Steaks with Fragrant Spices & Lime

### Serves 4

**INGREDIENTS**

| | | |
|---|---|---|
| 4 tuna steaks, 6 ounces each | 1 tsp ground cumin | TO SERVE: |
| ½ tsp finely grated lime rind | 1 tsp ground coriander | avocado relish (see Cook's Tip) |
| 1 garlic clove, crushed | pepper | lime wedges |
| 2 tsp olive oil | 1 tbsp lime juice | tomato wedges |
| | fresh cilantro, to garnish | |

1 Trim the skin from the tuna steaks, rinse, and pat dry on absorbent paper towels.

2 In a small bowl, mix together the lime rind, garlic, olive oil, cumin, ground coriander, and pepper to make a paste.

3 Spread the paste thinly on both sides of the tuna. Heat a nonstick, ridged skillet until hot and press the tuna steaks into the pan to seal them.

Lower the heat and cook for 5 minutes. Turn the fish over and cook for a further 4–5 minutes, until the fish is cooked through. Drain on absorbent paper towels and transfer to a warm serving plate.

4 Sprinkle the lime juice and chopped cilantro over the fish.

5 Serve with freshly made avocado relish (see Cook's Tip), lime wedges and tomato wedges.

## COOK'S TIP

*For low-fat avocado relish to serve with tuna, peel and remove the pit from one small ripe avocado. Toss in 1 tbsp lime juice. Mix in 1 tbsp freshly chopped cilantro and 1 small finely chopped red onion. Stir in some chopped fresh mango or a chopped medium tomato and season with salt and pepper to taste.*

# *Baked Trout Mexican-Style*

### Serves 4

**INGREDIENTS**

4 trout, 8 ounces each
1 small bunch fresh cilantro
4 shallots, finely shredded
1 small yellow bell pepper,
    seeded and very finely
    chopped

1 small red bell pepper, seeded
    and very finely chopped
2 green chiles, seeded and
    finely chopped
1–2 red chiles, seeded and
    finely chopped

1 tbsp lemon juice
1 tbsp white wine vinegar
2 tsp superfine sugar
salt and pepper
fresh cilantro, to garnish
salad leaves, to serve

1 Preheat the oven to 350°F. Wash the trout and pat dry with absorbent paper towels. Season the cavities and fill them with a few cilantro leaves.

2 Place the fish side by side in a shallow ovenproof dish. Sprinkle on the shallots, bell peppers, and chiles.

3 Mix together the lemon juice, vinegar, and sugar in a bowl. Spoon over the trout and season

with salt and pepper to taste. Cover the dish and bake for 30 minutes, or until the fish is tender and the flesh is opaque.

4 Remove the fish with a fish slice and drain thoroughly. Transfer the fish to warm serving plates and spoon the cooking juices over the fish. Garnish with fresh cilantro and serve immediately with chili bean rice, if you wish (see Cook's Tip) and salad leaves.

## COOK'S TIP

*To make chili bean rice to serve with this recipe, cook 1¼ cups long-grain white rice in boiling water. Drain and return to the pan. Drain and rinse a 14 ounce can kidney beans and stir into the rice along with 1 tsp each of ground cumin and ground coriander. Stir in 4 tbsp freshly chopped cilantro and season to taste.*

# Blackened Fish

### Serves 4

### INGREDIENTS

| | | |
|---|---|---|
| 4 white fish steaks | 1 tsp freshly ground black | $\frac{1}{2}$ tsp salt |
| 1 tbsp paprika | pepper | $\frac{1}{4}$ tsp ground allspice |
| 1 tsp dried thyme | $\frac{1}{2}$ tsp freshly ground white | 4 tbsp unsalted butter |
| 1 tsp cayenne pepper | pepper | 3 tbsp sunflower oil |

1 Rinse the fish steaks and pat them dry with absorbent paper towels.

2 Mix together the paprika, thyme, cayenne pepper, black and white peppers, salt, and allspice in a shallow dish.

3 Place the butter and oil in a small saucepan and heat, stirring occasionally, until the butter melts.

4 Brush the butter mixture liberally all over the fish steaks, on both sides.

5 Dip the fish into the spicy mix until well coated on both sides.

6 Broil the fish over hot coals for about 10 minutes on each side, turning it over once. Continue to baste the fish with the remaining butter mixture during the remaining cooking time.

## COOK'S TIP

*Basting the fish with the butter mixture will ensure that the fish remains moist during cooking.*

## VARIATION

*A whole fish—red mullet, for example—rather than steaks is also delicious cooked this way. The spicy seasoning can also be used to coat chicken portions, if you prefer.*

# Monkfish Skewers with Zucchini & Lemon

### Serves 4

## INGREDIENTS

| | | |
|---|---|---|
| 1 pound monkfish tail | SAUCE: | salt |
| 2 zucchini | 4 tbsp olive oil | |
| 1 lemon | 2 tbsp lemon juice | TO SERVE: |
| 12 cherry tomatoes | 1 tsp chopped, fresh thyme | salad greens |
| 8 bay leaves | $\frac{1}{2}$ tsp lemon pepper | fresh, crusty bread |

1 Cut the monkfish into 2-inch chunks. Cut the zucchini into thick slices and the lemon into wedges.

2 Thread the monkfish chunks, zucchini slices, lemon wedges, tomatoes, and bay leaves onto 4 skewers.

3 To make the basting sauce, combine the oil, lemon juice, thyme, lemon pepper, and salt to taste in a small bowl.

4 Brush the basting sauce liberally all over the fish, lemon, tomatoes, and bay leaves on the skewers.

5 Cook the skewers on the barbecue for about 15 minutes, basting frequently with the sauce, until the fish is cooked through.

6 Serve the kabobs with salad greens and warm, fresh crusty bread.

## VARIATION

*Use flounder fillets instead of the monkfish, if you prefer. Allow two fillets per person, and skin and cut each fillet lengthwise into two. Roll up each piece and thread them onto the skewers.*

# Monkfish Skewers with Coconut & Cilantro

### Serves 4

## INGREDIENTS

1 pound monkfish tails
8 ounces raw peeled shrimp
shredded coconut, toasted, to
    garnish (optional)

MARINADE:
1 tsp sunflower oil
¹/₂ small onion, finely grated
1 tsp fresh ginger root, grated

²/₃ cup canned coconut milk
2 tbsp chopped, fresh cilantro

1 To make the marinade, heat the oil in a wok or saucepan and sauté the onion and ginger for 5 minutes, until just softened but not browned.

2 Add the coconut milk to the pan and bring to a boil. Boil rapidly for about 5 minutes, or until reduced to the consistency of light cream.

3 Remove the pan from the heat and allow to cool completely. Once cooled, stir in the chopped cilantro and pour into a shallow dish.

4 Cut the fish into bite-size chunks and stir gently into the coconut mixture, together with the shrimp. Chill in the refrigerator for 1–4 hours.

5 Thread the fish and shrimp onto skewers and discard any remaining marinade. Broil the skewers over hot coals for 10–15 minutes, turning frequently. Garnish with toasted coconut, if desired.

## VARIATION

*Look for uncooked shrimp in the freezer section in large supermarkets. If you cannot obtain them, you can use cooked shrimp, but remember they only need heating through.*

# Charred Tuna Steaks

### Serves 4

**INGREDIENTS**

| | | |
|---|---|---|
| 4 tuna steaks | 1 tsp superfine sugar | TO GARNISH: |
| 3 tbsp soy sauce | 1 tbsp sunflower oil | parsley |
| 1 tbsp Worcestershire sauce | salad greens, to serve | lemon wedges |
| 1 tsp wholegrain mustard | | |

1 Place the tuna steaks in a shallow dish.

2 Mix together the soy sauce, Worcestershire sauce, mustard, sugar, and oil in a bowl. Pour the marinade over the tuna.

3 Gently turn the tuna steaks, using your fingers or a fork, so that they are well coated with the marinade.

4 Cover and place the tuna steaks in the refrigerator and chill for between 30 minutes and 2 hours.

5 Broil the marinated fish over hot coals for 10–15 minutes, turning once. Baste frequently with any of the marinade that is left in the dish.

6 Garnish with parsley and lemon wedges, and serve with salad greens.

### COOK'S TIP

*Tuna has a dark red flesh, which turns paler on cooking. Tuna has a good meaty texture, but if you are unable to obtain it, use swordfish steaks instead.*

### COOK'S TIP

*If a marinade contains soy sauce, the marinating time should be limited, usually to 2 hours. If allowed to marinate for too long, the fish will dry out and become tough.*

# *Charbroiled Bream*

### Serves 2

---
**INGREDIENTS**
---

| | | |
|---|---|---|
| 2 small sea bream, scaled, gutted, trimmed, and cleaned | BASTE: | TO GARNISH: |
| | 4 tbsp olive oil | fresh bay leaves |
| 2 slices lemon | 2 tbsp lemon juice | fresh thyme sprig |
| 2 bay leaves | 1/2 tsp chopped, fresh oregano | lemon wedges |
| salt and pepper | 1/2 tsp chopped, fresh thyme | |

1 Using a sharp knife, cut 2–3 deep slashes into the bodies of both fish in order to help them fully absorb the flavor of the basting sauce.

2 Place a slice of lemon and a bay leaf inside the cavity of each fish. Season inside the cavity with salt and pepper.

3 In a small bowl, mix together the ingredients for the baste using a fork. Alternatively, place the basting ingredients in a small screw-top jar and shake well to combine thoroughly.

4 Brush some of the baste liberally over the fish and place them on a rack over hot coals. Broil over hot coals for 20–30 minutes, turning and basting frequently.

5 Transfer the fish to a serving plate, garnish with fresh bay leaves, thyme, and lemon wedges, and serve.

## VARIATION

*If you prefer, use brill or a fish like gurnard instead of the sea bream.*

## COOK'S TIP

*The flavor of the dish will be enhanced if you use good fresh ingredients in the sauce. Dried herbs can be used, but remember that the flavor is much more intense, so only use half the quantity of the fresh herbs listed above.*

# Salmon Yakitori

### Serves 4

### INGREDIENTS

| | | |
|---|---|---|
| 12 ounces chunky salmon fillet | YAKITORI SAUCE: | 2 tbsp superfine sugar |
| 8 baby leeks | 5 tbsp light soy sauce | 5 tbsp dry white wine |
| | 5 tbsp fish stock | 3 tbsp sweet sherry |
| | | 1 clove garlic, crushed |

1 Skin the salmon and cut the flesh into 2-inch chunks. Trim the leeks and cut them into 2-inch lengths.

2 Thread the pieces of salmon and leek alternately onto 8 presoaked wooden skewers. Chill in the refrigerator until required.

3 To make the sauce, place all of the ingredients in a small pan and heat gently, stirring, until the sugar dissolves. Bring to a boil, then reduce the heat, and simmer for 2 minutes. Strain the sauce and leave to cool.

4 Pour about one-third of the sauce into a dish and then set aside to serve with the kabobs.

5 Brush plenty of the remaining sauce over the skewers and cook directly on the rack or, if preferred, place a sheet of greased foil on the rack and cook the salmon on that. Broil the skewers over hot coals for about 10 minutes, turning once. Baste the skewers frequently during cooking with the remaining sauce to prevent the fish and vegetables from drying out.

6 Serve the kabobs with the dish of reserved sauce for dipping.

## COOK'S TIP

*Soak the wooden skewers in cold water for at least 30 minutes to prevent them from burning during cooking. You can make the kabobs and sauce several hours ahead of time. Refrigerate until required.*

# *Salmon Brochettes*

### Serves 4

**INGREDIENTS**

| | | |
|---|---|---|
| 1 pound salmon, skinned and cut into large chunks | 1 green bell pepper, seeded and cut into chunks | ¼ cucumber, peeled, seeded, and chopped |
| 1 tbsp cornstarch | 4 tbsp olive oil | 8 basil leaves |
| ½ tsp salt | Italian bread, to serve | 6 tbsp olive oil |
| ½ tsp pepper | | 2 tbsp lemon juice |
| 1 small egg white, beaten | TOMATO SAUCE: | salt and pepper |
| 1 red bell pepper, seeded and cut into chunks | 4 tomatoes, seeded and quartered | |

1 Place the salmon in a shallow dish and sprinkle the cornstarch and salt and pepper on top. Add the beaten egg white and toss well to coat. Chill for 15 minutes.

2 Thread the pieces of salmon onto 4 skewers, alternating the fish pieces with the chunks of red and green bell peppers. Set the skewers aside while you make the tomato sauce.

3 To make the sauce, place all of the ingredients in a food processor and chop coarsely. Alternatively, chop the tomatoes, cucumber, and basil leaves by hand and mix with the oil, lemon juice, and seasoning. Let chill until required.

4 Broil the salmon brochettes over hot coals for 10 minutes, brushing frequently with olive oil to prevent them from drying out during the cooking time.

5 Slice the Italian bread at an angle to produce 4 long slices. Lightly toast on the barbecue.

6 Spread the sauce over each slice of bread and top with a salmon brochette. You can also serve the brochettes on toasted French baguettes.

# Japanese-Style Charbroiled Flounder

### Serves 4

#### INGREDIENTS

| | | |
|---|---|---|
| 4 small flounders | 1 tbsp lemon juice | TO GARNISH: |
| 6 tbsp soy sauce | 2 tbsp light brown sugar | 1 small carrot |
| 2 tbsp sake or dry white wine | 1 tsp fresh ginger root, grated | 4 scallions |
| 2 tbsp sesame oil | 1 clove garlic, crushed | |

1 Rinse the fish and pat dry on absorbent paper towels. Cut a few slashes into both sides of each fish.

2 Mix together the soy sauce, sake or wine, oil, lemon juice, sugar, ginger, and garlic in a large, shallow dish.

3 Place the fish in the marinade and turn them over so that they are well coated on both sides. Let stand in the refrigerator for 1–6 hours.

4 Meanwhile, prepare the garnish. Using a sharp knife, cut the carrot into even-size thin sticks and clean and shred the scallions.

5 Broil the fish over hot coals for 10 minutes, turning them once.

6 Scatter the chopped scallions and sliced carrot over the fish and then transfer the fish to a warm serving dish. Serve immediately.

## VARIATION

*Use sole instead of the flounders, and scatter over some toasted sesame seeds instead of the carrot and scallions, if you prefer.*

# Smoky Fish Skewers

### Serves 4

**INGREDIENTS**

| | | |
|---|---|---|
| 12 ounces smoked cod fillet | fresh dill, to garnish (optional) | 2 tbsp lemon or lime juice |
| 12 ounces cod fillet | | rind of ½ lemon or lime, grated |
| 8 large raw shrimp | MARINADE: | ¼ tsp dried dill |
| 8 bay leaves | 4 tbsp sunflower oil | salt and pepper |

1 Skin both types of cod and cut the flesh into bite-size pieces. Peel the shrimp, leaving the tail.

2 To make the marinade, combine the sunflower oil, lemon or lime juice, grated lemon or lime rind, dried dill, and salt and pepper to taste in a shallow, nonmetallic dish.

3 Place the prepared fish in the marinade and stir together until the fish is well coated on all sides. Marinate in the refrigerator for 1–4 hours.

4 Thread the fish onto 4 skewers, alternating the 2 types of cod with the shrimp and bay leaves.

5 Cover the rack with lightly buttered foil and place the fish skewers on top of the foil.

6 Broil the fish skewers over hot coals for 5–10 minutes, basting with any remaining marinade, turning once.

7 Garnish with fresh dill, if using, and serve immediately.

## COOK'S TIP

*Cod fillet is inclined to flake, so choose the thicker end which is easier to cut into chunky pieces. Line the rack with foil rather than cooking the fish directly on the rack so that, even if the fish does break away from the skewer, it is not wasted.*

# *Apricot Charbroiled Mackerel*

### Serves 4

## INGREDIENTS

| | | |
|---|---|---|
| 4 mackerel | 3 tbsp Worcestershire sauce | dash Tabasco sauce |
| 14 ounce can apricots in natural juice | 3 tbsp soy sauce | 1 clove garlic, crushed (optional) |
| 3 tbsp dark brown sugar | 2 tbsp tomato paste | salt and pepper |
| | 1 tsp ground ginger | |

1 Clean and gut the mackerel, removing the heads if preferred. Place the fish in a shallow dish.

2 Drain the apricots, reserving the juice. Roughly chop half of the apricots and set aside.

3 Place the remaining apricots in a food processor with the sugar, Worcestershire sauce, soy sauce, tomato paste, ginger, Tabasco sauce, and garlic (if using) and process until smooth. Alternatively, chop the apricots and mix with the other ingredients until well combined.

4 Pour the sauce over the fish, turning them so that they are well coated on both sides. Chill in the refrigerator until required.

5 Transfer the mackerel to the barbecue either directly on the rack or on a piece of greased kitchen foil. Broil the mackerel over hot coals for 5–7 minutes, turning once.

6 Spoon any remaining marinade into a saucepan. Add the reserved chopped apricots and about half of the reserved apricot juice, and bring to a boil. Reduce the heat and simmer for 2 minutes.

7 Transfer the mackerel to warm serving plates and serve with the apricot sauce.

## COOK'S TIP

*Use a hinged rack if you have one, as it will make it much easier to turn the fish while it is cooking.*

# *Mackerel with Lime & Cilantro*

### Serves 4

**INGREDIENTS**

4 small mackerel, trout, or
    sardines
1/4 tsp ground coriander
1/4 tsp ground cumin
4 sprigs fresh cilantro

3 tbsp chopped, fresh cilantro
1 red chili, seeded and chopped
grated rind and juice of 1 lime
2 tbsp sunflower oil
salt and pepper

1 lime, sliced, to garnish
chili flowers, to garnish
    (optional)
salad greens, to serve

1 To make the chili flowers (if using), cut the tip of a small chili lengthwise into thin strips, leaving the chili intact at the stem end. Remove the seeds and place in iced water until curled.

2 Clean and gut the mackerel, removing the heads if preferred. Transfer to a board.

3 Sprinkle the fish with the ground spices and salt and pepper to taste. Place a sprig of fresh cilantro inside the cavity of each fish.

4 Mix together the chopped cilantro, chili, lime rind and juice, and the oil in a small bowl. Brush the mixture liberally over the fish.

5 Place the fish in a hinged rack if you have one. Broil the fish over hot coals for 3–4 minutes on each side, turning once. Brush frequently with the remaining basting mixture.

6 Garnish with lime slices and chili flowers, if using, and serve with salad greens.

# Mediterranean-Style Sardines

### Serves 4

**INGREDIENTS**

| | | |
|---|---|---|
| 8–12 fresh sardines | 4 tbsp olive oil | TO GARNISH: |
| 8–12 sprigs of fresh thyme | salt and pepper | lemon wedges |
| 3 tbsp lemon juice | | tomato slices |
| | | fresh herbs |

1 Clean and gut the fish if this has not already been done.

2 Remove the scales by rubbing the back of a knife from head to tail along the body. Wash and pat the sardines dry on absorbent paper towels.

3 Tuck a sprig of fresh thyme into the body of each sardine. Transfer the sardines to a large, nonmetallic dish and season with salt and pepper.

4 Beat together the lemon juice and oil in a bowl and pour the mixture over the sardines. Let the sardines marinate in the refrigerator for about 30 minutes.

5 Remove the sardines from the marinade and place them in a hinged basket, if you have one, or on a rack. Broil the sardines over hot coals for 3–4 minutes on each side, basting frequently with any of the remaining marinade.

6 Serve the sardines garnished with lemon wedges, tomato slices, and fresh herbs.

## COOK'S TIP

*Look out for small sardines or sprats. Prepare them as above and use the same marinade. Place a piece of greased foil on the rack and cook over hot coals for 2–3 minutes on each side.*

## VARIATION

*For a slightly different flavor and texture, toss the sardines in dried bread crumbs and then baste them with a little olive oil for a crispy coating.*

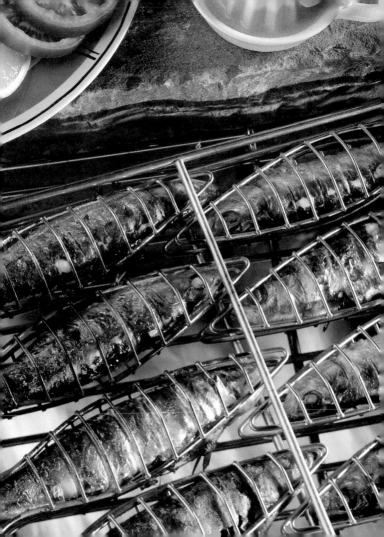

# Barbecued Herrings with Lemon

## Serves 4

### INGREDIENTS

| | | |
|---|---|---|
| 4 herrings, cleaned | 1 lemon, sliced | ½ tsp lemon pepper |
| 4 bay leaves | 4 tbsp unsalted butter | fresh crusty bread, to serve |
| salt | 2 tbsp chopped, fresh parsley | |

1 Season the prepared herrings inside and out with freshly ground salt to taste.

2 Place a bay leaf inside the cavity of each fish.

3 Place 4 squares of foil on the counter and divide the lemon slices evenly among them. Place one fish on top of the lemon slices.

4 Beat the butter until softened, then mix in the parsley and lemon pepper. Dot the flavored butter liberally all over the fish.

5 Wrap the fish tightly in the foil and cook over medium hot coals for about 15–20 minutes, or until the fish is cooked through—the flesh should be white in color and firm to the touch (unwrap the foil to check, then wrap up the fish again).

6 Carefully transfer the wrapped fish packets to individual, warm serving plates.

7 Unwrap the foil parcels just before serving and serve the fish with fresh, crusty bread with which to mop up the

deliciously flavored cooking juices.

## VARIATION

*For a main course use trout instead of herring. Cook for 20–30 minutes, until the flesh is firm to the touch and opaque.*

# Teriyaki Stir-Fried Salmon with Crispy Leeks

### Serves 4

**INGREDIENTS**

| | | |
|---|---|---|
| 1 pound salmon fillet, skinned | 1 tsp rice wine vinegar | 4 tbsp corn oil |
| 2 tbsp sweet soy sauce | 1 tbsp sugar | 1 leek, thinly shredded |
| 2 tbsp tomato ketchup | 1 clove garlic, crushed | finely chopped red chiles, to garnish |

1 Using a sharp knife, cut the salmon into slices. Place the slices of salmon in a shallow nonmetallic dish.

2 Mix together the soy sauce, tomato ketchup, rice wine vinegar, sugar, and garlic.

3 Pour the mixture over the salmon, toss well, and marinate for about 30 minutes.

4 Meanwhile, heat 3 tablespoons of the corn oil in a large preheated wok.

5 Add the leeks to the wok and stir-fry over a medium high heat for about 10 minutes, or until the leeks become crispy and tender.

6 Using a slotted spoon, carefully remove the leeks from the wok and transfer to warm serving plates.

7 Add the remaining oil to the wok. Add the salmon and the marinade to the wok and cook for 2 minutes. Spoon it over the leeks, garnish, and serve immediately.

## VARIATION

*You can use a fillet of beef instead of the salmon, if wished.*

# Stir-Fried Salmon with Pineapple

## Serves 4

### INGREDIENTS

| | | |
|---|---|---|
| 1 cup baby corn cobs, halved | 1 green bell pepper, seeded and sliced | ½ cup bean sprouts |
| 2 tbsp sunflower oil | 1 pound salmon fillet, skin removed | 2 tbsp tomato ketchup |
| 1 red onion, sliced | 1 tbsp paprika | 2 tbsp soy sauce |
| 1 orange bell pepper, seeded | 8 ounce can cubed | 2 tbsp medium sherry |
| and sliced | pineapple, drained | 1 tsp cornstarch |

1 Using a sharp knife, cut the baby corn cobs in half.

2 Heat the sunflower oil in a large preheated wok. Add the onion, bell peppers, and baby corn cobs to the wok and stir-fry for 5 minutes.

3 Rinse the salmon fillet under cold running water and pat dry with absorbent paper towels.

4 Cut the salmon flesh into thin strips and place in a large bowl.

Sprinkle with the paprika and toss until well coated.

5 Add the salmon to the wok, together with the pineapple, and stir-fry for a further 2–3 minutes or until the fish is tender.

6 Add the bean sprouts to the wok and toss well.

7 Mix together the tomato ketchup, soy sauce, sherry, and cornstarch. Add the mixture to the wok and cook until the juices thicken. Transfer to warm serving plates and serve immediately.

### VARIATION

*You can use trout fillets instead of the salmon as an alternative, if wished.*

# Tuna & Vegetable Stir-Fry

### Serves 4

### INGREDIENTS

| | | |
|---|---|---|
| 3–4 medium carrots | 1 pound fresh tuna | 2 tbsp sherry |
| 2 tbsp corn oil | 2 tbsp fish sauce | 1 tsp cornstarch |
| 1 onion, sliced | 1 tbsp palm sugar or brown sugar | rice or noodles, to serve |
| 2½ cups snow peas | finely grated zest and juice of | |
| 1¾ cups baby corn cobs, halved | 1 orange | |

1 Using a sharp knife, cut the carrots into thin sticks.

2 Heat the corn oil in a large preheated wok.

3 Add the onion, carrots, snow peas, and baby corn cobs to the wok and stir-fry for 5 minutes.

4 Using a sharp knife, thinly slice the tuna.

5 Add the tuna to the wok and stir-fry for 2–3 minutes, or until the tuna turns opaque.

6 Mix together the fish sauce, palm or brown sugar, orange zest and juice, sherry, and cornstarch.

7 Pour the mixture over the tuna and vegetables and cook for 2 minutes, or until the juices thicken. Serve with rice or noodles.

## VARIATION

*Try using swordfish steaks instead of the tuna. Swordfish steaks are now widely available and are similar in texture to tuna.*

## COOK'S TIP

*Baby corn cobs have a deliciously sweet fragrance and flavor. They are available both fresh and canned.*

# Stir-Fried Cod with Mango

### Serves 4

**INGREDIENTS**

| | | |
|---|---|---|
| 2–3 medium carrots | 1 pound skinless cod fillet | 1 tbsp lime juice |
| 2 tbsp vegetable oil | 1 ripe mango | 1 tbsp chopped cilantro |
| 1 red onion, sliced | 1 tsp cornstarch | |
| 1 red bell pepper, seeded and sliced | 1 tbsp soy sauce | |
| 1 green bell pepper, seeded and sliced | 1⅓ cup tropical fruit juice | |

1 Using a sharp knife, slice the carrots into thin sticks.

2 Heat the vegetable oil in a preheated wok.

3 Add the onions, carrots, and bell peppers to the wok and stir-fry for 5 minutes.

4 Using a sharp knife, cut the cod into small cubes.

5 Peel the mango, then carefully remove the flesh from the central pit. Cut the flesh into thin slices.

6 Add the cod and mango to the wok and stir-fry for a further 4–5 minutes, or until the fish is cooked through. Do not stir the mixture too much or you may break the fish up.

7 Mix the cornstarch, soy sauce, fruit juice, and lime juice in a small bowl.

8 Pour the cornstarch mixture over the stir-fry and allow the mixture to bubble and the juices to thicken. Scatter with cilantro, transfer to a warm serving dish, and serve immediately.

## VARIATION

*You can use papaya as an alternative to the mango, if wished.*

# *Stir-Fried Gingered Monkfish*

### Serves 4

**INGREDIENTS**

| | | |
|---|---|---|
| 1 pound monkfish | 1 tbsp corn oil | 3 scallions, sliced |
| 1 tbsp freshly grated ginger root | 1 cup fine asparagus | 1 tsp sesame oil |
| 2 tbsp sweet chili sauce | | |

1 Remove the membrane from the monkfish, then using a sharp knife, slice the flesh into thin flat rounds.

2 Mix the ginger with the chili sauce in a small bowl.

3 Brush the ginger and chili sauce mixture over the monkfish pieces.

4 Heat the corn oil in a large preheated wok.

5 Add the monkfish, asparagus, and scallions to the wok and stir-fry for about 5 minutes.

6 Remove the wok from the heat, drizzle the sesame oil over the stir-fry, and toss well to combine.

7 Transfer to warm serving plates and serve immediately.

## VARIATION

*Monkfish is quite expensive, but it is well worth using as it has a wonderful flavor and texture. Otherwise, could use cubes of chunky cod fillet instead.*

## COOK'S TIP

*Some recipes specify to grate ginger before it is cooked with other ingredients. To do this, just peel the flesh and rub it at a 45 degree angle up and down on the fine section of a metal grater, or use a special wooden or ceramic ginger grater.*

# *Braised Fish Fillets*

### Serves 4

**INGREDIENTS**

3–4 small Chinese dried mushrooms
10½–12 ounces fish fillets
1 tsp salt
½ egg white, lightly beaten
1 tsp cornstarch paste
2½ cups vegetable oil
1 tsp finely chopped ginger root

2 scallions, finely chopped
1 garlic clove, finely chopped
½ small green bell pepper, seeded
and cut into small cubes
½ small carrot, thinly sliced
½ cup canned sliced bamboo shoots,
rinsed and drained

½ tsp sugar
1 tbsp light soy sauce
1 tsp rice wine or dry sherry
1 tbsp chili bean sauce
2–3 tbsp Chinese stock or water
a few drops of sesame oil

1 Soak the dried mushrooms in a bowl of warm water for 30 minutes. Drain the mushrooms thoroughly on paper towels, reserving the soaking water for stock or soup. Squeeze the mushrooms to extract all of the moisture, cut off and discard any hard stems, and slice the caps thinly.

2 Cut the fish into bite-size pieces, then place in a shallow dish, and mix with a pinch of salt, the egg white, and cornstarch paste, turning the fish to coat well.

3 Heat the oil in a preheated wok. Add the fish pieces to the wok and deep-fry for about 1 minute. Remove the fish pieces with a slotted spoon and drain on paper towels.

4 Pour off the excess oil, leaving about 1 table-spoon in the wok. Add the ginger, scallions, and garlic to flavor the oil for a few seconds, then add the bell pepper, carrots, and bamboo shoots and stir-fry for about 1 minute.

5 Add the sugar, soy sauce, wine, chili bean sauce, stock or water, and the remaining salt and bring to a boil. Add the fish pieces, stir to coat well with the sauce, and braise for 1 minute.

6 Sprinkle with sesame oil, transfer to a warm serving dish, and serve immediately.

# Chinese Cabbage with Shiitake Mushrooms & Crab Meat

### Serves 4

### INGREDIENTS

| | | |
|---|---|---|
| 8 ounces shiitake mushrooms | 6 scallions, sliced | 6 tbsp coconut milk |
| 2 tbsp vegetable oil | 1 head Chinese cabbage, shredded | 7 ounce can white crab meat, drained |
| 2 cloves garlic, crushed | 1 tbsp mild curry paste | 1 tsp chili flakes |

1 Using a sharp knife, cut the the mushrooms into slices.

2 Heat the vegetable oil in a large preheated wok.

3 Add the mushrooms and garlic to the wok and stir-fry for 3 minutes, or until the mushrooms have softened.

4 Add the scallions and shredded Chinese cabbage to the wok and stir-fry until the leaves have wilted.

5 Mix together the mild curry paste and coconut milk in a small bowl.

6 Add the curry paste and coconut milk mixture to the wok, together with the crab meat and chili flakes. Mix together until thoroughly combined and heat through until the juices start to bubble.

7 Transfer to warm serving bowls and then serve immediately.

## COOK'S TIP

*Shiitake mushrooms are now readily available in the fresh vegetable section of most large supermarkets.*

# Stir-Fried Lettuce with Mussels & Lemon Grass

### Serves 4

## INGREDIENTS

| | | |
|---|---|---|
| 2¼ pounds mussels in their shells, scrubbed and debearded | 2 tbsp lemon juice | 1 iceberg lettuce |
| 2 stalks lemon grass, thinly sliced | ½ cup water | finely grated zest of 1 lemon |
| | 2 tbsp butter | 2 tbsp oyster sauce |

1 Discard any mussels that do not shut when sharply tapped. Place the mussels in a large saucepan.

2 Add the lemon grass, lemon juice, and water to the pan, cover, and cook for 5 minutes, or until the mussels have opened. Discard any that have not opened.

3 Carefully remove the cooked mussels from their shells.

4 Heat the butter in a large preheated wok.

5 Add the lettuce and lemon zest to the wok and stir-fry for 2 minutes, or until the lettuce begins to wilt.

6 Add the oyster sauce to the mixture in the wok, stir, and heat through. Serve immediately.

## COOK'S TIP

*Lemon grass with its citrus fragrance and lemon flavor looks like a fibrous scallion and is often used in Thai cooking.*

## COOK'S TIP

*When using fresh mussels, be sure to discard any opened mussels before scrubbing and any unopened mussels after cooking.*

# Mussels in Black Bean Sauce with Spinach

### Serves 4

**INGREDIENTS**

12 ounces leeks

12 ounces cooked green-lipped
   mussels, shelled

1 tsp cumin seeds

2 tbsp vegetable oil

2 cloves garlic, crushed

1 red bell pepper, seeded and sliced

3/4 cup canned bamboo shoots, drained

6 ounces baby spinach

5 3/4 ounce jar black bean sauce

1 Using a sharp knife, trim the leeks and shred them.

2 Place the mussels in a large bowl, sprinkle with the cumin seeds, and toss well to coat all over.

3 Heat the vegetable oil in a large preheated wok.

4 Add the leeks, garlic, and red bell pepper to the wok and stir-fry for 5 minutes, or until the vegetables are tender.

5 Add the bamboo shoots, baby spinach leaves, and cooked green-lipped mussels to the wok and stir-fry for about 2 minutes.

6 Pour the black bean sauce over the ingredients in the wok, toss well to coat all over, and simmer for a few seconds, stirring occasionally.

7 Transfer the stir-fry to warm serving bowls and serve immediately.

## COOK'S TIP

*If fresh green-lipped mussels are not available, they can be bought shelled in cans and jars from most large supermarkets.*

# *Shrimp with Bell Peppers*

### Serves 4

**INGREDIENTS**

1 pound frozen shrimp
½ bunch cilantro leaves
1 tsp fresh garlic, crushed

1 tsp salt
1 medium green bell pepper, sliced
1 medium red bell pepper

2³/₄ ounces unsalted butter

1 Defrost the shrimp. Once they are thawed, rinse them under cold running water twice. Drain the shrimp thoroughly and place in a large mixing bowl.

2 Using a sharp knife, finely chop the bunch of fresh cilantro leaves.

3 Add the garlic, salt, and fresh, chopped cilantro leaves to the shrimp, then set the bowl aside until required.

4 Deseed the bell peppers and cut into thin slices, using a sharp knife.

5 Melt the butter in a large skillet. Add the shrimp to the pan and stir-fry, stirring and tossing the shrimp gently, for 10-12 minutes.

6 Add the bell peppers to the pan and fry for a further 3-5 minutes, stirring occasionally.

7 Transfer the shrimp and bell pepper to a serving dish and serve hot.

## VARIATION

*You could use large shrimps in this dish, if you prefer.*

# *Shrimp with Spinach*

### Serves 4-6

**INGREDIENTS**

| | | |
|---|---|---|
| 8 ounces frozen shrimp | ²⁄₃ cup oil | 1 tsp fresh ginger root, finely |
| 12 ounces canned spinach purée | ½ tsp mustard seeds | chopped |
| or frozen spinach, thawed | ½ tsp onion seeds | 1 tsp fresh garlic, crushed |
| and chopped | | 1 tsp chili powder |
| 2 tomatoes | | 1 tsp salt |

1 Place the shrimp in a bowl of cold water and set aside to defrost.

2 Drain the can of spinach purée, if using.

3 Using a sharp knife, cut the tomatoes into slices and set aside.

4 Heat the oil in a large skillet. Add the mustard and onion seeds to the pan.

5 Reduce the heat and add the tomatoes, spinach, ginger, garlic, chili powder, and salt to the pan and stir-fry for about 5-7 minutes.

6 Drain the shrimp thoroughly.

7 Add the shrimp to the spinach mixture in the pan. Gently stir the shrimp and spinach mixture until well combined, cover, and leave to simmer over a low heat for about 7-10 minutes.

8 Transfer the cooked shrimp and spinach to a serving dish and serve hot.

## COOK'S TIP

*If using frozen spinach, it should be thawed and squeezed dry before using. You could use fresh spinach, if you prefer.*

# *Tandoori-Style Shrimp*

### Serves 4

---
**INGREDIENTS**

10-12 king shrimp

3¹/₂ ounces unsalted butter

1 tsp fresh ginger root, finely
chopped

1 tsp fresh garlic, crushed

1 tsp chili powder

¹/₂ tsp salt

1 tsp ground coriander

1 tsp ground cumin

fresh cilantro leaves, finely
chopped

a few drops of red food coloring

TO GARNISH:

8 lettuce leaves

1-2 green chiles, finely chopped

1 lemon, cut into wedges

---

1 Carefully remove the shells from the shrimp.

2 Transfer the shelled shrimp to a heatproof dish.

3 Melt the butter in a large saucepan.

4 Add the ginger, garlic, chili powder, salt, ground coriander, ground cumin, fresh cilantro leaves, and the red food coloring to the butter and mix together until well combined.

5 Brush the melted butter and spice mixture over the shrimp.

6 Cook the shrimp under a very hot pre-heated broiler for 10-12 minutes, turning once.

7 Serve the shrimp on a bed of lettuce and garnish with chopped green chiles and lemon wedges.

## COOK'S TIP

*Though not essential, it is best to shell the shrimp before cooking them as some people find it a bit awkward to shell them at the table.*

# Dried Shrimp

### Serves 4

---
**INGREDIENTS**
---

7 ounces dried shrimp
2 medium onions, sliced
3 green chiles, finely chopped
fresh cilantro leaves, finely
    chopped

½ cup oil
1½ tsp fresh ginger root, finely
    chopped
1½ tsp fresh garlic, crushed
pinch of turmeric

1 tsp salt
1 tsp chili powder, plus extra
    to garnish
2 tbsp lemon juice

---

1 Soak the shrimp in a bowl of cold water for about 2 hours. Drain the shrimp thoroughly and rinse under cold running water twice. Drain the shrimp again thoroughly.

2 Heat ¼ cup of the oil in a large saucepan. Add the onions, 2 of the green chiles, and half of the fresh cilantro to the pan and stir-fry until the onions are golden.

3 Add the ginger, garlic, turmeric, salt, and chili powder to the pan and stir-fry for a further 2 minutes over a low heat. Set aside until required.

4 Heat the remaining oil in a separate saucepan. Add the shrimp and fry, stirring occasionally, until the shrimp are crisp.

5 Add the fried shrimp to the onions and blend together. Return the shrimp and onion mixture to the heat, sprinkle with the lemon juice and stir-fry for 3-5 minutes.

6 Transfer to a serving dish, garnish with a pinch of chili powder, and serve with chapatis.

## VARIATION

*You could use 1 pound fresh shrimp instead of the dried shrimp, if you prefer.*

# Vegetables
# & Salads

Too frequently, leaf vegetables are overcooked
and limp, with all the goodness and flavor boiled
out, while salads are often nothing more than a
dismal leaf or two of pale green lettuce, with a slice
of tomato, and a dry ring of onion. Make the most
of the wonderful range of fresh produce that is
available in our shops and markets.

Steam broccoli and cabbage so that they
are colorful and crunchy. Enjoy the wonderfully
appetizing shades of orange and yellow bell peppers
and the purple-brown of eggplant. Try grating root
vegetables to add flavor and texture to garnishes and
casseroles. Look out for red and curly lettuces to
bring excitement to summer salads. Use sweet baby
tomatoes in salads and on skewers, and raid your
garden for sprigs of fresh mint and basil leaves.

Nuts and seeds are high in fat, so both should
be used in moderation. However, they are a
valuable source of protein and minerals, and
vegetarians and vegans in particular need to ensure
that their diets contain these valuable ingredients.

# *Vegetable Spaghetti with Lemon Dressing*

### Serves 4

**INGREDIENTS**

8 ounces celery root
2 medium carrots
2 medium leeks
1 small red bell pepper
1 small yellow bell pepper
2 garlic cloves
1 tsp celery seeds

1 tbsp lemon juice
10½ ounces spaghetti
celery leaves, chopped, to
    garnish

LEMON DRESSING:
1 tsp finely grated lemon rind

1 tbsp lemon juice
4 tbsp low-fat unsweetened
    yogurt
2 tbsp snipped fresh chives
salt and pepper

1 Peel the celery root and carrots and cut them into thin matchsticks, using a sharp knife. Place the celery root and carrots in a bowl. Trim and slice the leeks, rinse to flush out any trapped dirt, then shred finely. Halve, seed, and slice the bell peppers. Peel and thinly slice the garlic. Add all of the vegetables to the bowl containing the celery root and the carrots.

2 Toss the vegetables with the celery seeds and lemon juice.

3 Bring a large saucepan of water to a boil and cook the spaghetti according to the instructions on the packet. Drain and keep warm.

4 Meanwhile, bring another large saucepan of water to a boil, put the vegetables in a steamer or strainer and place over the boiling water. Cover and steam for 6–7 minutes or until tender.

5 When the spaghetti and vegetables are cooked, mix the ingredients for the lemon dressing together.

6 Transfer the spaghetti and vegetables to a warm serving bowl and mix with the dressing. Garnish with celery leaves and serve.

# *Pesto Pasta*

### Serves 4

**INGREDIENTS**

8 ounces crimini mushrooms,
    sliced
³/₄ cup fresh vegetable stock
6 ounces asparagus, trimmed
    and cut into 2-inch lengths
10¹/₂ ounces green and
    white tagliatelle

14 ounces canned artichoke
    hearts, drained and halved
bread sticks, to serve

TO GARNISH:
basil leaves, shredded
Parmesan shavings

PESTO:
2 large garlic cloves, crushed
¹/₂ ounce fresh basil leaves,
    washed
6 tbsp low-fat unsweetened
    yogurt
2 tbsp freshly grated
    Parmesan cheese
salt and pepper

1 Place the sliced mushrooms in a saucepan along with the stock. Bring to a boil, cover, and simmer for 3–4 minutes, until just tender. Drain and set aside.

2 Bring a small saucepan of water to a boil and cook the asparagus for 3–4 minutes, until just tender. Drain and set aside until required.

3 Bring a large pan of lightly salted water to a boil and cook the tagliatelle according to the instructions on the packet. Drain, return to the pan, and keep warm.

4 Meanwhile, make the pesto. Place all of the ingredients in a blender or food processor and process for a few seconds until smooth. Alternatively, finely

chop the basil and mix all the ingredients together.

5 Add the mushrooms, asparagus, and artichoke hearts to the past and cook, stirring, over a low heat for 2–3 minutes. Remove from the heat, mix with the pesto, and transfer to a warm bowl. Garnish with shredded basil leaves and Parmesan shavings and serve with bread sticks.

# *Rice-Stuffed Mushrooms*

### Serves 4

**INGREDIENTS**

4 large flat mushrooms
3¹/₂ ounces assorted exotic
  mushrooms, sliced
4 dry-pack, sun-dried
  tomatoes, shredded
²/₃ cup dry red wine

4 scallions, trimmed and
  finely chopped
1¹/₂ cups cooked red rice
2 tbsp freshly grated
  Parmesan cheese

4 thick slices whole grain or
  whole wheat bread
salt and pepper
scallion, shredded,
  to garnish

1 Preheat the oven to 375°F. Peel the flat mushrooms, pull out the stalks, and set aside. Finely chop the stalks and place in a saucepan.

2 Add the exotic mushrooms to the saucepan, along with the tomatoes and red wine. Bring to a boil, cover, and simmer gently for 2–3 minutes, until just tender. Drain, reserving the cooking liquid, and place in a small bowl.

3 Gently stir in the chopped scallions and cooked rice. Season well and spoon into the flat mushrooms, pressing the mixture down gently. Sprinkle with the grated Parmesan cheese.

4 Arrange the mushrooms in an ovenproof baking dish and pour the reserved cooking juices around them. Bake in the oven for 20–25 minutes, until they are just cooked.

5 Meanwhile, preheat the broiler. Trim the crusts from the bread and toast on each side until lightly browned.

6 Drain the mushrooms and place each one on a piece of toasted bread. Garnish with scallions and serve at once.

# *Biryani with Caramelized Onions*

### Serves 4

## INGREDIENTS

1 cup Basmati rice, rinsed
$\frac{1}{3}$ cup red lentils, rinsed
1 bay leaf
6 cardamom pods, split
1 tsp ground turmeric
6 cloves
1 tsp cumin seeds
1 cinnamon stick, broken

1 onion, chopped
8 ounces cauliflower, broken into
    small florets
1 large carrot, diced
$3\frac{1}{2}$ ounces frozen peas
2 ounces golden raisins
$2\frac{1}{2}$ cups fresh vegetable stock
salt and pepper

naan bread, to serve

CARAMELIZED ONIONS:
2 tsp vegetable oil
1 medium red onion, shredded
1 medium onion, shredded
2 tsp superfine sugar

1 Place the rice, lentils, bay leaf, spices, onion, cauliflower, carrot, peas, and golden raisins in a large saucepan. Season with salt and pepper and mix well.

2 Pour in the stock, bring to a boil, cover, and simmer for 15 minutes, stirring occasionally, until the rice is tender. Remove from the heat and let stand, covered, for 10 minutes to allow the stock to be absorbed. Discard the bay leaf, cardamom pods, cloves, and cinnamon stick.

3 Meanwhile, make the caramelized onions. Heat the oil in a skillet and sauté the onions over a medium heat for 3–4 minutes until just softened. Add the superfine sugar, raise the heat, and cook, stirring occasionally, for a further 2–3 minutes, until the onions are just golden.

4 Gently mix the rice and vegetables and transfer to warm serving plates. Spoon the caramelized onion on top, and serve with warmed naan bread.

# *Soft Pancakes with Stir-Fried Vegetables & Bean Curd*

### Serves 4

## INGREDIENTS

1 tbsp vegetable oil

1 garlic clove, crushed

1-inch piece fresh ginger root, grated

1 bunch scallions, trimmed and shredded lengthwise

3½ ounces snow peas, topped, tailed, and shredded

8 ounces bean curd, drained and cut into ½-inch pieces

2 tbsp dark soy sauce, plus extra to serve

2 tbsp hoisin sauce, plus extra to serve

2 ounces canned bamboo shoots, drained

2 ounces canned water chestnuts, drained and sliced

3½ ounces bean sprouts

1 small red chili, seeded and thinly sliced

1 small bunch fresh chives

12 soft Chinese pancakes

TO SERVE:

shredded Chinese cabbage leaves

1 cucumber, sliced

strips of red chili

1 Heat the oil in a nonstick wok or a large skillet and stir-fry the garlic and ginger for 1 minute. Add the scallions, snow peas, bean curd, soy sauce, and hoisin sauce to the wok or skillet. Stir-fry the vegetables for about 2 minutes.

2 Add the bamboo shoots, water chestnuts, bean sprouts, and red chili to the wok or skillet. Stir-fry for 2 minutes, until the vegetables are just tender, but still have bite. Snip the chives into 1-inch lengths and stir them into the mixture in the wok or skillet.

3 Meanwhile, heat the pancakes according to the instructions on the packet and keep warm.

4 Divide the vegetables and bean curd among the pancakes and roll up. Serve with the Chinese cabbage and extra sauce.

# Char-Grilled Mediterranean Vegetable Skewers

### Makes 8

**INGREDIENTS**

| | | |
|---|---|---|
| 1 large red bell pepper | 2 tbsp lemon juice | TO SERVE: |
| 1 large green bell pepper | 1 tbsp olive oil | cracked wheat, cooked |
| 1 large orange bell pepper | 1 garlic clove, crushed | tomato and olive relish |
| 1 large zucchini | 1 tbsp chopped, fresh rosemary | |
| 4 baby eggplants | or 1 tsp dried | |
| 2 medium red onions | salt and pepper | |

1 Halve and seed the bell peppers and cut into even sized pieces, about 1 inch wide. Trim the zucchini, cut in half lengthwise, and slice into 1-inch pieces. Place the bell peppers and zucchini into a large bowl and set aside.

2 Using a sharp knife, trim the eggplants and quarter them lengthwise. Peel the onions, then cut each one into 8 even-sized wedges. Add the eggplant and onion pieces to the bowl containing the bell peppers and zucchini.

3 In a small bowl, mix together the lemon juice, olive oil, garlic, rosemary, and salt and pepper to taste. Pour the mixture over the vegetables and stir well to coat.

4 Preheat the broiler. Thread the vegetables onto 8 skewers. Arrange the kabobs on the rack and cook for 10–12 minutes, turning frequently, until the vegetables are lightly charred and just softened.

5 Drain the vegetable kabobs and serve on a bed of cracked wheat accompanied with a tomato and olive relish, if desired.

# *Stuffed Vegetables Middle Eastern-Style*

### Serves 4

**INGREDIENTS**

| | | |
|---|---|---|
| 4 large beefsteak tomatoes | ¼ cucumber | TO SERVE: |
| 4 medium zucchini | 1 medium red onion | warm pita bread and low-fat |
| 2 orange bell peppers | 2 tbsp lemon juice | hummus |
| salt and pepper | 2 tbsp chopped fresh cilantro | |
| | 2 tbsp chopped fresh mint | |
| FILLING: | 1 tbsp olive oil | |
| 1¼ cups cracked wheat | 2 tsp cumin seeds | |

1 Preheat the oven to 400°F. Cut off the tops from the tomatoes and reserve. Using a teaspoon, scoop out the tomato pulp, chop, and place in a bowl. Season the tomato shells, then turn them upside down on absorbent paper towels to drain thoroughly.

2 Trim the zucchini and cut a V-shaped groove lengthwise down each one. Finely chop the cut-out zucchini flesh and add to the tomato pulp. Season the zucchini shells with salt and pepper to taste and set aside.

3 Halve the bell peppers. Leaving the stalks intact, cut out the seeds, and discard. Season the bell pepper shells and set aside.

4 To make the filling, soak the cracked wheat according to the instructions on the packet. Finely chop the cucumber and add to the reserved tomato pulp and zucchini mixture.

5 Finely chop the red onion, and add to the vegetable mixture with the lemon juice, herbs, olive oil, cumin, and seasoning, and mix together well.

6 When the wheat has soaked, mix with the vegetables and stuff into the tomato, zucchini, and bell pepper shells. Place the tops on the tomatoes, transfer to a roasting pan, and bake for 20–25 minutes, until cooked through. Drain and serve.

# *Fragrant Asparagus & Orange Risotto*

### Serves 4–6

## INGREDIENTS

4 ounces fine asparagus
spears, trimmed
5 cups vegetable stock
2 bulbs fennel
1 ounce low-fat spread

1 tsp olive oil
2 celery stalks, trimmed and
chopped
2 medium leeks, trimmed
and shredded

2 cups arborio rice
3 medium oranges
salt and pepper

1 Bring a small saucepan of water to a boil and cook the asparagus for 1 minute. Drain and set aside until required.

2 Pour the stock into a saucepan and bring to a boil. Reduce the heat to maintain a gentle simmer.

3 Meanwhile, trim the fennel, reserving the fronds, and cut into thin slices. Carefully melt the low-fat spread with the oil in a large saucepan, taking care that the water in the low-fat spread does not evaporate, and gently sauté the fennel, celery, and leeks for 3–4 minutes, until just softened. Add the rice and cook, stirring, for a further 2 minutes, until mixed.

4 Add a ladleful of stock to the pan and cook gently, stirring, until absorbed. Continue ladling the stock into the rice until the rice becomes creamy, thick, and tender. This process will take about 25 minutes and should not be hurried.

5 Finely grate the rind and extract the juice from 1 orange and mix into the rice. Carefully remove the peel and pith from the remaining oranges. Holding the fruit over the saucepan, cut out the orange segments and add to the rice, along with any juice that falls.

6 Stir the orange into the rice, along with the asparagus spears. Season with salt and pepper, garnish with the reserved fennel fronds, and serve.

# Spicy Black-Eyed Peas

### Serves 4

**INGREDIENTS**

2 cups black-eyed peas, soaked
overnight in cold water
1 tbsp vegetable oil
2 medium onions, chopped
1 tbsp clear honey
2 tbsp molasses
4 tbsp dark soy sauce

1 tsp dry mustard powder
4 tbsp tomato paste
2 cups fresh vegetable stock
1 bay leaf
1 sprig each of rosemary, thyme,
and sage
1 small orange

1 tbsp cornstarch
2 medium red bell peppers,
seeded and diced
pepper
2 tbsp chopped fresh flat-leaf
parsley, to garnish
crusty bread, to serve

1 Preheat the oven to 300°F. Rinse the peas and place in a saucepan. Cover with water, bring to a boil, and boil rapidly for 10 minutes. Drain and place in an ovenproof casserole dish.

2 Meanwhile, heat the oil in a skillet and sauté the onions for 5 minutes. Stir in the honey, molasses, soy sauce, mustard, and tomato paste. Pour in the stock, bring to a boil, and pour the mixture over the peas.

3 Tie the bay leaf, rosemary, thyme, and sage together with a clean piece of string and add to the pan containing the peas. Using a vegetable peeler, pare off 3 pieces of orange rind. Mix the orange rind into the pea mixture, along with plenty of freshly ground black pepper. Cover and bake for about 1 hour.

4 Extract the juice from the orange and blend with the cornstarch to form a paste. Stir into the peas, along with the red bell peppers. Cover and cook for 1 hour, until the sauce is rich and thick and the peas are tender. Discard the herbs and orange rind.

5 Garnish with chopped parsley and serve with lots of fresh crusty bread.

# Mexican-Style Pizzas

### Serves 4

---
**INGREDIENTS**
---

4 ready-made individual
   pizza bases
1 tbsp olive oil
7 ounce can chopped tomatoes
   with garlic and herbs
2 tbsp tomato paste

7 ounce can kidney beans,
   drained and rinsed
4 ounces corn kernels, thawed
   if frozen
1–2 tsp chili sauce
1 large red onion, shredded

3½ ounces reduced-fat cheddar
   cheese, grated
1 large green chili, sliced into
   rings
salt and pepper

---

1 Preheat the oven to 425°F. Arrange the pizza bases on a cookie sheet and brush them lightly with the oil.

2 In a bowl, mix together the chopped tomatoes, tomato paste, kidney beans, and corn, and add chili sauce to taste. Season with salt and pepper to taste.

3 Spread the tomato and kidney bean mixture evenly over each pizza base

to cover. Top each pizza with shredded onion and sprinkle with some grated cheese and a few slices of green chili according to taste. Bake in the oven for about 20 minutes until the vegetables are tender, the cheese has melted, and the base is crisp and golden.

4 Remove the pizzas from the cookie sheet and transfer to serving plates. Serve immediately.

## COOK'S TIP

*For a low-fat Mexican-style salad to serve with this pizza, arrange sliced tomatoes, fresh cilantro leaves, and a few slices of a small, ripe avocado. Sprinkle with fresh lime juice and coarse sea salt. Avocados have quite a high oil content, so eat in moderation.*

# *Eggplant Pasta Cake*

### Serves 6-8

**INGREDIENTS**

| | | |
|---|---|---|
| 1 medium eggplant | 4 ounces low-fat soft cheese | 4 tbsp grated Parmesan cheese |
| 10½ ounces tricolor pasta shapes | with garlic and herbs | 1½ tsp dried oregano |
| | 1⅓ cups sieved tomatoes | 2 tbsp dry white bread crumbs |
| | | salt and pepper |

1 Preheat the oven to 375°F. Grease and line an 8 inch round spring-form cake pan.

2 Trim the eggplant and slice lengthwise into slices about ¼ inch thick. Place in a bowl, sprinkle with salt, and set aside for 30 minutes to remove any bitter juices. Rinse well under cold running water and drain.

3 Bring a saucepan of water to a boil and blanch the eggplant slices for 1 minute. Drain and pat dry with paper towels. Set aside until required.

4 Cook the pasta shapes according to the instructions on the packet; for best results, the pasta should be slightly undercooked. Drain well and return to the saucepan. Add the soft cheese to the pan and allow it to melt over the pasta.

5 Stir in the sieved tomatoes, Parmesan cheese, oregano, and salt and pepper to taste. Set aside until required.

6 Arrange the eggplant over the base and sides of the prepared cake pan, overlapping the slices, and making sure there are no gaps between them.

7 Pile the pasta mixture into the pan, packing down well, and sprinkle with the bread crumbs. Bake for 20 minutes and let stand for 15 minutes.

8 Loosen the cake around the edge with a spatula and release from the pan. Turn out eggplant-side up and serve hot.

# *Mushroom Cannelloni*

### Serves 4

**INGREDIENTS**

12 ounces crimini mushrooms, finely chopped
1 medium onion, finely chopped
1 garlic clove, crushed
1 tbsp chopped fresh thyme
$\frac{1}{2}$ tsp ground nutmeg

4 tbsp dry white wine
4 tbsp fresh white bread crumbs
12 dried "quick-cook" cannelloni
salt and pepper
Parmesan cheese shavings, to garnish (optional)

TOMATO SAUCE:
1 large red bell pepper
$\frac{3}{4}$ cup dry white wine
2 cups sieved tomatoes
2 tbsp tomato paste
2 bay leaves
1 tsp superfine sugar

1 Preheat the oven to 400°F. Place the mushrooms, onion, and garlic in a pan. Stir in the thyme, nutmeg, and 4 tbsp wine. Bring to a boil, cover, and simmer for 10 minutes. Stir in the bread crumbs to bind the mixture and season. Leave to cool for 10 minutes.

2 Preheat the broiler. For the sauce, halve and seed the bell pepper, place

on the broiler rack, and cook for 8–10 minutes, until charred. Let cool.

3 Once the bell pepper has cooled, peel off the charred skin. Chop the flesh and place in a food processor with the wine. Blend until smooth and pour into a pan.

4 Mix the remaining sauce ingredients with the bell pepper and wine

and season. Bring to a boil and simmer for 10 minutes. Discard the bay leaves.

5 Cover the base of an ovenproof dish with a thin layer of sauce. Fill the cannelloni with the mushroom mixture and place in the dish. Spoon the remaining sauce on top, cover with foil, and bake for 35–40 minutes. Garnish with shavings of Parmesan (if using) and serve.

# Bean Curd & Garbanzo Bean Burgers

### Serves 4

## INGREDIENTS

1 small red onion, finely chopped

1 garlic clove, crushed

1 tsp ground cumin

1 tsp ground coriander

2 tbsp lemon juice

15 ounce can garbanzo beans, drained and rinsed

3 ounces soft silken bean curd, drained

4 ounces cooked potato, diced

4 tbsp freshly chopped cilantro

2 tbsp all-purpose flour (optional)

2³/₄ ounces dry brown bread crumbs

1 tbsp vegetable oil

burger rolls

2 medium tomatoes, sliced

1 large carrot, grated

salt and pepper

RELISH:

1 tsp sesame seed paste

4 tbsp low-fat unsweetened yogurt

1-inch piece cucumber, finely chopped

1 tbsp chopped, fresh cilantro

garlic salt, to season

1 Place the onion, garlic, spices, and lemon juice in a pan, bring to a boil, cover, and simmer for 5 minutes until softened.

2 Place the garbanzo beans, bean curd, and potato in a bowl and mash well. Stir in the onion mixture, cilantro, and seasoning, and mix together. Divide into 4 equal portions and form into patties 4 inches across, dusting the hands with flour, if necessary.

3 Sprinkle the bread crumbs onto a plate and press the burgers into the bread crumbs to coat both sides.

4 Heat the oil in a large nonstick skillet and fry the burgers for 5 minutes on each side, until heated through and golden. Drain on paper towels.

5 Meanwhile, mix all of the relish ingredients together in a bowl and chill.

6 Line the rolls with tomato and grated carrot and top each with a burger. Serve with the relish.

# Sweet Potato & Leek Patties

### Serves 4

**INGREDIENTS**

2 pounds sweet potato
4 tsp sunflower oil
2 medium leeks, trimmed and
    finely chopped
1 garlic clove, crushed
1-inch piece fresh ginger root,
    finely chopped
7 ounce can corn kernels,
    drained

2 tbsp low-fat unsweetened
    yogurt
2 ounces whole wheat flour
salt and pepper

GINGER SAUCE:
2 tbsp white wine vinegar
2 tsp superfine sugar
1 red chili, seeded and chopped

1-inch piece fresh ginger root,
    cut into thin strips
2 tbsp ginger wine
4 tbsp fresh vegetable stock
1 tsp cornstarch

TO SERVE:
lettuce leaves
scallions, shredded

1 Peel the potatoes and cut into ³/₄-inch thick pieces. Place in a saucepan, cover with water, and boil for 10–15 minutes. Drain well and mash. Let cool.

2 Heat 2 tsp of oil and sauté the leeks, garlic, and ginger for 2–3 minutes. Stir the leek mixture into the potato with the corn, seasoning, and yogurt.

Form into 8 patties and toss in flour to coat. Chill for 30 minutes.

3 Preheat the broiler. Place the patties on a broiler rack and brush with oil. Broil for 5 minutes, then turn over. Brush with oil and broil for a further 5 minutes, until golden. Drain thoroughly on paper towels.

4 To make the sauce, place the vinegar, sugar, chili, and ginger in a pan. Bring to a boil and simmer for 5 minutes. Stir in the ginger wine. Blend the stock and cornstarch to form a paste and stir into the sauce. Heat through, stirring, until thickened. Transfer the patties to serving plates, spoon over the sauce, and serve.

# *Ratatouille Vegetable Broil*

### Serves 4

**INGREDIENTS**

2 medium onions
1 garlic clove
1 medium red bell pepper
1 medium green bell pepper
1 medium eggplant
2 medium zucchini

2 14 ounce cans chopped
   tomatoes
1 bouquet garni
2 tbsp tomato paste
2 pounds potatoes

2¾ ounces reduced-fat cheddar
   cheese, grated
salt and pepper
2 tbsp snipped fresh chives,
   to garnish

1 Peel and finely chop the onions and garlic. Rinse, seed, and slice the bell peppers. Rinse, trim, and cut the eggplant into small dice. Rinse, trim, and thinly slice the zucchini.

2 Place the onion, garlic, and bell peppers into a large pan. Add the tomatoes and stir in the bouquet garni, tomato paste, and salt and pepper to taste. Bring to a boil, cover, and simmer for 10 minutes, stirring halfway through.

3 Stir in the eggplant and zucchini and cook, uncovered, for 10 minutes, stirring occasionally.

4 Meanwhile, peel the potatoes and cut into 1-inch cubes. Place the potatoes into another saucepan and cover with water. Bring to a boil and cook for 10–12 minutes, until tender. Drain thoroughly with a slotted spoon and set aside.

5 Transfer the vegetables to a heatproof gratin

dish. Arrange the cooked potato cubes evenly over the vegetables.

6 Preheat the broiler. Sprinkle grated cheese over the potatoes and place under the broiler for 5 minutes until golden, bubbling, and hot. Serve immediately garnished with snipped chives.

# *Cauliflower & Broccoli with Herb Sauce*

### Serves 4

**INGREDIENTS**

2 baby cauliflowers
8 ounces broccoli
salt and pepper

SAUCE:
8 tablespoons olive oil
4 tablespoons butter or
    vegetarian margarine

2 teaspoons grated ginger root
juice and rind of 2 lemons
5 tablespoons chopped cilantro
5 tablespoons grated cheddar

1 Using a sharp knife, cut the cauliflowers in half and the broccoli into very large florets.

2 Cook the cauliflower and broccoli in a saucepan of boiling salted water for about 10 minutes. Drain well, transfer to a shallow ovenproof dish, and keep warm until required.

3 To make the sauce, put the oil and butter or vegetarian margarine in a pan and heat gently until the butter melts. Add the grated ginger root, lemon juice, lemon rind, and chopped cilantro and simmer for 2–3 minutes, stirring occasionally.

4 Season the sauce with salt and pepper to taste, then pour it over the vegetables in the dish and sprinkle the cheese on top.

5 Cook under a preheated broiler for 2–3 minutes, or until the cheese is bubbling and golden. Let cool for 1–2 minutes and then serve.

## VARIATION

*Lime or orange could be used instead of the lemon for a fruity and refreshing sauce.*

# Steamed Vegetables with Vermouth

### Serves 4

**INGREDIENTS**

| | | |
|---|---|---|
| 1 carrot, cut into batons | 4 small onions, halved | pinch of paprika |
| 1 fennel bulb, sliced | 8 tablespoons vermouth | 4 sprigs tarragon |
| 3¹/₂ ounces zucchini, sliced | 4 tablespoons lime juice | salt and pepper |
| 1 red bell pepper, sliced | zest of 1 lime | fresh tarragon sprigs, to garnish |

1 Place all of the vegetables in a large bowl and mix well.

2 Cut 4 large squares of baking parchment and place a quarter of the vegetables in the center of each. Bring the sides of the parchment up and pinch together to make an open packet.

3 Mix together the vermouth, lime juice, lime zest, and paprika and pour a quarter of the mixture into each packet. Season with salt and pepper

and add a tarragon sprig to each. Pinch the tops of the packets together to seal.

4 Place in a steamer, cover, and cook for 15–20 minutes, or until the vegetables are tender. Garnish and serve.

## COOK'S TIP

*Seal the packets well to prevent them from opening during cooking and causing the juices to evaporate.*

## COOKS TIP

*Vermouth is a fortified white wine flavored with various herbs and spices. It its available in both sweet and dry forms.*

# Spicy Peas & Spinach

## Serves 4

### INGREDIENTS

1¼ cups green split peas
2 pounds spinach
4 tablespoons vegetable oil
1 onion, halved and sliced

1 teaspoon grated ginger root
1 teaspoon ground cumin
½ teaspoon chili powder
½ teaspoon ground coriander

2 garlic cloves, crushed
1¼ cups vegetable stock
salt and pepper
fresh cilantro sprigs and lime
wedges, to garnish

1 Rinse the peas under cold running water. Transfer to a mixing bowl, cover with cold water, and set aside to soak for 2 hours. Drain well.

2 Meanwhile, cook the spinach in a large saucepan for 5 minutes, until wilted. Drain well and roughly chop.

3 Heat the oil in a large saucepan and add the onion, spices, and garlic. Sauté for 2–3 minutes, stirring well.

4 Add the peas and spinach and stir in the stock. Cover and simmer for 10–15 minutes, or until the peas are cooked and the liquid has been absorbed. Season with salt and pepper to taste, garnish, and serve.

## VARIATION

*If you do not have time to soak the green peas, canned lentils are a good substitute, but remember to drain and rinse them first.*

## COOK'S TIP

*Once the peas have been added, stir occasionally to prevent them from sticking to the pan.*

# Curried Cauliflower & Spinach

### Serves 4

## INGREDIENTS

| | | |
|---|---|---|
| 1 medium cauliflower | 1 teaspoon turmeric | 6 tablespoons vegetable stock |
| 6 tablespoons vegetable oil | 2 garlic cloves, crushed | 1 tablespoon chopped cilantro |
| 1 teaspoon mustard seeds | 1 onion, halved and sliced | salt and pepper |
| 1 teaspoon ground cumin | 1 green chili, sliced | cilantro sprigs, to garnish |
| 1 teaspoon garam masala | 1 pound spinach | |

1 Break the cauliflower into small florets.

2 Heat the oil in a deep flameproof casserole . Add the mustard seeds and cook until they begin to pop.

3 Stir in the remaining spices, the garlic, onion, and chili and cook for 2–3 minutes, stirring.

4 Add the cauliflower, spinach, vegetable stock, cilantro, and seasoning and cook over gentle heat for 15 minutes, or until the cauliflower is tender. Uncover the dish and boil for 1 minute to thicken the juices. Garnish and serve at once.

## COOK'S TIP

*Mustard seeds are used throughout India and are particularly popular in southern vegetarian cooking. They are fried in oil first to bring out their flavor before the other ingredients are added.*

# Marinated Bean Curd Skewers

### Serves 4

**INGREDIENTS**

| | | |
|---|---|---|
| 12 ounces bean curd | slices of lemon, to garnish | 1 clove garlic, crushed |
| 1 red bell pepper | | 1/2 tsp fresh rosemary, chopped |
| 1 yellow bell pepper | MARINADE: | 1/2 tsp chopped, fresh thyme |
| 2 zucchini | grated rind and juice of | 1 tbsp walnut oil |
| 8 button mushrooms | 1/2 lemon | |

1 To make the marinade, combine the lemon rind and juice, garlic, rosemary, thyme, and oil in a shallow dish.

2 Drain the bean curd, pat it dry on paper towels, and cut it into squares. Add to the marinade and toss to coat. Marinate for 20–30 minutes.

3 Meanwhile, seed and cut the bell peppers into 1-inch pieces. Blanch in boiling water for 4 minutes, rinse in cold water, and drain.

4 Using a canelle knife or potato peeler, remove strips of peel from the zucchini. Cut the zucchini into 1-inch chunks.

5 Remove the bean curd from the marinade, reserving the liquid for basting. Thread the bean curd onto 8 skewers, alternating with the bell pepper pieces, zucchini chunks, and button mushrooms.

6 Broil the skewers over medium hot coals for about 6 minutes, turning and basting frequently with the marinade.

7 Transfer the skewers to warm serving plates, garnish with slices of lemon, and serve immediately.

## VARIATION

*For a spicy kabob, make a marinade by mixing together 1 tablespoon of curry paste, 2 tablespoons of oil and the juice of 1/2 lemon.*

# Crispy Potato Skins

### Serves 4-6

**INGREDIENTS**

| | | |
|---|---|---|
| 8 small baking potatoes, scrubbed | salt and pepper | $^1/_2$ cup grated Swiss cheese |
| 4 tbsp butter, melted | Optional Topping: | $1^3/_4$ ounces salami, cut into |
| | 6 scallions, sliced | thin strips |

1 Preheat the oven to 400°F. Prick the potatoes with a fork and bake for 1 hour, or until tender. Alternatively, cook in a microwave on High for 12–15 minutes.

2 Cut the potatoes in half and scoop out the flesh, leaving about $^1/_4$ inch potato flesh lining the skin.

3 Brush the insides of the potato with melted butter.

4 Place the skins, cut side down, over medium hot coals and broil for 10–15 minutes. Turn the potato skins over and broil for a further 5 minutes or until they are crispy. Take care that they do not burn.

5 Season the potato skins with salt and pepper to taste, transfer to serving plates and serve while they are still warm.

6 The skins can be filled with a variety of different toppings. Broil the potato skins as above for about 10 minutes, then turn cut side up and sprinkle with slices of scallion, grated cheese, and chopped salami. Broil for a further 5 minutes until the cheese just begins to melt. Serve the crispy potato skins hot.

## COOK'S TIP

*Potato skins can be served on their own, but they are delicious served with a dip. Try a spicy tomato or hummus dip.*

# Barbecued Garlic Potato Wedges

## Serves 4

### INGREDIENTS

| | | |
|---|---|---|
| 3 large baking potatoes, scrubbed | 2 tbsp butter | 1 tbsp chopped, fresh parsley |
| 4 tbsp olive oil | 2 garlic cloves, chopped | 1 tbsp chopped, fresh thyme |
| | 1 tbsp chopped, fresh rosemary | salt and pepper |

1 Bring a large pan of water to a boil, add the potatoes, and parboil them for 10 minutes. Drain the potatoes, rinse under cold water, and drain them again thoroughly.

2 Transfer the potatoes to a chopping board. When the potatoes are cold enough to handle, cut them into thick wedges, but do not remove the skins.

3 Heat the oil and butter in a small pan, together with the garlic. Cook gently until the garlic begins to brown, then remove the pan from the heat.

4 Stir the rosemary, parsley, thyme and salt and pepper to taste into the mixture in the pan.

5 Brush the herb mixture all over the potatoes.

6 Broil the potatoes over hot coals for 10–15 minutes, brushing liberally with any of the remaining herb and butter mixture, or until the potatoes are just tender and cooked through.

7 Transfer to a warm serving plate and serve as a starter or as a side dish.

## COOK'S TIP

*You may find it easier to barbecue these potatoes in a hinged rack or in a specially designed barbecue roasting tray.*

# *Vegetarian Sausages*

### Makes 8

---
### INGREDIENTS
---

1 tbsp sunflower oil
1 small onion, finely chopped
³/₄ cup finely chopped
 mushrooms
½ red bell pepper, seeded and
 finely chopped

14 ounce can cannolini beans,
 rinsed and drained
1²/₃ cups fresh bread crumbs
1 cup grated cheddar cheese
1 tsp dried mixed herbs
1 egg yolk

seasoned all-purpose flour
oil, to baste

TO SERVE:
rolls
slices of fried onion

---

1 Heat the oil in a saucepan and sauté the prepared onion, mushrooms, and bell peppers until softened.

2 Mash the cannolini beans in a large mixing bowl. Add the onion, mushroom, and bell pepper mixture, the bread crumbs, cheese, herbs, and egg yolk, and mix together well.

3 Press the mixture together with your

fingers and shape into 8 sausages.

4 Roll each sausage in the seasoned flour to coat well. Chill in the refrigerator for at least 30 minutes.

5 Broil the sausages on a sheet of oiled foil set over medium coals for 15–20 minutes, turning and basting frequently with oil, until golden.

6 Split a roll down the middle and insert a layer of fried onions. Place the sausage in the roll and serve.

## COOK'S TIP

*Take care not to break the sausages when you are turning them over. If you have a hinged rack, oil this and place the sausages inside, turning and oiling frequently.*

# Eggplant & Mozzarella Sandwiches

### Serves 2

## INGREDIENTS

1 large eggplant
1 tbsp lemon juice
3 tbsp olive oil

1 cup grated mozzarella cheese
2 sun-dried tomatoes, chopped
salt and pepper

TO SERVE:
Italian bread
mixed salad greens
slices of tomato

1 Slice the eggplant into thin rounds.

2 Mix the lemon juice and olive oil in a small bowl until well combined and season the mixture with salt and pepper to taste.

3 Brush the eggplant slices with the oil and lemon juice mixture and broil over medium hot coals for 2–3 minutes, without turning, until golden on the underside.

4 Turn half of the eggplant slices over and sprinkle with cheese and chopped sun-dried tomatoes.

5 Place the remaining eggplant slices on top of the cheese and tomatoes, turning them so that the pale side is uppermost.

6 Broil for 1–2 minutes, then carefully turn the whole sandwich over, and broil for 1–2 minutes. Baste with the oil mixture.

7 Serve with Italian bread, mixed salad greens, and a few slices of tomato.

## VARIATION

*Try feta cheese instead of mozzarella but omit the salt from the basting oil. A creamy goat cheese would be equally delicious.*

# *Charbroiled Eggplant*

### Serves 4

**INGREDIENTS**

| | | |
|---|---|---|
| 1 large eggplant | PESTO: | CUCUMBER SAUCE: |
| 3 tbsp olive oil | 1 clove garlic | $^2/_3$ cup unsweetened yogurt |
| 1 tsp sesame oil | $^1/_4$ cup pine nuts | 2-inch piece cucumber |
| salt and pepper | $^1/_4$ cup fresh basil leaves | $^1/_2$ tsp mint sauce |
| | 2 tbsp Parmesan cheese | |
| | 6 tbsp olive oil | |
| | salt and pepper | |

1 Remove the stalk from the eggplant, then cut it lengthwise into 8 thin slices.

2 Lay the eggplant slices on a plate or board and sprinkle them liberally with salt to remove the bitter juices. Set aside until required.

3 Meanwhile, prepare the baste. Combine the olive and sesame oils, season with pepper, and set aside.

4 To make the pesto, put the garlic, pine nuts, basil, and cheese in a food processor until finely chopped. With the machine running, gradually add the oil in a thin stream. Season to taste.

5 To make the minty cucumber sauce, place the yogurt in a mixing bowl. Remove the seeds from the cucumber and dice the flesh finely. Stir into the yogurt with the mint sauce.

6 Rinse the eggplant slices and pat them dry on absorbent paper towels. Baste with the oil mixture and broil over hot coals for about 10 minutes, turning once. The eggplant should be golden and tender.

7 Transfer the eggplant slices to warm individual serving plates and serve immediately with either the cucumber sauce or the pesto.

# Colorful Vegetable Skewers

### Serves 4

**INGREDIENTS**

| | |
|---|---|
| 1 red bell pepper, seeded | SEASONED OIL: |
| 1 yellow bell pepper, seeded | 6 tbsp olive oil |
| 1 green bell pepper, seeded | 1 clove garlic, crushed |
| 1 small onion 8 cherry tomatoes | $\frac{1}{2}$ tsp mixed dried herbs or |
| 3$\frac{1}{2}$ ounces mushrooms | herbes de Provence |

1 Cut the bell peppers into 1-inch pieces.

2 Peel the onion and cut it into wedges, leaving the root end just intact to help keep the wedges together.

3 Thread the bell peppers, onion wedges, tomatoes, and mushrooms onto skewers, alternating the colors of the bell peppers.

4 To make the seasoned oil, mix together the oil, garlic, and herbs in a small bowl until well combined. Brush the mixture liberally over the kabobs until well coated.

5 Broil the kabobs over medium hot coals for 10–15 minutes, brushing the vegetables with more of the seasoned oil and turning the skewers frequently.

6 Transfer the vegetable kabobs to warm individual serving plates. Serve with walnut sauce (see Cook's Tip), if you wish.

## COOK'S TIP

*These kabobs are delicious when accompanied with a walnut sauce. To make the sauce, process 1 cup walnuts in a food processor until they form a smooth paste. With the machine running, add $\frac{2}{3}$ cup heavy cream and 1 tablespoon of olive oil. Season to taste. Alternatively, finely chop the walnuts, then pound them in a mortar with a pestle to form a paste. Mix with the cream and oil, and season.*

# *Charbroiled Mixed Vegetables*

### Serves 4-6

**INGREDIENTS**

| | | |
|---|---|---|
| 8 baby eggplant | 4 tomatoes | BASTE: |
| 4 zucchini | salt and pepper | 6 tbsp butter |
| 2 red onions | 1 tsp balsamic vinegar, to serve | 2 tsp walnut oil |
| | | 2 cloves garlic, chopped |
| | | 4 tbsp dry white wine or cider |

1 To prepare the vegetables, cut the eggplant in half. Trim and cut the zucchini in half lengthwise. Thickly slice the onion and halve the tomatoes.

2 Season all of the vegetables with salt and black pepper to taste.

3 To make the baste, melt the butter with the oil in a saucepan. Add the garlic and cook gently for 1–2 minutes. Remove the pan from the heat and stir in the wine or cider.

4 Add the vegetables to the pan and toss them in the baste mixture. You may need to do this in several batches to ensure that all of the vegetables are coated evenly with the baste mixture.

5 Remove the vegetables from the baste mixture, reserving any excess baste. Place the vegetables on an oiled rack over medium hot coals. Broil for 15–20 minutes, basting with the reserved baste mixture and turning once or twice during cooking.

6 Transfer the vegetables to warm serving plates and serve sprinkled with balsamic vinegar.

## COOK'S TIP

*Use a long-handled brush for basting food on the barbecue.*

# Stuffed Mushrooms

### Makes 12

**INGREDIENTS**

12 open-cap mushrooms
4 scallions, chopped
4 tsp olive oil

2 cups fresh brown bread crumbs
1 tsp fresh oregano, chopped

3½ ounces feta cheese or
chorizo sausage

1 Remove the stalks from the mushrooms and chop the stalks finely.

2 Sauté the mushroom stalks and scallions in half of the oil.

3 Transfer the mushroom stalks and scallions to a large mixing bowl. Add the bread crumbs and oregano to the mushrooms and scallions, mix, and set aside.

4 If using feta cheese, crumble the cheese into small pieces in a small bowl, using a fork or your fingers.

5 If you are using chorizo sausage, remove the skin and chop the flesh finely.

6 Add the cheese or chorizo to the breadcrumb mixture and mix well.

7 Spoon the stuffing mixture into the mushroom caps. Carefully drizzle the oil over the mushrooms. Broil on an oiled rack over medium hot coals for 8–10 minutes. Transfer the mushrooms to serving plates and serve hot.

### COOK'S TIP

*If only small mushrooms are available, place a sheet of oiled foil on top of the barbecue rack and cook the mushrooms on this. This will stop the mushrooms from cooking too quickly and burning, and will stop any excess stuffing from dropping onto the coals.*

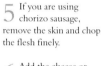

# Corn Cobs

### Serves 4

**INGREDIENTS**

| | | |
|---|---|---|
| 4 corn cobs, with husks<br>butter to taste | 1 tbsp chopped, fresh parsley<br>1 tsp chopped, fresh chives | 1 tsp chopped, fresh thyme<br>rind of 1 lemon, grated<br>salt and pepper |

1 To prepare the corn cobs, peel back the husks and remove the silken hairs.

2 Fold back the husks and secure them in place with string if necessary.

3 Blanch the corn cobs in a large saucepan of boiling water for about 5 minutes, in batches if necessary. Remove the cobs with a slotted spoon and drain thoroughly.

4 Broil the cobs over medium hot coals for 20–30 minutes, turning them frequently.

5 Meanwhile, soften the butter and beat in the parsley, chives, thyme, lemon rind, and salt and pepper to taste.

6 Transfer the corn cobs to serving plates, remove the string and pull back the husks. Serve with a generous portion of herb butter.

## COOK'S TIP

*When you are buying fresh corn, look for plump, tightly packed kernels. If you are unable to get fresh cobs, cook frozen corn cobs on the barbecue. Spread some of the herb butter onto a sheet of double thickness foil. Wrap the cobs in the foil and broil among the coals for about 20–30 minutes.*

# *Pumpkin Packets with Chili & Lime*

### Serves 4

**INGREDIENTS**

| | | |
|---|---|---|
| 1 pound 9 ounces pumpkin or squash | 2 tbsp sunflower oil | 1/2 tsp chili sauce |
| | 2 tbsp butter | rind of 1 lime, grated |
| | | 2 tsp lime juice |

1 Halve the pumpkin or squash and scoop out the seeds. Rinse the seeds and reserve. Cut the pumpkin into thin wedges and peel.

2 Heat the oil and butter together in a large pan, stirring continuously until melted. Stir in the chili sauce, lime rind, and juice.

3 Add the pumpkin or squash and seeds to the pan and toss to coat in the flavored butter.

4 Divide the mixture among 4 double-thickness sheets of foil.

Fold the foil to enclose the pumpkin or squash mixture completely.

5 Cook the foil packets over hot coals for 15–25 minutes, or until the pumpkin or squash is cooked through and tender.

6 Transfer the packets to warm serving plates. Open the packets at the table and serve at once.

## VARIATION

*Add 2 teaspoons of curry paste to the oil instead of the lime and chili.*

## COOK'S TIP

*It is a good idea to wear disposable gloves when slicing and seeding chiles. Alternatively, rub a little oil over your fingers—the oil will help to prevent your skin from absorbing the chili juice. Wash your hands thoroughly afterward.*

# Bean Curd with Soy Sauce, Green Bell Peppers, & Crispy Onions

### Serves 4

**INGREDIENTS**

| | | |
|---|---|---|
| 12 ounces bean curd | 1 tbsp sweet chili sauce | 1 green bell pepper, seeded and diced |
| 2 cloves garlic, crushed | 6 tbsp sunflower oil | 1 tbsp sesame oil |
| 4 tbsp soy sauce | 1 onion, sliced | |

1 Drain the bean curd and, using a sharp knife, cut it into bite-size pieces. Place the bean curd pieces in a shallow nonmetallic dish.

2 Mix together the garlic, soy sauce, and sweet chili sauce and drizzle over the bean curd. Toss well to coat each piece and set aside to marinate for about 20 minutes.

3 Meanwhile, heat the sunflower oil in a large preheated wok.

4 Add the onion slices to the wok and stir-fry over a high heat until they brown and become crispy. Remove the onion slices with a slotted spoon and drain on absorbent kitchen paper.

5 Add the bean curd to the hot oil and stir-fry for about 5 minutes.

6 Remove all but 1 tablespoon of the oil from the wok. Add the bell pepper to the wok and stir-fry for 2–3 minutes, or until it has softened.

7 Return the bean curd and onions to the wok and heat through, stirring occasionally. Drizzle with the sesame oil.

8 Transfer to serving plates and serve immediately.

## COOK'S TIP

*If you are in a real hurry, buy ready-marinated bean curd from your supermarket.*

# Stir-Fried Green Beans with Lettuce & Blackbean Sauce

### Serves 4

**INGREDIENTS**

| | | |
|---|---|---|
| 1 tsp chili oil | 1 clove garlic, crushed | 1 iceberg lettuce, shredded |
| 2 tbsp butter | 3½ ounces shiitake mushrooms, | 4 tbsp black bean sauce |
| 1½ cups fine green beans, sliced | thinly sliced | 4 shallots, sliced |

1 Heat the chili oil and butter in a large preheated wok.

2 Add the green beans, shallots, garlic, and mushrooms to the wok and stir-fry for 2–3 minutes.

3 Add the shredded lettuce to the wok and stir-fry until the leaves have wilted.

4 Stir the black bean sauce into the mixture in the wok and heat through, tossing to mix, until the sauce is bubbling. Serve.

## COOK'S TIP

*To make your own black bean sauce, soak ⅓ cup dried black beans overnight in cold water. Drain and place in a pan of cold water, boil for 10 minutes, then drain. Return the beans to the pan with 2 cups vegetable stock and boil. Blend 1 tablespoon each of malt vinegar, soy sauce, sugar, 1½ teaspoons cornstarch, 1 chopped red chili, and ½ inch ginger root. Add to the pan and simmer for 40 minutes.*

## COOK'S TIP

*If possible, use Chinese green beans, which are tender and can be eaten whole. They are available from specialty Chinese stores.*

# *Aspagarus & Red Bell Pepper Packets*

### Serves 4

| INGREDIENTS | | |
|---|---|---|
| 3½ ounces fine tip asparagus | ¼ cup bean sprouts | 1 egg yolk, beaten |
| 1 red bell pepper, seeded and thinly sliced | 2 tbsp plum sauce | oil, for deep-frying |
| | 8 sheets filo pastry | |

1 Place the asparagus, bell pepper, and bean sprouts in a large mixing bowl.

2 Add the plum sauce to the vegetables and mix until well combined.

3 Spread out the sheets of filo pastry on a clean counter or chopping board.

4 Place a little of the asparagus and red bell pepper filling at the top end of each filo pastry sheet. Brush the edges of the filo pastry with a little of the beaten egg yolk.

5 Roll up the filo pastry, tucking in the ends and enclosing the filling like a spring roll.

6 Heat the oil for deep-frying in a large preheated wok.

7 Carefully cook the packets, 2 at a time, in the hot oil for 4–5 minutes, or until crispy.

8 Remove the packets with a slotted spoon and drain on absorbent paper towels.

9 Transfer the packets to individual warm serving plates and serve immediately.

## COOK'S TIP

*Be sure to use fine-tipped asparagus, as it is more tender than the larger stems.*

# Carrot & Orange Stir-Fry

### Serves 4

**INGREDIENTS**

2 tbsp sunflower oil

1 pound carrots, grated

8 ounces leeks, shredded

2 oranges, peeled and segmented

2 tbsp tomato ketchup

1 tbsp sugar

2 tbsp light soy sauce

1 cup chopped peanuts

1 Heat the sunflower oil in a large preheated wok.

2 Add the grated carrot and leeks to the wok and stir-fry for 2–3 minutes, or until the vegetables have just softened.

3 Add the orange segments to the wok and heat through gently, ensuring that you do not break up the orange segments as you stir the mixture.

4 Mix the tomato ketchup, sugar and soy sauce together in a small bowl.

5 Add the tomato and sugar mixture to the wok and stir-fry for a further 2 minutes.

6 Transfer the stir-fry to warm serving bowls and scatter with the chopped peanuts. Serve immediately.

## VARIATION

*Scatter with toasted sesame seeds instead of the peanuts, if wished.*

## VARIATION

*You could use pineapple instead of orange, if wished. If using canned pineapple, make sure that it is in natural juice not syrup, as it will spoil the fresh taste of this dish.*

# Spinach Stir-Fry with Shiitake & Honey

### Serves 4

## INGREDIENTS

3 tbsp peanut oil

12 ounces shiitake mushrooms, sliced

2 cloves garlic, crushed

12 ounces baby leaf spinach

2 tbsp dry sherry

2 tbsp clear honey

4 scallions, sliced

1 Heat the peanut oil in a large preheated wok.

2 Add the shiitake mushrooms to the wok and stir-fry for about 5 minutes, or until the mushrooms have softened.

3 Add the crushed garlic and baby leaf spinach to the mushrooms in the wok and stir-fry for a further 2–3 minutes, or until the spinach leaves have just begun to wilt.

4 Mix together the dry sherry and clear honey in a small bowl until well combined.

5 Drizzle the sherry and honey mixture over the spinach and heat through.

6 Transfer the stir-fry to warm serving dishes and scatter with scallion slices. Serve immediately, while hot.

## COOK'S TIP

*Nutmeg complements the flavour of spinach and it is a classic combination. Add a pinch of nutmeg to the dish in step 3, if you wish.*

## COOK'S TIP

*A good quality, dry pale sherry should be used in this recipe. Cream or sweet sherry should not be substituted. Rice wine is often used in Chinese cooking, but sherry can be used instead.*

# Chinese Vegetable Rice

### Serves 4

#### INGREDIENTS

| | | |
|---|---|---|
| 1³⁄4 cups long grain white rice | 1 green bell pepper, seeded | ³⁄4 cup bean sprouts |
| 1 tsp ground turmeric | and sliced | 6 scallions, sliced, plus extra to |
| 2 tbsp sunflower oil | 1 green chili, seeded and | garnish |
| 8 ounces zucchini, sliced | finely chopped | 2 tbsp soy sauce |
| 1 red bell pepper, seeded | 1 medium carrot, coarsely grated | salt |
| and sliced | | |

1 Place the rice and ground turmeric in a large saucepan of lightly salted water and bring to a boil. Reduce the heat and simmer until the rice is just tender. Drain the rice thoroughly and press out any excess water with a sheet of double thickness paper towels.

2 Heat the sunflower oil in a large preheated wok.

3 Add the zucchini to the wok and stir-fry for about 2 minutes.

4 Add the bell peppers and chili to the wok and stir-fry for 2–3 minutes.

5 Add the cooked rice to the mixture in the wok, a little at a time, tossing well after each addition.

6 Add the carrots, bean sprouts, and scallions to the wok and stir-fry for a further 2 minutes. Drizzle the Chinese vegetable rice with soy sauce and serve at once, garnished with extra scallions, if desired.

## VARIATION

*For real luxury, add a few saffron strands infused in boiling water instead of the turmeric.*

# *Vegetable Stir-Fry with Hoisin Sauce*

### Serves 4

#### INGREDIENTS

| | | |
|---|---|---|
| 2 tbsp sunflower oil | 1 yellow bell pepper, seeded | 6 ounces snow peas |
| 1 red onion, sliced | and diced | $^3/_4$ cup bean sprouts |
| 1–2 medium carrots, sliced | 1 cup cooked brown rice | 4 tbsp hoisin sauce |
| | | 1 tbsp snipped fresh chives |

1 Heat the sunflower oil in a large preheated wok.

2 Add the red onion slices, carrots, and yellow bell pepper to the wok and stir-fry for about 3 minutes.

3 Add the cooked brown rice, snow peas, sliced diagonally, if wished, and bean sprouts to the mixture in the wok and stir-fry for a further 2 minutes.

4 Stir the hoisin sauce into the vegetables and mix until well combined and completely heated through.

5 Transfer to warm serving dishes and scatter with the snipped fresh chives. Serve immediately.

## COOK'S TIP

*Hoisin sauce is a dark brown, reddish sauce made from soy beans, garlic, chili, and various other spices, and is commonly used in Chinese cookery. It may also be used as a dipping sauce.*

## VARIATION

*Almost any vegetables could be used in this dish: other good choices would be broccoli florets, baby corn cobs, green peas, Chinese cabbage, and young spinach leaves. Either white or oyster mushrooms can also be used to give a greater diversity of textures. In addition, make sure that there is a good variety of color in this dish.*

# Sweet & Sour Cauliflower & Cilantro Stir-Fry

### Serves 4

**INGREDIENTS**

| | | |
|---|---|---|
| 1 pound cauliflower florets | 3½ ounces snow peas | 3 tbsp fresh lime juice |
| 2 tbsp sunflower oil | 1 ripe mango, sliced | 1 tbsp clear honey |
| 1 onion, sliced | ½ cup bean sprouts | 6 tbsp coconut milk |
| 3–4 medium carrots, sliced | 3 tbsp chopped fresh cilantro | salt |

1 Bring a large saucepan of lightly salted water to a boil. Lower the heat slightly, add the cauliflower flowerets to the pan and cook for about 2 minutes. Remove from the heat and drain the cauliflower thoroughly in a colander.

2 Heat the sunflower oil in a large preheated wok.

3 Add the onion and carrots to the wok and stir-fry for about 5 minutes.

4 Add the drained cauliflower and snow peas to the wok and stir-fry for 2–3 minutes.

5 Add the mango and bean sprouts to the wok and stir-fry for about 2 minutes.

6 Mix together the cilantro, lime juice, honey, and coconut milk in a bowl.

7 Add the cilantro mixture and stir-fry for about 2 minutes or until the juices are bubbling.

8 Transfer the stir-fry to serving dishes and serve immediately.

## VARIATION

*Use broccoli instead of the cauliflower as an alternative, if wished.*

# Broccoli & Chinese Cabbage with Black Bean Sauce

### Serves 4

### INGREDIENTS

| | | |
|---|---|---|
| 1 pound broccoli florets | 2 cloves garlic, thinly sliced | 1 head Chinese cabbage, shredded |
| 2 tbsp sunflower oil | 1/4 cup slivered almonds | 4 tbsp black bean sauce |
| 1 onion, sliced | | |

1 Bring a large saucepan of water to a boil. Add the broccoli florets to the pan and cook for 1 minute. Drain the broccoli thoroughly.

2 Meanwhile, heat the sunflower oil in a large preheated wok.

3 Add the onion and garlic to the wok and stir-fry until just beginning to brown.

4 Add the drained broccoli florets and the flaked almonds to the mixture in the wok and stir-fry for a further 2–3 minutes.

5 Add the Chinese cabbage to the wok and stir-fry for a further 2 minutes.

6 Stir the black bean sauce into the vegetables in the wok, tossing to mix, and cook until the juices are just beginning to bubble.

7 Transfer the vegetables to warm serving bowls and serve immediately.

## VARIATION

*Use unsalted cashew nuts instead of the almonds, if wished.*

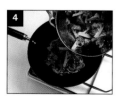

# Quorn with Ginger & Mixed Vegetables

## Serves 4

### INGREDIENTS

| | | |
|---|---|---|
| 1 tbsp grated fresh ginger root | 1 clove garlic, crushed | ³/₄ cup green beans, sliced |
| 1 tsp ground ginger | 2 tbsp soy sauce | 4 stalks celery, sliced |
| 1 tbsp tomato paste | 12 ounces Quorn or | 1 red bell pepper, seeded and sliced |
| 2 tbsp sunflower oil | mycoprotein cubes | boiled rice, to serve |
| | 3–4 medium carrots, sliced | |

1 Place the grated fresh ginger, ground ginger, tomato paste, 1 tablespoon of the sunflower oil, garlic, soy sauce, and Quorn or mycoprotein in a large bowl. Mix well to combine, stirring carefully so that you don't break up the Quorn or mycoprotein. Cover and marinate for 20 minutes.

2 Heat the remaining sunflower oil in a large preheated wok.

3 Add the marinated Quorn mixture to the wok and stir-fry for about 2 minutes.

4 Add the carrots, green beans, celery, and red bell pepper to the wok and stir-fry for a further 5 minutes.

5 Transfer the stir-fry to warm serving dishes and serve immediately with freshly cooked boiled rice.

## COOK'S TIP

*Ginger root will keep for several weeks in a cool, dry place. Ginger root can also be kept frozen— break off lumps as needed.*

## VARIATION

*Use bean curd instead of the Quorn, if you prefer.*

# Leeks with Baby Corn Cobs & Yellow Bean Sauce

### Serves 4

**INGREDIENTS**

3 tbsp peanut oil
1 pound leeks, sliced

8 ounces Chinese cabbage, shredded
6 ounces baby corn cobs, halved

6 scallions, sliced
4 tbsp yellow bean sauce

1 Heat the peanut oil in a large preheated wok.

2 Add the leeks, shredded Chinese cabbage, and baby corn cobs to the wok and stir-fry over a high heat for about 5 minutes, or until the edges of the vegetables are beginning to brown slightly.

3 Add the scallions to the wok, stirring to combine.

4 Add the yellow bean sauce to the mixture in the wok and stir-fry for a further 2 minutes, or until heated through.

5 Transfer to warm serving dishes and serve immediately.

## COOK'S TIP

*Yellow bean sauce adds an authentic Chinese flavor to stir-fries. It is made from crushed salted soy beans mixed with flour and spices to make a thick paste. It is mild in flavor and is excellent with a range of vegetables.*

## COOK'S TIP

*Baby corn cobs are sweeter and have a more delicate flavor than the larger corn cobs and are therefore perfect for stir-frying.*

# Vegetable Stir-Fry

### Serves 4

## INGREDIENTS

3 tbsp olive oil

8 baby onions, halved

1 eggplant, cubed

8 ounces zucchini, sliced

8 ounces open-cap mushrooms, halved

2 cloves garlic, crushed

14 ounce can chopped tomatoes

2 tbsp sun-dried tomato paste

freshly ground black pepper

fresh basil leaves, to garnish

1 Heat the olive oil in a large preheated wok.

2 Add the baby onions and eggplant to the wok and stir-fry for 5 minutes, or until the vegetables are golden and just beginning to soften.

3 Add the zucchini, mushrooms, garlic, tomatoes, and tomato paste to the wok and stir-fry for about 5 minutes. Reduce the heat and simmer for 10 minutes, or until the vegetables are tender.

4 Season with freshly ground black pepper and scatter with fresh basil leaves. Serve immediately.

## VARIATION

*If you want to serve this as a vegetarian main meal, add cubed bean curd in step 3.*

## COOK'S TIP

*Wok cooking is an excellent means of cooking for vegetarians as it is a quick and easy way of serving up delicious dishes of crisp, tasty vegetables. All ingredients should be cut into uniform sizes with as many cut surfaces e xposed as possible for quick cooking.*

# *Spiced Eggplant Stir-Fry*

### Serves 4

**INGREDIENTS**

| | | |
|---|---|---|
| 3 tbsp peanut oil | 2 red chiles, seeded and very | 3 tbsp mango chutney |
| 2 onions, sliced | finely chopped | oil, for deep-frying |
| 2 cloves garlic, chopped | 2 tbsp sugar | 2 cloves garlic, sliced, to garnish |
| 2 eggplants, diced | 6 scallions, sliced | |

1 Heat the peanut oil in a large preheated wok.

2 Add the onions and chopped garlic to the wok, stirring well.

3 Add the eggplants and chiles to the wok and stir-fry for 5 minutes.

4 Add the sugar, scallions, and mango chutney to the wok, stirring well. Reduce the heat slightly, cover, and simmer, stirring from time to time, for about 15 minutes or until the eggplants are tender.

5 Transfer the stir-fry to warm serving bowls and keep warm. Heat the oil for deep-frying in the wok and quickly stir-fry the slices of garlic. Garnish the bowls of stir-fry with the deep-fried garlic and serve immediately.

## COOK'S TIP

*Keep the vegetables moving around the wok as the eggplant will soak up the oil very quickly and may begin to burn if left unattended.*

## COOK'S TIP

*The "hotness" of chiles varies enormously, so always use with caution, but as a general guide the smaller they are the hotter they will be. The seeds are the hottest part and so are usually discarded.*

# Vegetable Kabobs

### Makes 10-12

**INGREDIENTS**

2 large potatoes, sliced
1 medium onion, sliced
½ medium cauliflower, cut into
    small florets
1¾ ounces peas

1 tbsp spinach paste
2-3 green chiles
cilantro leaves
1 tsp fresh ginger root, finely
    chopped
1 tsp fresh garlic, crushed

1 tsp ground coriander
1 pinch turmeric
1 tsp salt
1 cup breadcrumbs
1¼ cups oil
fresh chili strips, to garnish

1 Place the potatoes, onion, and cauliflower florets in a pan of water and bring to the boil. Reduce the heat and leave to simmer until the potatoes are cooked through. Remove the vegetables from the pan with a perforated spoon and drain them thoroughly.

2 Add the peas and spinach to the vegetables and mix together, mashing down with a fork.

3 Using a sharp knife, finely chop the green chiles and cilantro leaves.

4 Mix the chiles and cilantro with the ginger, garlic, ground coriander, turmeric, and salt. Then blend the spice mixture into the vegetables, mixing with a fork to make a paste.

5 Scatter the breadcrumbs on to a large plate.

6 Break off 10-12 small balls from the spice paste. Flatten them with the palm of your hand to make flat, round shapes.

7 Dip each kabob in the breadcrumbs, coating well.

8 Heat the oil in a heavy skillet and fry the kabobs in batches until golden brown. Transfer to serving plates and garnish with fresh chili strips.

# Okra Curry

### Serves 4

**INGREDIENTS**

| | | |
|---|---|---|
| 1 pound lady's fingers | 3 green chiles, finely chopped | 1 tomato, sliced |
| ⅔ cup oil | 2 curry leaves | 2 tbsp lemon juice |
| 2 medium onions, sliced | 1 tsp salt | cilantro leaves |

1 Rinse the okra and drain thoroughly. Using a sharp knife, chop and discard the ends of the okra. Cut the okra into 1-inch long pieces.

2 Heat the oil in a large, heavy skillet. Add the onions, green chiles, curry leaves, and salt and mix together. Stir-fry the vegetables for 5 minutes.

3 Gradually add the okra, mixing in gently with a perforated spoon. Stir-fry the vegetable mixture over a medium heat for 12-15 minutes.

4 Add the sliced tomato to the mixture and sprinkle over the lemon juice sparingly.

5 Garnish with cilantro leaves, cover, and leave to simmer for 3-5 minutes.

6 Transfer to serving plates and serve hot.

## COOK'S TIP

*Okra have a remarkable glutinous quality which naturally thickens curries and casseroles.*

## COOK'S TIP

*When you buy fresh okra, make sure they are not shriveled and that they do not have any brown spots. Fresh okra will keep, tightly wrapped, for up to 3 days in the refrigerator.*

# *Vegetable Curry*

### Serves 4

**INGREDIENTS**

8 ounces turnip or swede, peeled
1 eggplant, leaf end trimmed
12 ounces new potatoes, scrubbed
8 ounces cauliflower
8 ounces button mushrooms
1 large onion
8 ounces carrots, peeled
6 tbsp vegetable ghee or oil
2 garlic cloves, crushed

2 inch ginger root, chopped finely
1-2 fresh green chiles, seeded and chopped
1 tbsp paprika
2 tsp ground coriander
1 tbsp mild or medium curry powder or paste
$1^3/4$ cups vegetable stock
14 ounce can chopped tomatoes

1 green bell pepper, seeded and sliced
1 tbsp cornstarch
$^2/_3$ cup coconut milk
2-3 tbsp ground almonds
salt
cilantro sprigs, to garnish

1 Cut the turnips or swede, eggplant, and potatoes into $\frac{1}{2}$ inch cubes. Divide the cauliflower into small florets. Leave the mushrooms whole and slice the onion and carrots.

2 Heat the ghee or oil in a large saucepan, add the onion, turnip, potato, and cauliflower, and cook gently for 3 minutes, stirring frequently. Add the garlic, ginger, chiles, paprika, ground coriander, and curry powder or paste and cook for 1 minute.

3 Add the stock, tomatoes, eggplant, and mushrooms, and season with salt. Cover and simmer for 30 minutes or until tender. Add the bell pepper and carrots, cover, and cook for a further 5 minutes.

4 Blend the cornstarch with the coconut milk and stir into the mixture. Add ground almonds and simmer for 2 minutes, stirring all the time. Transfer to serving plates and garnish with fresh cilantro.

# Zucchini
# & Fenugreek Seeds

### Serves 4

## INGREDIENTS

6 tbsp oil
1 medium onion, finely chopped
3 green chiles, finely chopped
1 tsp fresh ginger root, chopped finely

1 tsp fresh garlic, crushed
1 tsp chili powder
1 pound zucchini, sliced
2 tomatoes, sliced

cilantro leaves, plus extra to garnish
2 tsp fenugreek seeds

1 Heat the oil in a large skillet.

2 Add the onion, green chiles, ginger, garlic, and chili powder to the pan, stirring to combine.

3 Add the sliced zucchini, and the sliced tomatoes to the pan, and stir-fry for 5-7 minutes.

4 Add the cilantro and fenugreek seeds to the zucchini mixture in the pan and stir-fry for 5 minutes.

5 Remove the pan from the heat and transfer the zucchini and fenugreek seed mixture to serving dishes. Garnish and serve hot with chapatis.

## COOK'S TIP

*Both the leaves and seeds of fenugreek are used, but the stalks and root should be discarded, as they have a bitter taste. Fresh fenugreek is sold in bunches. Fenugreek seeds are flat and yellowish brown in color. You could use coriander seeds instead of the fenugreek seeds, if you prefer.*

# Mixed Vegetables

### Serves 4

**INGREDIENTS**

1¼ cups oil
1 tsp mustard seeds
1 tsp onion seeds
½ tsp white cumin seeds
3-4 curry leaves, chopped
1 pound onions, finely chopped
3 medium tomatoes, chopped
½ red, ½ green bell pepper, sliced

1 tsp fresh ginger root, finely chopped
1 tsp fresh garlic, crushed
1 tsp chili powder
¼ tsp turmeric
1 tsp salt
2 cups water
2 medium potatoes, peeled and cut into pieces

½ cauliflower, cut into small florets
4 medium carrots, peeled and sliced
3 green chiles, finely chopped
cilantro leaves
1 tbsp lemon juice

1 Heat the oil in a large saucepan. Add the mustard, onion, and white cumin seeds along with the curry leaves and fry until they turn a shade darker.

2 Add the onions to the pan and fry over a medium heat until golden.

3 Add the tomatoes and bell peppers and stir-fry for about 5 minutes.

4 Add the ginger, garlic, chili powder, turmeric, and salt and mix well.

5 Add 1¼ cups of the water, cover, and leave to simmer for 10-12 minutes.

6 Add the potatoes, cauliflower, carrots, green chiles, and cilantro leaves, and stir-fry for about 5 minutes.

7 Add the remaining ⅔ cup of water and the lemon juice, stirring to combine. Cover and leave to simmer for about 15 minutes, stirring occasionally.

8 Transfer the mixed vegetables to serving plates and serve at once.

# Dry Split Okra

### Serves 4

#### INGREDIENTS

| | | |
|---|---|---|
| 1 pound okra | 2 tsp dried mango powder | 1 tsp chili powder |
| 2/3 cup oil | 1 tsp ground cumin | 1 tsp salt |
| 1/2 cup dried onions | | |

1 Prepare the okra by cutting the ends off and discarding them. Using a sharp knife, carefully split the okra down the middle without cutting through them completely.

2 Heat the oil in a large saucepan. Add the dried onions and fry until they are crisp.

3 Remove the fried onions from the pan with a perforated spoon and leave them to drain thoroughly on sheets of paper towel.

4 When cool enough to handle, roughly tear the dried onions and place in a large bowl.

5 Add the dried mango, ground cumin, chili powder, and salt to the dried onions and blend well together.

6 Spoon the onion and spice mixture into the split okra.

7 Re-heat the oil in the saucepan.

8 Gently add the okra to the hot oil and cook

over a low heat for about 10-12 minutes.

9 Transfer the cooked okra to a serving dish and serve immediately.

## COOK'S TIP

*Ground cumin has a warm, pungent aromatic flavor and is used extensively in Indian cooking. It is a good storecupboard standby.*

# Tomato Curry

### Serves 4

**INGREDIENTS**

| | | |
|---|---|---|
| 14 ounce can tomatoes | ¹/₂ tsp ground cumin | 2 tbsp lemon juice |
| 1 tsp fresh ginger root, chopped finely | 4 tbsp oil | 3 eggs, hard-cooked |
| 1 tsp fresh garlic, crushed | ¹/₂ tsp onion seeds | fresh cilantro leaves |
| 1 tsp chili powder | ¹/₂ tsp mustard seeds | |
| 1 tsp salt | ¹/₂ tsp fenugreek seeds | |
| ¹/₂ tsp ground coriander | 1 pinch white cumin seeds | |
| | 3 dried red chiles | |

1 Place the tomatoes in a large mixing bowl.

2 Add the ginger, garlic, chili powder, salt, ground coriander, and ground cumin to the tomatoes and blend well.

3 Heat the oil in a saucepan. Add the onion, mustard, fenugreek, white cumin seeds, and the dried red chiles, and stir-fry for about 1 minute. Remove the pan from the heat.

4 Add the tomato mixture to the spicy oil mixture and return to the heat. Stir-fry the mixture for about 3 minutes, then reduce the heat and cook with the lid ajar for 7-10 minutes, stirring occasionally.

5 Sprinkle over the lemon juice sparingly.

6 Transfer the tomato curry to a serving dish, set aside, and keep warm until required.

7 Shell and halve the hard-cooked eggs, then gently add them, yolk end down, to the tomato curry.

8 Garnish with cilantro leaves and serve hot.

## COOK'S TIP

*This tomato curry can be made in advance and frozen, as it freezes particularly well.*

# Mussel & Red Bell Pepper Salad

### Serves 4

## INGREDIENTS

| | | |
|---|---|---|
| 2 large red bell peppers | DRESSING: | salt and pepper |
| 12 ounces cooked shelled mussels, thawed if frozen | 1 tbsp olive oil | |
| 1 head of radicchio | 1 tbsp lemon juice | TO SERVE: |
| 1 ounce arugula leaves | 1 tsp finely grated lemon rind | lemon wedges |
| 8 cooked New Zealand mussels in their shells | 2 tsp clear honey | crusty bread |
| | 1 tsp French mustard | |
| | 1 tbsp snipped fresh chives | |

1 Preheat the broiler. Halve and seed the bell peppers and place them skin side up on the rack. Cook for 8–10 minutes, until the skin is charred and blistered and the flesh is soft. Let cool for 10 minutes, then peel off the skin.

2 Slice the bell pepper flesh into thin strips and place in a bowl. Gently mix in the shelled mussels and set aside.

3 To make the dressing, mix all of the ingredients until well blended. Mix into the bell pepper and mussel mixture until coated.

4 Remove the central core of the radicchio and shred the leaves. Place in a serving bowl with the arugula leaves and toss together.

5 Spoon the mussel mixture into the center of the leaves and arrange the cooked New Zealand mussels around the edge of the dish. Serve with lemon wedges and crusty bread.

## VARIATION

*Replace the shelled mussels with peeled shrimp and the New Zealand mussels with large crevettes, if you prefer. Lime could be used instead of lemon for a different citrus flavor.*

# *Sweet & Sour Fish Salad*

### Serves 4

## INGREDIENTS

8 ounces trout fillets
8 ounces white fish fillets
 (such as haddock or cod)
1¼ cups water
1 stalk lemon grass
2 lime leaves
1 large red chili
1 bunch scallions, trimmed
 and shredded

4 ounces fresh pineapple
 flesh, diced
1 small red bell pepper, seeded
 and diced
1 bunch watercress, washed
 and trimmed
fresh snipped chives, to garnish

DRESSING:
1 tbsp sunflower oil
1 tbsp rice wine vinegar
pinch of chili powder
1 tsp clear honey
salt and pepper

1 Rinse the fish, place in a skillet, and add the water. Bend the lemon grass in half to bruise it and add to the pan with the lime leaves. Prick the chili with a fork and add to the pan. Bring to a boil and simmer for 7–8 minutes. Let cool.

2 Drain the fish fillet, discarding the lemon grass, lime leaves and chili. Flake the fish flesh away from the skin, and place in a bowl. Gently stir in the scallions, pineapple, and bell pepper.

3 Arrange the washed watercress on 4 serving plates, spoon the cooked fish mixture on top, and set aside until required.

4 To make the dressing, mix all the ingredients together and season with salt and pepper to taste.

Spoon the dressing over the fish and serve garnished with chives.

## VARIATION

*This recipe also works very well if you replace the fish with 12 ounces white crabmeat. Add a dash of Tabasco sauce if you like it hot!*

# Beef & Peanut Salad

### Serves 4

**INGREDIENTS**

½ head Chinese cabbage leaves
1 large carrot
4 ounces radishes
3½ ounces baby corn cobs
1 tbsp ground nut oil
1 red chili, seeded and
    finely chopped

1 clove garlic, finely chopped
12 ounces lean beef (such as
    fillet, sirloin, or rump),
    trimmed and finely shredded
1 tbsp dark soy sauce
1 ounce fresh peanuts (optional)
red chili, sliced, to garnish

DRESSING:
1 tbsp smooth peanut butter
1 tsp superfine sugar
2 tbsp light soy sauce
1 tbsp sherry vinegar
salt and pepper

1 Finely shred the Chinese cabbage leaves and arrange on a platter. Peel the carrot and cut into thin, matchstick-like strips. Wash, trim, and quarter the radishes, and halve the baby corn cobs lengthwise. Arrange these ingredients around the edge of the dish and set aside.

2 Heat the oil in a nonstick wok or large skillet and stir-fry the chili, garlic, and beef for

5 minutes. Add the dark soy sauce and stir-fry for a further 1–2 minutes until tender and cooked through.

3 Meanwhile, make the dressing. Place all of the ingredients in a small bowl and blend them together until smooth.

4 Place the hot cooked beef in the center of the salad ingredients. Spoon over the dressing and sprinkle with a few

peanuts, if using. Garnish with the slices of red chili and serve the salad immediately.

## VARIATION

*If preferred, use chicken, turkey, lean pork, or even strips of venison instead of beef in this recipe. Cut off all visible fat before you begin.*

# Chicken & Spinach Salad

### Serves 4

**INGREDIENTS**

4 boneless, skinless chicken
   breasts, 5½ ounces each
2 cups fresh chicken stock
1 bay leaf
8 ounces fresh young
   spinach leaves

1 small red onion, shredded
4 ounces fresh raspberries
salt and freshly ground
   pink peppercorns
fresh toasted croûtons, to
   garnish

DRESSING:
4 tbsp low-fat unsweetened
   yogurt
1 tbsp raspberry vinegar
2 tsp clear honey

1 Place the chicken breasts in a skillet. Add the chicken stock and the bay leaf. Bring to a boil, cover, and simmer for 15–20 minutes, turning halfway through, until the chicken is completely cooked through. Allow to cool in the liquid.

2 Arrange the spinach leaves on 4 serving plates and top with the shredded red onion. Cover and leave to chill in the refrigerator.

3 Drain the cooked chicken and pat dry on absorbent paper towels. Slice the chicken breasts thinly and arrange, fanned out, over the spinach and onion. Sprinkle with the raspberries.

4 To make the dressing, mix all the ingredients together in a small bowl.

5 Drizzle a spoonful of dressing over each chicken breast and season with salt and ground pink peppercorns to taste. Serve the salad with freshly toasted croûtons.

## VARIATION

*This recipe is delicious with smoked chicken, but it will be more expensive and richer, so use slightly less. It would make an impressive starter for a dinner party.*

# Pasta Provençale

### Serves 4

## INGREDIENTS

8 ounces penne (pasta quills)
1 tbsp olive oil
1 ounce pitted black olives, drained and chopped
1 ounce dry-pack sun-dried tomatoes, soaked, drained, and chopped
14 ounce can artichoke hearts, drained and halved

4 ounces baby zucchini, trimmed and sliced
4 ounces baby plum tomatoes, halved
3½ ounces assorted baby salad greens
salt and pepper
shredded basil leaves, to garnish

DRESSING:
4 tbsp sieved tomatoes
2 tbsp low-fat unsweetened yogurt
1 tbsp unsweetened orange juice
1 small bunch fresh basil, shredded

1 Cook the penne (pasta quills) according to the instructions on the packet. Do not overcook the pasta—it should still have bite. Drain well and return to the pan. Stir in the olive oil, salt and pepper, olives, and sun-dried tomatoes. Let cool.

2 Gently mix the artichokes, zucchini, and plum tomatoes into the cooked pasta. Arrange the salad greens in a large serving bowl.

3 To make the dressing, mix all the ingredients together until well combined and toss into the vegetables and pasta.

4 Spoon the mixture on top of the salad greens and garnish with shredded basil leaves.

## VARIATION

*For a nonvegetarian version, stir 8 ounces canned tuna in brine, drained and flaked, into the pasta together with the vegetables. Other pasta shapes can be included—try farfalle (bows) and rotelle (spoked wheels).*

# Root Vegetable Salad

### Serves 4

## INGREDIENTS

12 ounces carrots
8 ounces daikon (white radish)
4 ounces radishes
12 ounces celery root
1 tbsp orange juice
2 celery stalks with leaves,
    washed and trimmed

3½ ounces assorted salad greens
1 ounce chopped walnuts

DRESSING:
1 tbsp walnut oil
1 tbsp white wine vinegar
1 tsp wholegrain mustard

½ tsp finely grated orange rind
1 tsp celery seeds
salt and pepper

1 Peel and coarsely grate or very finely shred the carrots, daikon (white radish), and radishes. Set these vegetables aside in separate bowls until required.

2 Peel and coarsely grate or finely shred the celery root and mix with the orange juice.

3 Remove the celery leaves and reserve for garnishing. Finely chop the celery stalks.

4 Divide the salad greens among 4 serving plates and arrange the carrots, daikon (white radish), and radishes in small piles on top. Set aside while you make the dressing.

5 Mix all of the dressing ingredients together and season with salt and pepper to taste. Drizzle a little of the dressing over each salad. Shred the reserved celery leaves and sprinkle over the salad with the chopped walnuts.

## COOK'S TIP

*Also known as Chinese white radish and mooli, daikon resembles a large white parsnip. It has crisp, slightly pungent flesh, which can be eaten raw or cooked. It is a useful ingredient in stir-fries. Fresh daikon tend to have a stronger flavor than store-bought ones.*

# Beet & Orange Rice Salad

### Serves 4

**INGREDIENTS**

1⅓ cups long-grain and wild
   rices (see Cook's Tip)
4 large oranges
1 pound cooked beet, peeled
2 heads of chicory
salt and pepper

fresh snipped chives, to garnish

DRESSING:
4 tbsp low-fat unsweetened
   yogurt
1 garlic clove, crushed

1 tbsp wholegrain mustard
½ tsp finely grated orange rind
2 tsp clear honey

1 Cook the rices according to the instructions on the packet. Drain and set aside to cool.

2 Slice the top and bottom off each orange and remove the skin and pith. Holding the orange over a bowl to catch the juice, carefully slice between each segment. Place the segments in a separate bowl. Cover the juice and chill in the refrigerator until required.

3 Drain the beet if necessary and dice into cubes. Mix with the orange segments, cover, and chill.

4 When the rice has cooled, mix in the reserved orange juice and season with salt and pepper to taste.

5 Line 4 serving bowls or plates with the chicory leaves. Spoon the rice over the leaves and top with the beet and oranges.

6 Mix all the dressing ingredients together and spoon over the salad, or serve separately in a bowl, if preferred. Garnish with fresh snipped chives.

## COOK'S TIP

*Look for boxes of ready-mixed long-grain and wild rices. Alternatively, you can cook 1 cup white rice and ¼ cup wild rice separately.*

# Red Hot Slaw

### Serves 4

### INGREDIENTS

½ small red cabbage
1 large carrot
2 red-skinned apples
1 tbsp lemon juice
1 medium red onion
3½ ounces reduced-fat Cheddar
  cheese, grated

TO GARNISH:
red chili strips
carrot strips

DRESSING:
3 tbsp reduced-calorie
  mayonnaise

3 tbsp low-fat unsweetened
  yogurt
1 garlic clove, crushed
1 tsp paprika
1–2 tsp chili powder
pinch cayenne pepper (optional)
salt and pepper

1 Cut the red cabbage in half and remove the central core. Finely shred the leaves and place in a large bowl. Peel and coarsely grate or finely shred the carrot and mix into the cabbage.

2 Core the apples and finely dice, leaving on the skins. Place in another bowl and toss in the lemon juice to prevent the apple browning. Mix the apple into the cabbage and carrot.

3 Peel and finely shred or grate the onion. Stir into the other vegetables, along with the cheese, and mix together.

4 To make the dressing, mix together the mayonnaise, yogurt, garlic, and paprika in a small bowl. Add chili powder according to taste, and the cayenne pepper, if using—this will add more spice to the dressing. Season well.

5 Toss the dressing into the vegetables and mix well. Cover and chill in the refrigerator for 1 hour to allow the flavors to develop. Serve garnished with strips of red chili and carrot.

# Pasta Niçoise Salad

### Serves 4

## INGREDIENTS

8 ounces farfalle (pasta bows)
6 ounces green beans, topped
   and tailed
12 ounces fresh tuna steaks
4 ounces baby plum
   tomatoes, halved

8 anchovy fillets, drained on
   absorbent paper towels
2 tbsp capers in water, drained
1 ounce pitted black olives in
   water, drained
fresh basil leaves, to garnish
salt and pepper

DRESSING:
1 tbsp olive oil
1 garlic clove, crushed
1 tbsp lemon juice
$\frac{1}{2}$ tsp finely grated lemon rind
1 tbsp shredded fresh basil
   leaves

1 Cook the pasta in a pan of lightly salted boiling water according to the instructions on the packet until just cooked. Drain well, set aside, and keep warm.

2 Bring a small saucepan of lightly salted water to a boil and cook the green beans for 5–6 minutes, until just tender. Drain well and toss into the pasta. Set aside and keep warm.

3 Preheat the broiler. Rinse and pat the tuna steaks dry on absorbent paper towels. Season on both sides with black pepper. Place the tuna steaks on the broiler rack and cook for 4–5 minutes on each side, until cooked through.

4 Drain the tuna on absorbent paper towels and flake into bite-size pieces. Toss the tuna into the pasta, along with the tomatoes, anchovies, capers, and olives. Set aside and keep warm.

5 Meanwhile, prepare the dressing. Mix all the ingredients together and season well. Pour the dressing over the pasta mixture and mix carefully. Transfer to a warmed serving bowl and serve sprinkled with fresh basil leaves.

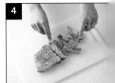

# *Coconut Couscous Salad*

### Serves 4

**INGREDIENTS**

12 ounces couscous

6 ounces dried apricots

1 small bunch fresh chives

2 tbsp unsweetened
 shredded coconut

1 tsp ground cinnamon

salt and pepper

shredded mint leaves, to garnish

DRESSING:

1 tbsp olive oil

2 tbsp unsweetened orange juice

1/2 tsp finely grated orange rind

1 tsp wholegrain mustard

1 tsp clear honey

2 tbsp chopped fresh mint leaves

1 Soak the couscous according to the instructions on the packet.

2 Bring a large pan of water to a boil. Transfer the couscous to a steamer or large strainer lined with cheesecloth and place over the water. Cover and steam as directed. Remove from the heat, place in heatproof bowl, and set aside to cool.

3 Meanwhile, slice the apricots into thin strips and place in a small bowl. Using kitchen scissors, snip the chives over the apricots.

4 When the couscous is cool, mix in the apricots, chives, coconut, and cinnamon. Season well.

5 To make the dressing, mix all the ingredients together and season. Pour over the couscous and mix until well combined. Cover and leave to chill for 1 hour to allow the flavors to develop. Serve the salad garnished with shredded mint leaves.

## COOK'S TIP

*To serve this salad hot, when the couscous has been steamed, mix in the apricots, chives, coconut, cinnamon, and seasoning, along with 1 tbsp olive oil. Transfer to a warmed serving bowl and serve.*

# *Bulgur Pilau*

### Serves 4

**INGREDIENTS**

6 tablespoons butter or
  vegetarian margarine
1 red onion, halved and sliced
2 garlic cloves, crushed
2 cups bulgur wheat
6 ounces tomatoes, seeded
  and chopped

1³/₄ ounces baby corn,
  halved lengthwise
2³/₄ ounces small broccoli florets
3³/₄ cups vegetable stock
2 tablespoons honey
¹/₃ cup golden raisins

¹/₂ cup pine nuts
¹/₂ teaspoon ground cinnamon
¹/₂ teaspoon ground cumin
salt and pepper
sliced scallions,
  to garnish

1 Melt the butter or vegetarian margarine in a large flameproof casserole.

2 Add the onion and garlic and sauté for 2–3 minutes, stirring occasionally.

3 Add the bulgur wheat, tomatoes, corn, broccoli florets, and stock and bring to a boil. Reduce the heat, cover, and simmer for 15–20 minutes, stirring occasionally.

4 Stir in the honey, golden raisins, pine nuts, ground cinnamon, cumin, and salt and pepper to taste, mixing well. Remove the casserole from the heat, cover, and set aside for 10 minutes.

5 Spoon the bulgur pilau into a warm serving dish.

6 Garnish the bulgur pilau with sliced scallions and serve at once.

## COOK'S TIP

*The dish is left to stand for 10 minutes in order for the bulgur to finish cooking and the flavors to mingle.*

# Caesar Salad

### Serves 6-8

### INGREDIENTS

| | | |
|---|---|---|
| 2 thick slices of white bread | 1 clove garlic | DRESSING: |
| 2 tbsp sunflower oil | 1¾ ounces Parmesan cheese | 1 small egg |
| 2 slices fatty bacon, or | 1 large romaine lettuce | juice 1 lemon |
|    6 chopped anchovies | | 6 tbsp olive oil |
| | | salt and white pepper |

1 To make the croutons, remove the crusts from the bread and discard. Cut the bread into small cubes. Heat the sunflower oil in a skillet and fry the bread cubes until a golden brown color. Drain the bread cubes thoroughly on absorbent paper towels.

2 Chop the slices of bacon and fry until crisp. Drain on absorbent paper towels.

3 Cut the garlic in half and rub all around the inside of a serving dish. This will give the salad just a hint of garlic.

4 Wash the lettuce, tear into bite-size pieces, and place in the serving dish.

5 Using a vegetable peeler, shave peelings off the cheese.

6 To make the dressing, whisk the egg in a small bowl. Gradually whisk in the lemon juice and oil. Season with salt and pepper to taste.

7 Pour the salad dressing over the lettuce and toss to coat. Serve sprinkled with the croutons, bacon or anchovies, and Parmesan.

## COOK'S TIP

*Pregnant women, children, and people with weak immune systems may wish to avoid eating recipes containing raw egg.*

# Coleslaw

### Serves 10-12

**INGREDIENTS**

²/₃ cup mayonnaise
²/₃ cup low-fat unsweetened
   yogurt

dash of Tabasco sauce
1 medium head white cabbage
4 carrots

1 green bell pepper
2 tbsp sunflower seeds
salt and pepper

1 To make the dressing, combine the mayonnaise, yogurt, Tabasco sauce, and salt and pepper to taste in a small bowl. Leave to chill in the refrigerator until required.

2 Cut the cabbage in half and then into quarters. Remove and discard the tough center stalk. Shred the cabbage leaves finely. Wash the leaves and dry them thoroughly.

3 Peel the carrot and shred in a food processor. Alternatively, coarsely grate the carrot.

4 Quarter and seed the bell pepper and cut the flesh into thin strips.

5 Combine the vegetables in a large serving bowl and toss to mix. Pour the dressing on and toss until the vegetables are well coated. Let chill.

6 Just before serving, place the sunflower seeds on a cookie sheet and toast in the oven or under the broiler until golden.

7 Scatter the sesame seeds over the coleslaw and serve.

## COOK'S TIP

*You can make coleslaw a few days in advance. To ensure that the sunflower seeds are crispy, add them just before serving.*

## VARIATION

*For a slightly different taste, add one or more of the following ingredients to the coleslaw: raisins, grapes, grated apple, chopped walnuts, cubes of cheese, or roasted peanuts.*

# Green Bean & Carrot Salad

### Serves 4

**INGREDIENTS**

| | | |
|---|---|---|
| 12 ounces green beans | DRESSING: | ¼ tsp superfine sugar |
| 8 ounces carrots | 2 tbsp extra virgin olive oil | salt and pepper |
| 1 red bell pepper | 1 tbsp red wine vinegar | |
| 1 red onion | 2 tsp sun-dried tomato paste | |

1 Top and tail the beans and blanch them in boiling water for 4 minutes, until just tender. Drain the beans and rinse them under cold water until they are cool. Drain the beans again thoroughly.

2 Transfer the beans to a large salad bowl.

3 Peel the carrots and cut them into matchsticks.

4 Halve and seed the bell pepper and cut the flesh into thin strips.

5 Peel the onion and cut it into thin slices.

6 Add the carrot, bell pepper, and onion to the beans and toss to mix.

7 To make the dressing, place the oil, wine vinegar, sun-dried tomato paste, sugar, and salt and pepper to taste in a small screw-top jar and shake well.

8 Pour the dressing over the vegetables and serve or chill in the refrigerator until required.

### COOK'S TIP

*Use canned beans if fresh ones are unavailable. Rinse off the salty liquid and drain well. There is no need to blanch canned beans.*

# Spinach & Orange Salad

### Serves 4–6

## INGREDIENTS

| | | |
|---|---|---|
| 8 ounces baby spinach leaves | DRESSING: | 2 tsp lemon juice |
| 2 large oranges | 3 tbsp extra virgin olive oil | 1 tsp clear honey |
| ½ red onion | 2 tbsp freshly squeezed orange juice | ½ tsp wholegrain mustard |
| | | salt and pepper |

1 Wash the spinach leaves under cold running water and then dry them thoroughly on absorbent paper towels. Remove any tough stalks and tear the larger leaves into smaller pieces.

2 Slice the top and bottom off each orange with a sharp knife, then remove the peel.

3 Carefully slice between the membranes of the orange to remove the individual segments.

4 Using a sharp knife, finely chop the onion.

5 Mix together the spinach leaves and orange segments and arrange in a serving dish. Scatter the chopped onion over the salad.

6 To make the dressing, whisk together the olive oil, orange juice, lemon juice, honey, mustard, and salt and pepper to taste.

7 Pour the dressing over the salad just before serving. Toss the salad well to coat the leaves.

## COOK'S TIP

*Tear the spinach leaves into bite-size pieces rather than cutting them because cutting bruises the leaves.*

## VARIATION

*Use a mixture of spinach and watercress leaves, if you prefer a slightly more peppery flavor.*

# *Potato Salad*

### Serves 4

**INGREDIENTS**

| | | |
|---|---|---|
| 1 pound 9 ounces tiny new potatoes | generous 1 cup mayonnaise | TO GARNISH: |
| 8 scallions | 1 tsp paprika | 2 tbsp snipped chives |
| 1 hard-boiled egg (optional) | salt and pepper | pinch of paprika |

1 Bring a large pan of lightly salted water to a boil. Add the potatoes to the pan and cook for 10–15 minutes, or until they are just tender.

2 Drain the potatoes in a colander and rinse them under cold running water until they are completely cold. Drain them again thoroughly. Transfer the potatoes to a mixing bowl and set aside until required.

3 Using a sharp knife, trim and slice the scallions thinly on the diagonal.

4 Shell and chop the hard-boiled egg.

5 Combine the mayonnaise, paprika, and salt and pepper to taste in a bowl. Pour the mixture over the potatoes.

6 Add the scallions and egg (if using) to the potatoes and toss together.

7 Transfer the potato salad to a serving bowl, sprinkle with snipped chives and a pinch of paprika. Cover and chill in the refrigerator until required.

## VARIATION

*To make a lighter dressing, use a mixture of half mayonnaise and half unsweetened yogurt.*

## VARIATION

*Add cubes of cheese to the potato salad, if liked.*

# *Tabouleh*

### Serves 4

**INGREDIENTS**

| | | |
|---|---|---|
| 1½ cups cracked wheat | 4 tbsp chopped, fresh parsley | 2 cloves garlic, crushed |
| 8 ounces tomatoes | 3 tbsp chopped, fresh mint | salt and pepper |
| 1 small onion | 2 tbsp pine nuts | |
| ¼ cucumber | 4 tbsp lemon juice | |
| ½ red bell pepper | 4 tbsp extra virgin olive oil | |

1 Place the cracked wheat in a large bowl and cover with plenty of boiling water. Let stand for about 30 minutes, or until the grains are tender and have swelled in size.

2 Drain the wheat through a large strainer. Press down with a plate in order to remove as much water as possible. Transfer the wheat to a large mixing bowl.

3 Cut the tomatoes in half, scoop out the seeds, and discard them.

Chop the flesh into fine dice. Using a sharp knife, finely chop the onion.

4 Scoop out the seeds from the cucumber and discard them. Finely dice the cucumber flesh.

5 Seed the bell peppers and chop the flesh. Add the prepared vegetables to the wheat, with the herbs and pine nuts. Toss until mixed.

6 Mix together the lemon juice oil, garlic, and salt and pepper to taste.

7 Pour the mixture over the wheat and vegetables and toss together. Chill in the refrigerator until required.

## COOK'S TIP

*This salad is best made a few hours before it is required to allow time for the flavors to develop and blend together. It can even be made a few days ahead, if wished.*

# Hot Lentil Salad with Balsamic Dressing

### Serves 6-8

**INGREDIENTS**

³/₄ cup Puy lentils, cooked
4 tbsp olive oil
1 small onion, sliced
4 stalks celery, sliced
2 cloves garlic, crushed

2 zucchini, trimmed and diced
4¹/₂ ounces green beans, trimmed
and cut into short lengths
¹/₂ red bell pepper, seeded and
diced

¹/₂ yellow bell pepper, seeded
and diced
1 tsp Dijon mustard
1 tbsp balsamic vinegar
salt and pepper

1 Place the lentils in a large mixing or serving bowl. The lentils can still be warm, if wished.

2 Heat the oil in a saucepan and sauté the onion and celery for 2–3 minutes, until softened but not browned.

3 Add the garlic, zucchini, and green beans to the pan and cook for 2 minutes, stirring.

4 Add the bell peppers to the pan and cook for 1 minute.

5 Stir the mustard and the balsamic vinegar into the pan and mix until warm and thoroughly combined.

6 Pour the warm mixture over the lentils and toss together to mix well. Season with salt and pepper and serve immediately.

## COOK'S TIP

*To cook the lentils, rinse them well and place in a large saucepan. Cover with plenty of cold water and bring to a boil. Boil rapidly for 10 minutes, then reduce the heat, and simmer for 35 minutes, until the lentils are tender. Drain well.*

# Italian Mozzarella Salad

### Serves 6

### INGREDIENTS

| | | |
|---|---|---|
| 7 ounces baby spinach leaves | 8 ounces cherry tomatoes | salt and freshly ground black |
| 4½ ounces watercress | 2 tsp balsamic vinegar | pepper |
| 4½ ounces mozzarella cheese | 1½ tbsp extra virgin olive oil | |

1 Wash the spinach and watercress and drain thoroughly on absorbent paper towels. Remove any tough stalks. Place the spinach and watercress leaves in a serving dish.

2 Cut the mozzarella cheese into small pieces and scatter them over the spinach and watercress leaves.

3 Cut the cherry tomatoes in half and scatter them over the salad.

4 Sprinkle with the balsamic vinegar and oil, and season with salt and pepper to taste. Toss the mixture together to coat the leaves. Serve at once or chill in the refrigerator until required.

## VARIATION

*Include feta or halloumi cheese instead of mozzarella for a change, and use sherry vinegar instead of balsamic vinegar, if preferred.*

## COOK'S TIP

*Mozzarella is a highly popular cheese. It is a soft, fresh cheese with a piquant flavor, traditionally made from water buffalo's milk. It is usually sold surrounded by whey to keep it moist. Buffalo milk is now scarce, and so nowadays this cheese is often made with cow's milk. Mozzarella combines well with tomatoes, and this combination is now a classic.*

# Artichoke & Prosciutto Salad

### Serves 4

**INGREDIENTS**

9 ½ ounce can artichoke hearts
in oil, drained
4 small tomatoes
½ cup sun-dried tomatoes
in oil
1 ½ ounces prosciutto

½ cup pitted black olives,
halved
few basil leaves

Dressing:
3 tbsp olive oil

1 tbsp white wine vinegar
1 clove garlic, crushed
½ tsp mild mustard
1 tsp clear honey
salt and pepper

1 Make sure the artichoke hearts are thoroughly drained, then cut them into quarters, and place in a bowl.

2 Cut each fresh tomato into wedges. Slice the sun-dried tomatoes into thin strips. Cut the prosciutto into thin strips and add to the bowl containing the artichokes together with the tomatoes and olive halves.

3 Keeping a few basil leaves whole for garnishing, tear the remainder of the leaves into small pieces and add to the bowl containing the other salad ingredients.

4 Put the oil, wine vinegar, garlic, mustard, honey, and salt and pepper to taste in a screw-top jar and shake vigorously until well blended.

5 Pour the dressing over the salad and toss.

6 Serve the salad garnished with a few whole basil leaves.

### COOK'S TIP

*Use bottled artichokes in oil as they have a better flavor. Rinse canned artichokes to remove the salty liquid.*

# Pear & Roquefort Salad

### Serves 4

## INGREDIENTS

| | | |
|---|---|---|
| 1³/₄ ounces Roquefort cheese | 2 tbsp snipped chives | few leaves of corn salad |
| ²/₃ cup low-fat unsweetened yogurt | few leaves of lollo rosso | 2 ripe pears |
| | few leaves of radiccio | pepper |
| | | whole chives, to garnish |

1 Place the cheese in a bowl and mash with a fork. Gradually blend the yogurt into the cheese to make a smooth dressing. Add the snipped chives and season with pepper according to taste.

2 Tear the lollo rosso, radiccio, and corn salad leaves into manageable pieces. Arrange the salad greens on a serving platter or on individual serving plates.

3 Quarter and core the pears, and then cut them into slices.

4 Arrange the pear slices over the salad greens.

5 Drizzle the dressing over the pears and garnish with a few whole chives. Serve at once.

## COOK'S TIP

*Arrange the Pear & Roquefort Salad on individual plates for an attractive starter, or on one large serving platter for a side salad.*

## COOK'S TIP

*Look for bags of mixed salad greens, as these are generally more economical than buying lots of different greens separately. If you are using greens that have not been prewashed, rinse them well and dry them thoroughly on absorbent paper towels or in a salad spinner. Alternatively, wrap the greens in a clean dish cloth and shake dry.*

# Pasta Salad with Basil Vinaigrette

### Serves 4

## INGREDIENTS

2 cups fusilli (pasta spirals)
4 tomatoes
<sup>1</sup>/<sub>3</sub> cup black olives
<sup>1</sup>/<sub>2</sub> cup sun-dried tomatoes in oil
2 tbsp pine nuts

2 tbsp grated Parmesan cheese
fresh basil, to garnish

VINAIGRETTE:
1/4 cup basil leaves

1 clove garlic
2 tbsp grated Parmesan cheese
4 tbsp extra virgin olive oil
2 tbsp lemon juice
salt and pepper

1 Cook the pasta in lightly salted boiling water for 10–12 minutes, until just tender, or according to the instructions on the packet. Drain the pasta, rinse under cold water, then drain again thoroughly. Place the pasta in a large bowl.

2 To make the vinaigrette, place the basil leaves, garlic, cheese, oil, and lemon juice in a food processor. Season with salt and pepper to taste. Process until the leaves are well chopped and the ingredients are combined. Alternatively, finely chop the basil leaves by hand and combine with the other vinaigrette ingredients. Pour the vinaigrette over the pasta and toss to coat.

3 Cut the tomatoes into wedges. Pit and halve the olives. Slice the sun-dried tomatoes. Toast the pine nuts on a cookie sheet under the broiler until golden brown.

4 Add the tomatoes (fresh and sun-dried) and the olives to the pasta and mix until combined.

5 Transfer the pasta to a serving dish, scatter over the Parmesan and pine nuts, and garnish with a few basil leaves.

# *Mango & Wild Rice Salad*

### Serves 6

**INGREDIENTS**

| | | |
|---|---|---|
| ½ cup wild rice | ¼ cup ready-to-eat dried | sprigs of fresh cilantro or mint, |
| 1 cup Basmati rice | apricots, chopped | to garnish |
| 3 tbsp hazelnut oil | ¾ cup slivered almonds | |
| 1 tbsp sherry vinegar | 2 tbsp chopped, fresh cilantro | |
| 1 ripe mango | or mint | |
| 3 stalks celery | salt and pepper | |

1 Cook the rice in separate pans in lightly salted boiling water. Cook the wild rice for 45–50 minutes, and the Basmati rice for 10–12 minutes. Drain, rinse, and drain again. Put the rice in a bowl.

2 Mix the oil, vinegar, and seasoning together. Pour the mixture over the rice and toss well.

3 Cut the mango in half lengthwise, as close to the pit as possible. Remove and discard the pit.

4 Peel the skin from the mango and cut the flesh into slices.

5 Slice the celery thinly and add to the cooled rice with the mango, apricots, almonds, and chopped herbs. Toss together and transfer to a serving dish. Garnish with sprigs of fresh herbs.

## COOK'S TIP

*To toast almonds, place them on a cookie sheet in a preheated oven at 350°F for 5–10 minutes. Alternatively, toast them under the broiler, turning frequently and keeping a close eye on them because they will quickly burn.*

# Mixed Bean Salad

### Serves 6-8

**INGREDIENTS**

| | | |
|---|---|---|
| 14 ounce can small navy beans, drained | 1 small red onion, thinly sliced | DRESSING: |
| 14 ounce can red kidney beans, drained | 6 ounces green beans, topped and tailed | 4 tbsp olive oil |
| 14 ounce can dried lima beans, drained | 1 red bell pepper, halved and seeded | 2 tbsp sherry vinegar |
| | | 2 tbsp lemon juice |
| | | 1 tsp light brown sugar |
| | | 1 tsp chili sauce (optional) |

1 Put the canned beans in a large mixing bowl. Add the sliced onion and mix together.

2 Cut the green beans in half and cook in lightly salted boiling water for about 8 minutes, until just tender. Rinse under cold water and drain again. Add to the mixed beans and onions.

3 Place the bell pepper halves, cut side down, on a broiler rack and cook until the skin blackens and chars. Cool slightly, then put them into a plastic bag for about 10 minutes. Peel away the skin from the bell peppers and discard. Roughly chop the bell pepper flesh and add it to the beans.

4 To make the dressing, place the oil, sherry vinegar, lemon juice, sugar, and chili sauce (if using) in a screw-top jar and shake vigorously.

5 Pour the dressing over the mixed bean salad and toss well. Chill in the refrigerator until required.

## VARIATION

*You can use any combination of beans in this salad. For a distinctive flavor, add 1 teaspoon of curry paste instead of the chili sauce.*

# *Mediterranean Bell Pepper Salad*

### Serves 4

**INGREDIENTS**

| | | |
|---|---|---|
| 2 red bell peppers, halved and seeded | 3 tbsp extra virgin olive oil | 1³/₄ ounces anchovy fillets, chopped |
| 2 yellow bell peppers, halved and seeded | 1 onion, cut into wedges | ¹/₄ cup pitted black olives, quartered |
| | 2 large zucchini, sliced | fresh basil leaves |
| | 2 garlic cloves, sliced | |
| | 1 tbsp balsamic vinegar | |

1 Place the bell pepper halves, cut side down, on a broiler pan and cook until the skin blackens and chars. Cool slightly, then put them into a plastic bag for about 10 minutes.

2 Peel away the skin from the bell peppers and discard. Cut the flesh into thick strips.

3 Heat the oil in a large skillet, add the onion, and sauté gently for 10 minutes, or until softened. Add the zucchini slices, garlic, and bell pepper strips to the skillet and cook, stirring occasionally, for another 10 minutes.

4 Add the vinegar, anchovies, and olives to the pan. Season to taste. Mix well and let cool.

5 Reserve a few basil leaves for garnishing, then tear the remainder into small pieces. Stir them into the salad.

6 Transfer the bell pepper salad to a serving dish and garnish with a few fresh, whole basil leaves.

### COOK'S TIP

*Balsamic vinegar is made in and around Modena in Italy. Its rich, mellow flavor is perfect for Mediterranean-style salads, but if it is unavailable, use sherry vinegar or white wine vinegar instead.*

# Hot Salad

### Serves 4

**INGREDIENTS**

| | | |
|---|---|---|
| 1/2 medium-sized cauliflower | 1/2 cucumber | 2 tbsp butter |
| 1 green bell pepper | 4 carrots | salt and pepper |
| 1 red bell pepper | | |

1 Rinse the cauliflower and cut into small florets, using a sharp knife.

2 Cut the bell peppers into thin slices.

3 Cut the cucumber into thin slices.

4 Peel the carrots and cut them into thin slices.

5 Melt the butter in a large saucepan, stirring constantly so that it doesn't burn.

6 Add the cauliflower, bell peppers, cucumber, and carrots and stir-fry for 5-7 minutes. Season with salt and pepper to taste, cover the pan with a lid, reduce the heat and leave to simmer for about 3 minutes.

7 Transfer the vegetables to a serving dish, toss to mix, and serve immediately.

## VARIATION

*You can replace the vegetables in this recipe with those of your choice, if you prefer.*

## COOK'S TIP

*In India, you can buy snacks and accompaniments along the roadside while elswhere you can either buy them from Indian or Pakistani grocers. However, they are fresher and more satisfying made at home.*

# Cool Cucumber Salad

### Serves 4

**INGREDIENTS**

8 ounces cucumber
1 green chili (optional)
fresh cilantro leaves, finely
    chopped

2 tbsp lemon juice
½ tsp salt
1 tsp sugar

fresh mint leaves and red bell
    pepper strips, to garnish

1 Using a sharp knife, slice the cucumber thinly. Arrange the cucumber slices on a round serving plate.

2 Using a sharp knife, chop the green chili (if using).

3 Scatter the chopped chili over the cucumber.

4 To make the dressing, place the chopped cilantro leaves, lemon juice, salt and sugar into a bowl, mix together and set aside.

5 Place the cucumber in the refrigerator and leave to chill for at least 1 hour, or until required.

6 Transfer the cucumber to a serving dish.

7 Pour the dressing over the cucumber just before serving and garnish with fresh mint leaves.

## COOK'S TIP

*To store fresh cilantro, put the roots in a glass of water and keep in a cool place for up to 4 days.*

## COOK'S TIP

*Much of the heat in Indian dishes comes from fresh green chiles, although dried and ground red chiles are also commonplace. In southern India, with its searingly hot temperatures, large quantities of chiles are used because they cause the body to perspire, which has a cooling effect. Numerous varieties of fresh chili grow in India. As a general rule, the smaller the chili, the hotter it will be. Fresh chiles will keep for about 5 days in the refrigerator.*

# *Indian-Style Omelet*

### Serves 2-4

**INGREDIENTS**

| | | |
|---|---|---|
| 1 small onion, very finely chopped | cilantro leaves, finely chopped | 2 tbsp oil |
| 2 green chiles, finely chopped | 4 medium eggs | |
| | 1 tsp salt | |

1 Place the onion, chiles, and cilantro in a large mixing bowl. Mix together, ideally with your fingers.

2 Place the eggs in a separate bowl and whisk together.

3 Add the onion mixture to the eggs and mix together well.

4 Add the salt to the egg and onion mixture and whisk together well.

5 Heat 1 tbsp of the oil in a large skillet. Place a ladleful of the omelet batter into the heated pan.

6 Fry the omelet, turning once, and pressing down with a flat spoon to make sure that the egg is cooked right through, until the omelet is a golden brown color.

7 Repeat the same process for the remaining batter. Set the omelets aside and keep warm while you make the remaining batches of omelets.

8 Serve the omelets immediately with paratas or toasted bread. Alternatively, simply serve the omelets with a crisp green salad for a light lunch.

## COOK'S TIP

*Indian cooks use a variety of vegetable oils, and groundnut or sunflower oils make good alternatives for most dishes, although sometimes more specialist ones, such as coconut oil, mustard oil, and sesame oil, are called for.*

# Sweet & Sour Fruit

### Serves 4

## INGREDIENTS

14 ounce can mixed fruit cocktail
14 ounce can guavas
2 large bananas
3 apples

1 tsp ground black pepper
1 tsp salt

2 tbsp lemon juice
$\frac{1}{2}$ tsp ground ginger
fresh mint leaves, to garnish

1 Drain the can of fruit cocktail and pour the fruit pieces into a deep mixing bowl.

2 Mix the guavas and their syrup with the drained fruit cocktail.

3 Peel the bananas and cut into slices.

4 Peel and core the apples (optional) and cut into dice.

5 Add the pieces of fresh fruit to the bowl containing the canned fruit and mix together.

6 Add the ground black pepper, salt, lemon juice, and ginger and stir well to mix.

7 Serve as a snack garnished with a few fresh mint leaves.

## COOK'S TIP

*The lemon juice in this recipe serves to add a sharp flavor to the dish but it also prevents the banana and apple from dicoloring and turning brown when the flesh is exposed to the air.*

## COOK'S TIP

*Ginger is one of the most popular spices in India and also one of the oldest. It can be bought as fresh ginger root in most large supermarkets. It should always be peeled before use and can be finely chopped or puréed. Ground ginger is also useful to have in your storecupboard.*

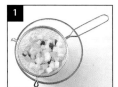

# *Baking & Desserts*

The ideal ending to a meal is fresh fruit topped with low-fat yogurt or fromage frais. Fruit contains no fat and is sweet enough not to need extra sugar, and it is also a valuable source of vitamins and fiber—ideal in every way for anyone who cares about their own and their family's health.

There are, however, dozens of other ways in which fruit can be used as the basis for desserts and bakes, and thanks to modern transportation systems the range of unusual and exotic fruits available in supermarkets seems to expand every week. Experiment with some of these unfamiliar fruits in delicious warm desserts, sophisticated mousses and fools, and satisfying cakes, and use old favorites in enticing new ways.

# *Paper-Thin Fruit Pies*

### Serves 4

**INGREDIENTS**

| | | |
|---|---|---|
| 1 medium eating apple | 4 rectangular sheets of filo | 1 tbsp orange juice |
| 1 medium ripe pear | pastry, thawed if frozen | 2 tsp confectioner's sugar, |
| 2 tbsp lemon juice | 2 tbsp low-sugar apricot | for dusting |
| 2 ounces low-fat spread | preserve | low-fat custard, to serve |

1 Preheat the oven to 400°F. Core and thinly slice the apple and pear and toss them in the lemon juice to prevent discoloration.

2 Gently melt the low-fat spread in a pan set over a low heat.

3 Cut the sheets of pastry into 4 and cover with a clean, damp dish cloth. Brush 4 nonstick large muffin pans, measuring 4 inches across, with a little of the low-fat spread.

4 Working on each pie, separately, brush 4 sheets of pastry with low-fat spread. Press a small sheet of pastry into the base of one large muffin pan. Arrange the other sheets of pastry on top at slightly different angles. Repeat with the other sheets of pastry to make another 3 pies.

5 Arrange the apple and pear slices alternately in the center of each pastry case and lightly crimp the edges of the pastry of each pie.

6 Mix the preserve and orange juice together until smooth and brush over the fruit. Bake for 12–15 minutes. Dust lightly with confectioner's sugar, and serve hot with low-fat custard.

## VARIATION

*Other combinations of fruit are equally delicious. Try peach and apricot, raspberry and apple, or pineapple and mango.*

# *Almond Trifles*

### Serves 4

**INGREDIENTS**

8 Amaretti di Saronno cookies

4 tbsp brandy or Amaretto
   liqueur

8 ounces raspberries

1¼ cups low-fat custard

1¼ cups low-fat unsweetened
   yogurt

1 tsp almond extract

½ ounce toasted
   almonds, slivered

1 tsp cocoa powder

1 Using the end of a rolling pin, carefully crush the cookies into small pieces.

2 Divide the crushed cookies among 4 serving glasses. Sprinkle in the brandy or liqueur and let stand for about 30 minutes to allow the cookies to soften.

3 Top the layer of cookies with a layer of raspberries, reserving a few raspberries for decoration, and spoon over enough custard to just cover.

4 Mix the unsweetened yogurt with the almond extract and spoon over the custard. Chill in the refrigerator for about 30 minutes.

5 Just before serving, sprinkle with the toasted slivered almonds and dust with a little cocoa powder. Decorate with the reserved raspberries and serve at once.

## VARIATION

*Try this trifle with assorted summer fruits. If they are a frozen mix, use them frozen and allow them to thaw so that the juices soak into the cookie base—it will taste delicious.*

# Cheese Hearts with Strawberry Sauce

### Serves 4

**INGREDIENTS**

15½ ounces low-fat cottage cheese
⅔ cup low-fat unsweetened yogurt
1 medium egg white

2 tbsp superfine sugar
1–2 tsp vanilla extract
rose-scented geranium leaves, to decorate (optional)

SAUCE:
8 ounces strawberries
4 tbsp unsweetened orange juice
2–3 tsp confectioner's sugar

1 Line 4 heart-shaped molds or ramekins with clean cheesecloth. Place a strainer over a mixing bowl and using the back of a metal spoon, press the cottage cheese through. Mix in the unsweetened yogurt.

2 Whisk the egg white until stiff. Fold into the cheeses, along with the superfine sugar and vanilla extract.

3 Place the molds on a wire rack set over a baking pan. Spoon the cheese mixture into the molds and smooth over the tops. Leave to chill for 1 hour or until firm and drained.

4 Meanwhile, make the sauce. Wash the strawberries under cold running water. Reserving a few strawberries for decoration, hull and chop the remainder. Place the strawberries in a blender or food processor with the orange juice and process until smooth. Alternatively, push through a strainer to purée. Mix with the confectioner's sugar to taste. Cover and chill until the sauce is required.

5 Remove the cheese hearts from the molds and transfer to serving plates. Remove the cheesecloth, decorate with the reserved strawberries and geranium leaves (if using), and serve with the sauce.

# Almond & Golden Raisin Cheesecake

## Serves 4

### INGREDIENTS

| | | |
|---|---|---|
| 12 Amaretti di Saronno cookies | ½ tsp finely grated lime rind | 2 tbsp lime juice |
| 1 medium egg white, lightly beaten | 1 ounce ground almonds | |
| 8 ounces skimmed-milk soft cheese | 1 ounce superfine sugar | TO DECORATE: |
| | 2 ounces golden raisins | 1 ounces slivered toasted almonds |
| ½ tsp almond extract | 2 tsp powdered gelatin | strips of lime rind |
| | 2 tbsp boiling water | |

1 Preheat the oven to 350°F. Place the cookies in a clean plastic bag, seal the bag, and using a rolling pin, crush them into small pieces. Place the crumbs in a bowl and bind together with the egg white.

2 Arrange 4 nonstick pastry rings or poached egg rings, 3½ inches across, on a cookie sheet lined with baking parchment. Divide the cookie mixture into 4 equal portions and spoon it into the rings,

pressing down well. Bake for 10 minutes, until crisp, and allow to cool in the rings.

3 Beat together the soft cheese, almond extract, lime rind, ground almonds, sugar, and golden raisins until well mixed.

4 Dissolve the gelatin in the boiling water and stir in the lime juice. Fold into the cheese mixture and spoon over the cookie bases. Smooth over the tops

and chill for 1 hour, or until set.

5 Loosen the cheesecakes from the rings, using a small spatula, and transfer to serving plates. Decorate with toasted almonds and lime rind, and serve.

## VARIATION

*If you prefer, substitute chopped dried apricots for the golden raisins.*

# Red Fruits with Foaming Sauce

## Serves 4

### INGREDIENTS

| | | |
|---|---|---|
| 8 ounces redcurrants, washed and trimmed, thawed if frozen | ³/₄ cup unsweetened apple juice | SAUCE: |
| | 1 cinnamon stick, broken | 8 ounces raspberries, thawed if frozen |
| 8 ounces cranberries | 10¹/₂ ounces small strawberries, washed, hulled, and halved | 2 tbsp fruit cordial |
| 3 ounces light brown sugar | | 3¹/₂ ounces marshmallows |

1 Place the redcurrants, cranberries, and sugar in a saucepan. Pour in the apple juice and add the cinnamon stick. Bring the mixture to a boil and simmer gently for 10 minutes, until the fruit has just softened.

2 Stir the strawberries into the cranberry and sugar mixture and mix well. Transfer the mixture to a bowl, cover, and chill in the refrigerator for about 1 hour. Remove and discard the cinnamon stick.

3 Just before serving, make the sauce. Place the raspberries and fruit cordial in a small pan, bring to a boil, and simmer for 2–3 minutes, until the fruit is just beginning to soften. Stir the marshmallows into the raspberry mixture and heat through, stirring, until the marshmallows begin to melt.

4 Transfer the fruit salad to serving bowls. Top with the raspberry and marshmallow sauce and serve at once.

## VARIATION

*This sauce is delicious poured over low-fat ice cream. For an extra-colorful sauce, replace the raspberries with an assortment of summer berries.*

# Brown Bread Ice Cream

### Serves 4

**INGREDIENTS**

6 ounces fresh whole
wheat bread crumbs
1 ounce finely chopped walnuts
2 ounces superfine sugar
½ tsp ground nutmeg

1 tsp finely grated orange rind
2 cups low-fat unsweetened
yogurt
2 large egg whites

TO DECORATE:

walnut halves
orange slices
fresh mint leaves

1 Preheat the broiler. Mix the bread crumbs, walnuts, and sugar together and spread over a sheet of foil in the broiler pan. Broil, stirring frequently, for 5 minutes until crisp and evenly browned. (Take care that the sugar does not burn.) Remove from the heat and allow to cool.

2 When the mixture is cool, transfer to a mixing bowl and mix in the nutmeg, orange rind, and yogurt. In another bowl, whisk the egg whites until stiff. Gently fold the egg whites into the bread crumb mixture using a metal spoon.

3 Spoon the mixture into 4 mini-basins, smooth over the tops, and freeze for 1½–2 hours until firm.

4 To serve, hold the bases of the molds in hot water for a few seconds, then turn onto serving plates. Serve immediately, decorated with walnut halves, orange rind, and fresh mint leaves.

## COOK'S TIP

*If you don't have mini-basins, use ramekins or cups or, if you prefer, use one large bowl. Alternatively, spoon the mixture into a large, freezing container to freeze and serve the ice cream in scoops.*

# Chocolate Cheese Pots

### Serves 4

**INGREDIENTS**

1¼ cups low-fat ricotta cheese
⅔ cup low-fat unsweetened
    yogurt
1 ounce confectioner's sugar
4 tsp low-fat drinking
    chocolate powder

4 tsp cocoa powder
1 tsp vanilla extract
2 tbsp dark rum (optional)
2 medium egg whites
4 chocolate cake decorations

TO SERVE:
pieces of kiwi fruit, orange,
    and banana
whole strawberries and
    raspberries

1 Combine the ricotta cheese and low-fat yogurt in a mixing bowl. Sift in the confectioner's sugar, chocolate powder, and cocoa powder and mix until well combined. Add the vanilla extract and rum, if using.

2 In another bowl, whisk the egg whites until stiff. Using a metal spoon, fold the egg whites into the ricotta cheese, unsweetened yogurt, and chocolate mixture.

3 Spoon the ricotta cheese, unsweetened yogurt, and chocolate mixture into 4 small china dessert pots and chill in the refrigerator for about 30 minutes. Decorate each chocolate cheese pot with a chocolate cake decoration.

4 Serve each chocolate cheese pot with an assortment of fresh fruit, such as pieces of kiwi fruit, orange, and banana, and a few whole strawberries and raspberries.

## VARIATION

*This chocolate mixture would make an excellent filling for a cheesecake. Make the base out of crushed Amaretti di Saronno cookies and egg white, and set the filling with 2 tsp powdered gelatin dissolved in 2 tbsp boiling water. Make sure you use cookies made from apricot kernels, which are virtually fat free.*

# *Citrus Meringue Crush*

### Serves 4

## INGREDIENTS

8 ready-made meringue nests
1¼ cups low-fat natural
    unsweetened yogurt
½ tsp finely grated orange rind
½ tsp finely grated lemon rind
½ tsp finely grated lime rind
2 tbsp orange liqueur or
    unsweetened orange juice

TO DECORATE:
sliced kumquat
lime rind, grated

SAUCE:
2 ounces kumquats
8 tbsp unsweetened orange juice
2 tbsp lemon juice

2 tbsp lime juice
2 tbsp water
2–3 tsp superfine sugar
1 tsp cornstarch mixed with
    1 tbsp water

1 Place the meringues in a clean plastic bag, seal the bag, and using a rolling pin, crush the meringues into small pieces. Transfer to a mixing bowl.

2 Stir the yogurt, grated citrus rinds, and the liqueur or juice into the crushed meringue. Spoon the mixture into 4 mini-basins, smooth over the tops, and freeze for 1½–2 hours, until firm.

3 To make the sauce, thinly slice the kumquats and place them in a pan with the fruit juices and water. Bring gently to a boil and then simmer over a low heat for 3–4 minutes, until the kumquats have just softened.

4 Sweeten with sugar to taste, stir in the cornstarch mixture, and cook, stirring, until thickened. Pour into a small bowl, cover the surface with a layer of plastic wrap, and allow to cool—the film will help prevent a skin forming. Chill in the refrigerator.

5 To serve, dip the meringue basins in hot water for 5 seconds, or until they loosen, and turn onto serving plates. Spoon on a little sauce, decorate with slices of kumquat and lime rind, and serve.

# Tropical Fruit Fool

### Serves 4

**INGREDIENTS**

1 medium ripe mango
2 kiwi fruit
1 medium banana
2 tbsp lime juice

1/2 tsp finely grated lime rind,
plus extra to decorate
2 medium egg whites
15 ounce can low-fat custard

1/2 tsp vanilla extract
2 passion fruit

1. To peel the mango, slice either side of the smooth, flat central pit. Roughly chop the flesh and blend the fruit in a food processor or blender until smooth. Alternatively, mash the chopped mango flesh with a fork.

2. Peel the kiwi fruit, chop the flesh into small pieces, and place in a bowl. Peel and chop the banana and add to the bowl. Toss all of the fruit in the lime juice and rind and mix well to prevent discoloration.

3. In a grease-free bowl, whisk the egg whites until stiff and then gently fold in the custard and vanilla extract until thoroughly mixed.

4. In 4 tall glasses, alternately layer the chopped fruit, mango purée, and custard mixture, finishing with the custard on top. Chill in the refrigerator for 20 minutes.

5. Halve the passion fruits, scoop out the seeds, and spoon the passion fruit over the fruit fools.

6. Decorate each serving with the extra lime rind and serve.

## VARIATION

*Other tropical fruits to try include papaya puree, with chopped pineapple and dates, and tamarillo or pomegranate seeds to decorate. Or make a summer fruit fool by using strawberry puree, topped with raspberries and blackberries, with cherries to finish.*

# Brown Sugar Pavlovas

### Serves 4

## INGREDIENTS

2 large egg whites
1 tsp cornstarch
1 tsp raspberry vinegar
3½ ounces light brown sugar,
   crushed free of lumps

2 tbsp redcurrant jelly
2 tbsp unsweetened orange juice
¾ cup low-fat unsweetened yogurt
6 ounces raspberries, thawed
   if frozen

rose-scented geranium leaves,
   to decorate (optional)

1 Preheat the oven to 300°F. Line a large cookie sheet with baking parchment. In a large, grease-free bowl, whisk the egg whites until very stiff and dry. Fold in the cornstarch and vinegar.

2 Gradually whisk in the sugar, a spoonful at a time, until the mixture is thick and glossy.

3 Divide the mixture into 4 and spoon onto the cookie sheet, spaced well apart. Smooth each

into a round, about 4 inches across, and bake in the oven for 40–45 minutes until lightly browned and crisp. Leave to cool on the cookie sheet.

4 Place the redcurrant jelly and orange juice in a small saucepan and heat, stirring, until the jelly has melted. Cool for 10 minutes.

5 Meanwhile, using a spatula, carefully remove each pavlova from the baking parchment and

transfer to a serving plate. Top with unsweetened yogurt and raspberries. Spoon on the redcurrant jelly mixture to glaze. Decorate and serve.

## VARIATION

*Make a large pavlova by forming the meringue into a round, measuring 7 inches across, on a lined cookie sheet and bake for 1 hour.*

# *Apricot & Orange Jellies*

### Serves 4

**INGREDIENTS**

| | | |
|---|---|---|
| 8 ounces no-need-to-soak dried apricots | 1 tbsp powdered gelatin | CINNAMON CREAM: |
| 1¼ cups unsweetened orange juice | 4 tbsp boiling water | 4 ounces medium fat ricotta cheese |
| 2 tbsp lemon juice | TO DECORATE: | 4 ounces low-fat unsweetened yogurt |
| 2–3 tsp clear honey | orange segments | 1 tsp ground cinnamon |
| | sprigs of mint | 1 tbsp clear honey |

1 Place the apricots in a saucepan and pour in the orange juice. Bring to a boil, cover, and simmer for 15–20 minutes, until the apricots are plump and soft. Set aside and cool for 10 minutes.

2 Transfer the mixture to a blender or food processor and blend until smooth. Stir in the lemon juice and add the honey. Measure the mixture and make 2½ cups with cold water.

3 Dissolve the gelatin in the boiling water and stir into the apricot mixture.

4 Pour the mixture into 4 individual molds, each measuring ⅔ cup, or 1 large mold, measuring 2½ cups. Chill until set.

5 Meanwhile, make the cinnamon cream. Thoroughly mix all the ingredients together and place in a small bowl. Cover and chill.

6 To turn out the jellies, dip the molds in hot water for a few seconds to loosen, and invert onto serving plates. Decorate and serve with the cinnamon cream dusted with extra cinnamon.

## VARIATION

*Other fruits that would work well in this recipe instead of the apricots are dried peaches, mangoes, and pears.*

# *Sticky Sesame Bananas*

### Serves 4

### INGREDIENTS

| | | |
|---|---|---|
| 4 ripe medium bananas | 2 tbsp sesame seeds | 1 tsp vanilla extract |
| 3 tbsp lemon juice | $^2/_3$ cup low-fat unsweetened | lemon and lime rind, shredded, |
| 4 ounces superfine sugar | yogurt | to decorate |
| 4 tbsp cold water | 1 tbsp confectioner's sugar | |

1 Peel the bananas and cut into 2-inch pieces. Place the banana pieces in a bowl, add the lemon juice, and stir well to coat—this will help prevent the bananas from discoloring.

2 Place the sugar and water in a small saucepan and heat gently, stirring, until the sugar dissolves. Bring to a boil and cook for 5–6 minutes, until the mixture turns golden-brown.

3 Meanwhile, drain the bananas and blot with absorbent paper towels to dry. Line a cookie sheet or board with baking parchment and arrange the bananas, well spaced out, on top.

4 When the caramel is ready, drizzle it over the bananas, working quickly because the caramel sets almost instantly. Sprinkle with the sesame seeds and cool for about 10 minutes.

5 Mix the yogurt with the confectioner's sugar and vanilla extract.

6 Peel the bananas away from the paper and arrange on serving plates. Serve the unsweetened yogurt as a dip, decorated with the shredded lemon and lime rind.

## COOK'S TIP

*For the best results, use a cannelle knife or a potato peeler to peel away thin strips of rind from the fruit, taking care not to include any bitter pith. Blanch the shreds in boiling water for 1 minute, then refresh in cold water.*

# *Mocha Swirl Mousse*

### Serves 4

**INGREDIENTS**

1 tbsp coffee and chicory extract

2 tsp cocoa powder, plus extra
   for dusting

1 tsp low-fat drinking
   chocolate powder

²/₃ cup half-fat crème fraîche,
   plus 4 tsp to serve (see
   Cook's Tip)

2 tsp powdered gelatin

2 tbsp boiling water

2 large egg whites

2 tbsp superfine sugar

4 chocolate coffee beans,
   to serve

1 Place the coffee and chicory extract in one bowl, and 2 tsp of cocoa powder and the chocolate powder in another bowl. Divide the crème fraîche between the 2 bowls and mix both until well combined.

2 Dissolve the gelatin in the boiling water and set aside. In a grease-free bowl, whisk the egg whites and sugar until stiff, and divide this mixture evenly between the coffee mixture and the chocolate mixture.

3 Divide the dissolved gelatin between the 2 mixtures and, using a large metal spoon, gently fold until well mixed.

4 Spoon small amounts of the 2 mousses alternately into 4 serving glasses and swirl together gently. Chill for 1 hour or until set.

5 To serve, top each mousse with 1 tsp crème fraîche, a chocolate coffee bean, and a light dusting of cocoa powder.

## COOK'S TIP

*Traditional crème fraîche is sour cream and has a fat content of around 40 percent. It is thick and has a slightly sour and nutty flavor. Lower-fat versions have a reduced fat content and are slightly looser in texture, but they should be used in a low-fat diet only occasionally. If you want to use a lower-fat alternative, a reduced fat, unsweetened yogurt would be more suitable.*

# Fruit & Fiber Layers

## Serves 4

### INGREDIENTS

| | | |
|---|---|---|
| 4 ounces dried apricots | 6 cardamom pods | TO DECORATE: |
| 4 ounces dried prunes | 6 cloves | apricot slices |
| 4 ounces dried peaches | 1 cinnamon stick, broken | |
| 2 ounces dried apple | 1¼ cups low-fat | |
| 1 ounce dried cherries | unsweetened yogurt | |
| 2 cups unsweetened apple juice | 14 ounces crunchy oat cereal | |

1 To make the fruit compote, place the dried apricots, prunes, peaches, apples, and cherries in a saucepan and pour in the apple juice.

2 Add the cardamom pods, cloves, and cinnamon stick to the pan, bring to a boil, and simmer for 10–15 minutes, until the fruits are plump and tender.

3 Allow the mixture to cool completely in the pan, then transfer the mixture to a bowl, and leave to chill in the refrigerator for 1 hour. Remove and discard the spices from the fruits.

4 Spoon the compote into 4 dessert glasses, layering it alternately with yogurt and oat cereal, finishing with the oat cereal on top.

5 Decorate each dessert with slices of apricot and serve at once.

## COOK'S TIP

*There are many dried fruits available, including mangoes and pears, some of which need soaking, so read the instructions on the packet before use. Also, check the ingredients label, because several types of dried fruit have added sugar or are rolled in sugar, and this will affect the sweetness of the dish that you use them in.*

# *Pan-Cooked Apples in Red Wine*

### Serves 4

**INGREDIENTS**

| | | |
|---|---|---|
| 4 eating apples | 2 ounces light brown sugar | $^2/_3$ cup red wine |
| 2 tbsp lemon juice | 1 small orange | 8 ounces raspberries, hulled and |
| 1$^1/_2$ ounces low-fat spread | 1 cinnamon stick, broken | thawed if frozen |
| | | sprigs of fresh mint, to decorate |

1 Peel and core the apples, then cut them into thick wedges. Place the apples in a bowl and toss in the lemon juice to prevent the fruit from discoloring.

2 In a skillet, gently melt the low-fat spread over a low heat, add the sugar, and stir to form a paste.

3 Stir the apple wedges into the skillet and cook, stirring occasionally, for 2 minutes, or until the apples are well coated in the sugar paste.

4 Using a vegetable peeler, pare off a few strips of orange rind. Add the orange rind to the pan, along with the cinnamon pieces. Extract the juice from the orange and pour into the pan with the red wine. Bring to a boil, then simmer for 10 minutes, stirring.

5 Add the raspberries to the pan and cook for 5 minutes, or until the apples are tender.

6 Discard the orange rind and cinnamon pieces. Transfer the apple and raspberry mixture to a serving plate, together with the wine sauce. Decorate with a sprig of fresh mint and serve hot.

## VARIATION

*For other fruity combinations, cook the apples with blackberries, blackcurrants, or red-currants. You may need to add more sugar if you use currants, as they are not as sweet as raspberries.*

# *Mixed Fruit Brûlées*

### Serves 4

**INGREDIENTS**

1 pound prepared, assorted
summer fruits (such as
strawberries, raspberries,
blackcurrants, redcurrants,
and cherries), thawed if
frozen

³/₄ cup half-fat heavy
cream alternative
³/₄ cup low-fat unsweetened
yogurt
1 tsp vanilla extract
4 tbsp raw crystal sugar

1 Divide up each of
the strawberries,
raspberries, blackcurrants,
redcurrants, and cherries
evenly among 4 small,
heatproof ramekin dishes.

2 Mix together the half-
fat cream alternative,
unsweetened yogurt, and
vanilla extract. Generously
spoon the mixture over
the fruit.

3 Preheat the broiler.
Top each serving with
1 tablespoon of brown
crystal sugar and broil the
desserts for 2–3 minutes,
until the sugar melts and
just begins to caramelize.
Serve the fruit brûlées
piping hot.

## VARIATION

*If you are making this
dessert for a special occasion,
soak the fruits in 2–3 tbsp
fruit liqueur before topping
with the cream mixture.*

## COOK'S TIP

*Look for half-fat
creams, in light and
heavy varieties. They
are good substitutes for
occasional use.
Alternatively, in this
recipe, omit the cream
and double the
quantity of yogurt for a
lower-fat version.*

# Broiled Fruit Platter with Lime Butter

## Serves 4

### INGREDIENTS

| | | |
|---|---|---|
| 1 baby pineapple | 4 tbsp dark rum | LIME BUTTER: |
| 1 ripe papaya | 1 tsp ground allspice | 2 ounces low-fat spread |
| 1 ripe mango | 2 tbsp lime juice | ½ tsp finely grated lime rind |
| 2 kiwi fruit | 4 tbsp dark brown sugar | 1 tbsp confectioner's sugar |
| 4 finger bananas | | |

1 Quarter the pineapple, trimming away most of the leaves, and place in a shallow dish. Peel the papaya, cut it in half, and scoop out the seeds. Cut the flesh into thick wedges and place in the same dish as the pineapple.

2 Peel the mango, cut either side of the smooth, central flat pit and remove the pit. Slice the flesh into thick wedges. Peel the kiwi fruit and cut in half. Peel the bananas. Add all of these fruits to the dish.

3 Sprinkle with the rum, allspice, and lime juice, cover, and leave at room temperature for about 30 minutes, turning occasionally, to allow the flavors to develop.

4 Meanwhile, make the lime butter. Place the low-fat spread in a small bowl and beat in the lime rind and sugar until well mixed. Chill until the butter is required.

5 Preheat the broiler. Drain the fruit, reserving the juices, and arrange in the broiler pan. Sprinkle with the sugar and broil for 3–4 minutes until hot and just beginning to char.

6 Transfer the fruit to a serving plate and spoon the juices on top. Serve the fruit with the lime butter.

## VARIATION

*Serve with a light sauce of 1¼ cups tropical fruit juice thickened with 2 tsp arrowroot.*

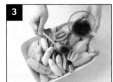

# *Baked Pears with Cinnamon & Brown Sugar*

### Serves 4

**INGREDIENTS**

| | | |
|---|---|---|
| 4 ripe pears | 1 tsp ground cinnamon | lemon rind, finely grated, to |
| 2 tbsp lemon juice | 2 ounces low-fat spread | decorate |
| 4 tbsp light brown sugar | low-fat custard, to serve | |

1 Preheat the oven to 400°F. Core and peel the pears, then slice them in half lengthwise, and brush all over with the lemon juice to prevent the pears from discoloring. Place the pears, cored side down, in a small nonstick roasting pan.

2 Place the sugar, cinnamon, and low-fat spread in a small saucepan and heat gently, stirring, until the sugar has melted. Keep the heat low to stop too much water evaporating from the low-fat spread as it gets hot. Spoon the mixture over the pears.

3 Bake in the oven for 20–25 minutes, or until the pears are tender and golden, occasionally spooning the sugar mixture over the fruit during the cooking time.

4 To serve, heat the custard until it is piping hot and spoon over the bases of 4 warm dessert plates. Arrange 2 pear halves on each plate. Decorate and serve.

## VARIATION

*This recipe also works well if you use cooking apples. For alternative flavors, replace the cinnamon with ground ginger, and serve the pears sprinkled with chopped, preserved ginger in syrup. Alternatively, use ground allspice and spoon warm dark rum on top.*

# Baked Apples with Blackberries

### Serves 4

## INGREDIENTS

| | | |
|---|---|---|
| 4 medium-size cooking apples | $\frac{1}{2}$ tsp ground allspice | 2 tsp cornstarch blended with |
| 1 tbsp lemon juice | $\frac{1}{2}$ tsp finely grated lemon rind | 2 tbsp cold water |
| 3$\frac{1}{2}$ ounces prepared blackberries, | 2 tbsp raw crystal sugar | low-fat custard, to serve |
| thawed if frozen | 1$\frac{1}{4}$ cups ruby port | |
| $\frac{1}{2}$ ounce slivered almonds | 1 cinnamon stick, broken | |

1 Preheat the oven to 400°F. Wash and dry the apples. Using a small sharp knife, make a shallow cut through the skin around the middle of each apple—this will help the apples to cook through.

2 Core the apples, brush the centers with the lemon juice to prevent browning, and stand in a shallow ovenproof dish.

3 In a bowl, mix together the blackberries, almonds, allspice, lemon rind, and sugar. Using a teaspoon, spoon the mixture into the center of each apple.

4 Pour the port into the dish, add the cinnamon stick, and bake the apples in the oven for 35–40 minutes, or until tender. Drain the cooking juices into a pan and keep the apples warm.

5 Discard the cinnamon and add the cornstarch mixture to the cooking juices. Heat, stirring, until thickened.

6 Heat the custard until piping hot. Pour the sauce over the apples and serve with the custard.

## VARIATION

*Use raspberries instead of blackberries and, if you prefer, replace the port with unsweetened orange juice.*

# White Lace Crêpes with Oriental Fruits

### Serves 4

**INGREDIENTS**

| | | |
|---|---|---|
| 3 medium egg whites | FRUIT FILLING: | ¹/₂-inch piece fresh root ginger |
| 4 tbsp cornstarch | 12 ounces fresh lychees | 2 pieces preserved ginger in |
| 3 tbsp cold water | ¹/₄ Galia melon | syrup |
| 1 tsp vegetable oil | 6 ounces seedless green grapes | 2 tbsp ginger wine or dry sherry |

1 To make the fruit filling, peel the lychees and remove the pits. Place the lychees in a bowl. Scoop out the seeds from the melon and remove the skin. Cut the melon flesh into small pieces and place in the bowl.

2 Wash and dry the grapes, remove from the stalks, and add to the bowl. Peel the ginger root and cut into thin shreds or grate finely. Drain the preserved ginger pieces, reserving the syrup, and chop the ginger finely.

3 Mix the gingers into the bowl, along with the ginger wine or sherry and the reserved preserved ginger syrup. Cover and set aside.

4 Meanwhile, prepare the crêpes. In a small pitcher, mix together the egg whites, cornstarch, and cold water until very smooth.

5 Brush a small nonstick crêpe pan with oil and heat until hot. Drizzle the surface of the pan with a quarter of the cornstarch

mixture to give a lacy effect. Cook for a few seconds until set, then carefully lift out, and transfer to absorbent paper towels to drain. Set aside and keep warm. Repeat with the remaining mixture to make 4 crêpes in total.

6 To serve, place a crêpe on each serving plate and top with the fruit filling. Fold over the pancake and serve hot.

# Fruit Loaf with Strawberry & Apple Spread

### Serves 8

---
**INGREDIENTS**
---

6 ounces oatmeal

3½ ounces light brown
    sugar

1 tsp ground cinnamon

4½ ounces golden raisins

6 ounces seedless raisins

2 tbsp malt extract

1¼ cups unsweetened apple
    juice

6 ounces self-rising whole
    wheat flour

1½ tsp baking powder

strawberries and apple wedges,
    to serve

FRUIT SPREAD:

8 ounces strawberries, washed
    and hulled

2 eating apples, cored, chopped,
    and mixed with 1 tbsp lemon
    juice to prevent browning

1¼ cups unsweetened apple juice

---

1 Preheat the oven to 350°F. Grease and line a 2-pound loaf pan. Place the oatmeal, sugar, cinnamon, golden raisins, raisins, and malt extract in a mixing bowl. Pour in the apple juice, stir well, and let soak for 30 minutes.

2 Sift in the flour and baking powder, adding any husks that remain in the strainer, and fold in using a metal spoon. Spoon the mixture into the pan and bake for 1½ hours, until firm or until a skewer inserted into the center comes out clean. Cool for 10 minutes, then turn onto a rack, and cool completely.

3 Meanwhile, make the fruit spread. Place the strawberries and apples in a saucepan and pour in the apple juice. Bring to a boil, cover, and simmer for 30 minutes. Beat the sauce well and spoon into a clean, warmed jar. Set aside and let cool, then seal the jar.

4 Serve the loaf with 1–2 tablespoons of the fruit spread and an assortment of strawberries and apple wedges.

# Banana & Lime Cake

## Serves 10

### INGREDIENTS

| | | |
|---|---|---|
| 10½ ounces all-purpose flour | ⅔ cup low-fat unsweetened | TO DECORATE: |
| 1 tsp salt | yogurt | banana chips |
| 1½ tsp baking powder | 4 ounces golden raisins | lime rind, finely grated |
| 6 ounces light brown sugar | | |
| 1 tsp lime rind, grated | TOPPING: | |
| 1 medium egg, beaten | 4 ounces confectioner's sugar | |
| 1 medium banana, mashed with | 1–2 tsp lime juice | |
| 1 tbsp lime juice | ½ tsp lime rind, finely grated | |

1 Preheat the oven to 350°F. Grease and line a deep 7-inch round cake pan with baking parchment. Sift the flour, salt, and baking powder into a mixing bowl and stir in the sugar and lime rind until well combined.

2 Make a well in the center of the dry ingredients and add the egg, banana, yogurt, and golden raisins. Mix until thoroughly incorporated.

3 Spoon the mixture into the pan and smooth the surface. Bake for 40–45 minutes, until firm to the touch or until a skewer inserted in the center comes out clean. Cool for 10 minutes, then turn out onto a wire rack.

4 To make the topping, sift the confectioner's sugar into a small bowl and mix with the lime juice to form a soft, but not too runny, frosting. Stir in the lime rind. Drizzle the frosting over the cake, letting it run down the sides.

5 Decorate with banana chips and lime rind. Let stand for 15 minutes, so that the frosting sets.

## VARIATION

*Replace the lime rind and juice with orange, and the golden raisins with chopped apricots, if preferred.*

# *Crispy Sugar-Topped Blackberry & Apple Cake*

### Serves 10

### INGREDIENTS

12 ounces cooking apples
3 tbsp lemon juice
10$\frac{1}{2}$ ounces self-rising whole
  wheat flour
$\frac{1}{2}$ tsp baking powder
1 tsp ground cinnamon, plus
  extra for dusting

6 ounces prepared blackberries,
  thawed if frozen, plus extra
  to decorate
6 ounces light brown sugar
1 medium egg, beaten
$\frac{3}{4}$ cup low-fat unsweetened
  yogurt

2 ounces white or brown sugar
  cubes, lightly crushed
sliced eating apple,
  to decorate

1 Preheat the oven to 375°F. Grease and line a 2-pound loaf pan. Core, peel, and finely dice the apples. Place them in a saucepan with the lemon juice, bring to a boil, cover, and simmer for 10 minutes, until soft and pulpy. Beat well and set aside to cool.

2 Sift the flour, baking powder, and 1 tsp cinnamon into a bowl, adding any husks that remain in the strainer. Stir in 4 ounces blackberries and the sugar.

3 Make a well in the center of the ingredients and add the egg, unsweetened yogurt, and cooled apple purée. Mix well to incorporate thoroughly. Spoon the mixture into the prepared loaf pan and smooth over the top.

4 Sprinkle with the blackberries, pressing them down into the mixture, and top with the crushed sugar. Bake for 40–45 minutes. Cool in the pan.

5 Remove the cake from the pan and peel away the lining paper. Serve dusted with cinnamon.

# *Rich Fruit Cake*

### Serves 12

**INGREDIENTS**

6 ounces unsweetened pitted
    dates
4 ounces dried prunes
³/₄ cup unsweetened orange juice
2 tbsp molasses
1 tsp finely grated lemon rind
1 tsp finely grated orange rind

8 ounces self-rising whole
    wheat flour
1 tsp apple pie spice
4 ounces seedless raisins
4 ounces golden sultanas
4 ounces currants
4 ounces dried cranberries
3 large eggs, separated

confectioner's sugar, to dust

TO DECORATE:
1 tbsp apricot preserves,
    softened
6 ounces sugar paste
strips of orange rind
strips of lemon rind

1 Preheat the oven to 325°F. Grease and line a deep 8-inch round cake pan. Chop the dates and prunes and place in a pan. Add the orange juice and bring to a boil. Simmer for 10 minutes until soft. Remove from the heat and beat the mixture until puréed. Stir in the molasses and citrus rinds until combined. Let cool.

2 Sift the flour and apple pie spice into a bowl, adding any husks that remain in the strainer. Mix in the dried fruits.

3 When the date and prune mixture is cool, whisk in the egg yolks. In a separate bowl, whisk the egg whites until stiff. Spoon the fruit and egg yolk mixture into the dry ingredients, and mix.

4 Gently fold in the egg whites, using a metal spoon. Transfer to the pan and bake for 1½ hours. Cool completely in the pan.

5 Remove the cake from the pan and brush the top with preserves. Dust the counter with confectioner's sugar and roll out the sugar paste thinly. Lay the sugar paste over the top of the cake and trim the edges. Decorate the cake with orange and lemon rind.

# *Carrot & Ginger Cake*

### Serves 10

**INGREDIENTS**

8 ounces all-purpose flour
1 tsp baking powder
1 tsp baking soda
2 tsp ground ginger
$\frac{1}{2}$ tsp salt
6 ounces light brown sugar
8 ounces carrots, grated
2 pieces of preserved ginger in
    syrup, drained and chopped

1 ounce fresh ginger root, grated
2 ounces seedless raisins
2 medium eggs, beaten
3 tbsp corn oil
juice of 1 medium orange

FROSTING:

8 ounces low-fat soft cheese
4 tbsp confectioner's sugar

1 tsp vanilla extract

TO DECORATE:

grated carrot
preserved ginger
ground ginger

1 Preheat the oven to 350°F. Grease and line an 8-inch round cake pan with baking parchment.

2 Sift the flour, baking powder, baking soda, ground ginger, and salt into a mixing bowl. Stir in the sugar, carrots, preserved ginger, fresh root ginger, and raisins. Make a well in the center of the dry ingredients.

3 Beat together the eggs, oil, and orange juice, then pour into the center of the well. Combine until well mixed.

4 Spoon the mixture into the pan and smooth the surface. Bake in the oven for 1–1¼ hours, until firm to the touch, or until a skewer inserted into the center comes out clean. Cool in the pan.

5 To make the frosting, place the soft cheese in a bowl and beat to soften. Sift in the confectioner's sugar and add the vanilla extract. Stir until combined.

6 Remove the cake from the pan and smooth the frosting over the top. Serve decorated with grated carrot, preserved ginger, and a dusting of ground ginger.

# Strawberry Roulade

### Serves 8

## INGREDIENTS

3 large eggs
4 ounces superfine sugar
4 ounces all-purpose flour
1 tbsp hot water

FILLING:
$^3/_4$ cup low-fat unsweetened
    yogurt
1 tsp almond extract

8 ounces small strawberries
$^1/_2$ ounce toasted
    almonds, slivered
1 tsp confectioner's sugar

1 Preheat the oven to 425°F. Line a 14 × 10-inch jelly roll pan with baking parchment. Place the eggs in a mixing bowl with the superfine sugar. Place the bowl over a pan of hot water and whisk until pale and thick.

2 Remove the bowl from the pan. Sift in the flour and fold into the eggs with the hot water. Pour the mixture into the pan and bake for 8–10 minutes, until golden and set.

3 Transfer the mixture to a sheet of baking parchment. Peel off the lining paper and roll up the sponge tightly along with the baking parchment. Wrap in a dish cloth and let cool.

4 To make the filling, mix together the yogurt and almond extract. Reserving a few strawberries for decoration, wash, hull, and slice the rest. Leave the filling mixture to chill until ready to assemble.

5 Unroll the sponge, spread the yogurt mixture over the sponge, and sprinkle with strawberries. Roll the sponge up again and transfer to a serving plate. Sprinkle with the almonds and dust with confectioner's sugar. Decorate with the reserved strawberries.

## VARIATION

*Serve the roulade with a fruit puree, sweetened with a little sugar.*

# Fruity Muffins

## Makes 10

### INGREDIENTS

8 ounces self-rising whole
    wheat flour
2 tsp baking powder
1 ounce light muscovado sugar
3½ ounces dried apricots,
    finely chopped

1 medium banana, mashed with
    1 tbsp orange juice
1 tsp orange rind, grated finely
1¼ cups skim milk
1 medium egg, beaten

3 tbsp corn oil
2 tbsp oatmeal
fruit spread, honey, or maple
    syrup, to serve

1 Preheat the oven to 400°F. Place 10 paper muffin cups in a deep muffin pan.

2 Sift the flour and baking powder into a mixing bowl, adding any husks that remain in the strainer. Stir in the sugar and chopped apricots and mix until well combined.

3 Make a well in the center of the dry ingredients and add the banana, orange rind, milk, beaten egg, and oil. Mix well to form a thick batter. Divide the batter evenly among the 10 paper cups.

4 Sprinkle with a little oatmeal and bake for 25–30 minutes, until well risen and firm to the touch, or until a toothpick inserted into the center comes out clean. Transfer the muffins to a wire rack to cool slightly.

5 Serve the muffins warm with fruit spread, honey, or maple syrup.

## VARIATION

*If you like dried figs, they make a deliciously crunchy alternative to the apricots; they also go very well with the flavor of orange. Other no-need-to-soak dried fruits, chopped up finely, can be used as well. Store these muffins in an airtight container for 3-4 days. They also freeze well in sealed bags or in freezer containers for up to 3 months.*

# *Chocolate Brownies*

## Makes 12

### INGREDIENTS

2 ounces unsweetened pitted
    dates, chopped
2 ounces dried prunes, chopped
6 tbsp unsweetened apple juice
4 medium eggs, beaten
10½ ounces dark brown sugar

1 tsp vanilla extract
4 tbsp low-fat drinking chocolate
    powder, plus extra for dusting
2 tbsp cocoa powder
6 ounces all-purpose flour
2 ounces dark chocolate chips

FROSTING:
4 ounces confectioner's sugar
1–2 tsp water
1 tsp vanilla extract

1 Preheat the oven to 350°F. Grease and line a 7 × 11-inch cake pan with baking parchment. Place the dates and prunes in a small saucepan and add the apple juice. Bring to a boil, cover, and simmer for 10 minutes, until soft. Beat to form a smooth paste, then set aside to cool.

2 Place the cooled fruit in a mixing bowl and stir in the eggs, sugar, and vanilla extract. Sift in 4 tablespoons of chocolate powder, the cocoa, and the flour, and fold in, along with the chocolate chips, until well incorporated.

3 Spoon the mixture into the prepared pan and smooth over the top. Bake for 25–30 minutes until firm to the touch or until a toothpick inserted into the center of the cake comes out clean. Cut into 12 bars and cool in the pan for 10 minutes. Transfer the brownies to a wire rack to cool completely.

4 To make the frosting, sift the sugar into a bowl and mix with enough water and the vanilla extract to form a soft, but not too runny, frosting.

5 Drizzle the frosting over the chocolate brownies and allow to set. Dust with the extra chocolate powder just before serving.

# *Cheese & Chive Biscuits*

## Makes 10

### INGREDIENTS

9 ounces self-rising flour
1 tsp powdered mustard
½ tsp cayenne pepper
½ tsp salt

3½ ounces low-fat soft cheese
  with added herbs
2 tbsp fresh snipped chives, plus
  extra to garnish

3½ fl ounces and 2 tbsp
  skim milk
2 ounces reduced-fat vheddar
  cheese, grated
low-fat soft cheese, to serve

1 Preheat the oven to 400°F. Sift the self-rising flour, mustard, cayenne pepper, and salt into a mixing bowl.

2 Add the soft cheese to the mixture and mix together until well incorporated. Stir in the snipped chives.

3 Make a well in the center of the ingredients and gradually pour in 3½ fl ounces milk, stirring as you pour, until the mixture forms a soft dough.

4 Turn the dough onto a floured counter and knead lightly. Roll out until ¾ inch thick and use a 2-inch plain pastry cutter to stamp out as many rounds as you can. Transfer the rounds to a cookie sheet.

5 Re-knead the dough trimmings together and roll out again. Stamp out more rounds—you should be able to make 10 biscuits in total.

6 Brush the biscuits with the remaining milk and sprinkle with the grated

cheese. Bake for 15–20 minutes, until risen and golden. Transfer to a wire rack to cool. Serve warm with low-fat soft cheese, garnished with chives.

## VARIATION

*For a sweet variation omit the mustard, cayenne, chives, and grated cheese and add 3 ounces currants or raisins and 1 ounce sugar, and use plain low-fat soft cheese.*

# Savory Tomato & Bell Pepper Bread

### Serves 8

**INGREDIENTS**

| | | |
|---|---|---|
| 1 small red bell pepper | 2 tsp dried yeast | $^2/_3$ cup low-fat unsweetened |
| 1 small green bell pepper | 1 tsp superfine sugar | yogurt |
| 1 small yellow bell pepper | $^2/_3$ cup tepid water | 1 tbsp coarse salt |
| 2 ounces dry-pack sun- | 4 cups strong white bread flour | 1 tbsp olive oil |
| dried tomatoes | 2 tsp dried rosemary | |
| $^1/_4$ cup boiling water | 2 tbsp tomato paste | |

1 Preheat the oven to 425°F and the broiler to hot. Halve and seed the bell peppers, arrange on the broiler rack, and cook until the skin is charred. Cool for 10 minutes, peel off the skin, and chop the flesh.

2 Slice the tomatoes into strips, place in a heatproof bowl, and add the boiling water. Let soak.

3 Place the yeast and sugar in a small pitcher, add the water, and

leave for 10–15 minutes, until frothy. Sift the flour into a bowl and add 1 tsp dried rosemary. Make a well in the center and pour in the yeast mixture. Add the tomato paste, the tomatoes and soaking liquid, the bell peppers, yogurt, and half the salt. Mix together to form a soft dough.

4 Knead the dough on a floured counter for 3–4 minutes, until smooth and elastic. Place in a floured

bowl, cover, and leave in a warm room for 40 minutes, until doubled in size. Knead the dough again and place in a greased, 9-inch round, spring-form cake pan. Using a wooden spoon, form "dimples" in the surface. Cover and leave for 30 minutes.

5 Brush with oil and sprinkle with rosemary and salt. Bake for 35–40 minutes, cool, and release from the pan.

# *Exotic Fruity Packets*

### Serves 4

**INGREDIENTS**

1 papaya
1 mango
1 star fruit

1 tbsp grenadine
3 tbsp orange juice

light cream or unsweetened
yogurt, to serve

1 Cut the papaya in half, scoop out the seeds with a spoon, and then discard the seeds. Peel the papaya and cut the flesh into thick slices.

2 Prepare the mango by cutting it lengthwise in half either side of the central pit.

3 Score each mango half in a criss-cross pattern. Push each mango half inside out to separate the cubes and cut them away from the peel.

4 Using a sharp knife, slice the star fruit.

5 Place all of the fruit in a bowl and mix them together.

6 Mix the grenadine and orange juice together and pour over the fruit. Marinate for at least 30 minutes.

7 Divide the fruit among 4 double-thickness squares of foil and gather up the edges to form a packet that encloses the fruit.

8 Place the foil packet on a rack set over warm coals and barbecue the fruit for 15–20 minutes.

9 Serve the fruit in the packet, with light cream or yogurt.

## COOK'S TIP

*Grenadine is a sweet syrup made from pomegranates. If you prefer, you could use pomegranate juice instead of the grenadine for this recipe. To extract the juice, cut the pomegranate in half and squeeze gently with a lemon squeezer—do not press too hard or the juice may become bitter.*

# Index